IMAGES
of America

CASSIA COUNTY

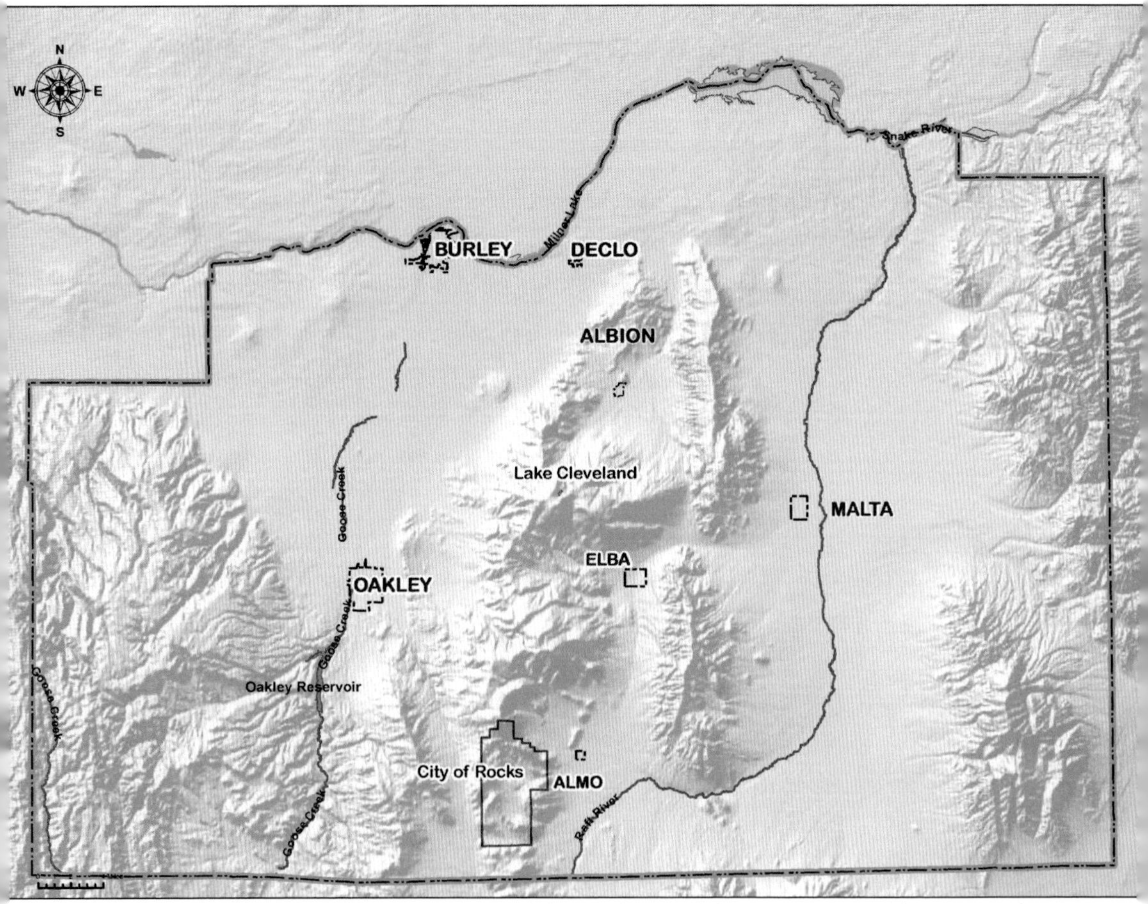

Cassia County, located in south central Idaho, is the ninth largest county in the state and covers 2,500 square miles. (Courtesy of Sarah Wright.)

ON THE COVER: Three students from the Albion Normal School hiked up to an overlook above the town of Albion. This was taken about 1900. (Courtesy of the Cassia County Museum.)

IMAGES
of America

Cassia County

Valerie K. Bowen and
the Cassia County Historical Society

ARCADIA
PUBLISHING

ISBN 978-0-7385-6928-4

Published by Arcadia Publishing
Charleston SC, Chicago IL, Portsmouth NH, San Francisco CA

Printed in the United States of America

Library of Congress Control Number: 2008938276

For all general information contact Arcadia Publishing at:
Telephone 843-853-2070
Fax 843-853-0044
E-mail sales@arcadiapublishing.com
For customer service and orders:
Toll-Free 1-888-313-2665

Visit us on the Internet at www.arcadiapublishing.com

Contents

Acknowledgments		6
Introductions		7
1.	Albion	9
2.	Almo	23
3.	Burley	35
4.	Declo	59
5.	Elba	69
6.	Malta	79
7.	Oakley	87
8.	Irrigation, Farming, and Ranching	101
9.	Transportation	117
10.	Recreation	121
Bibliography		127

ACKNOWLEDGMENTS

The Cassia County Historical Society and Museum was organized by a group of Cassia County citizens who realized the need to preserve the wonderful history of this area. It was their dedication to historic preservation that has kept this institution going. Every caretaker of this museum has added his or her touch to improve and expand the collections. A motto hanging in the museum says, "He who has no respect for the past, has no regard for the future." By remembering the past and learning from it, we can appreciate what we have and leave it better for the future generations.

On behalf of the Cassia County Historical Society, I would like to thank those people who took the time to search through their private collections of photographs and histories to contribute to this book. Family photographs are precious and irreplaceable, and I appreciate the trust they had in us to safeguard their treasures. I would like to thank Ann Wight, Mable Pierce, Pat Gebauer, Ada Parke, Penny Thompson, Alvin and Rosella Neddo, Jeanette Durfee Babbitt, Maxine Adams, Martell Holland, Cleone Moncur, James Peterson, Dick and Ilene Fuqua, Sherry Funk, Jamie Larsen, Leah Beck, Mary Lynne Bristol, Vermoyne Ridenour, Deborah Jones, Janis Carnahan, Pati Christensen, Phyllis Tracy, and Bessie Nye for sharing their family collections. Thank you to Betty Warr from the Oakley Valley Museum for opening up their collection to us and to Verlene Powell for sharing her collection from the Albion Valley. All photographs not credited came from collections we have at the museum that have been donated through the years. The dedication of early photographers such as George Klink, M. B. Martin, ? Tsunami, and Otto Paulson, who preserved the everyday happenings of life in Cassia County, has given us a peek into what it was like to live just a few short years ago.

This project could not have been completed without great support from many people. I give thanks to Kim Seely and Donna Tracy for their critical eye for detail and way with words. A special thanks to Jamie Larsen for her computer expertise and to Lyn Ann Arnell for her many hours of sorting and organizing what seemed to be an endless assortment of great photographs.

INTRODUCTION

Cassia County is located along the Snake River in south-central Idaho. It has a diversity of natural beauty. The City of Rocks National Reserve, with its towering formations growing up from the high desert valley floor, was a landmark for pioneer wagons traveling through the area. It has beautiful mountain peaks that soar to 10,000 feet in elevation and the beautiful Snake River, which flows smooth and wide.

Cassia County has a rich history with early settlers. Some parts of the county were settled in the 1870s as a result of the stage and wagon routes between Salt Lake City, Utah, and Boise, Idaho. As time and progress came to the area, railroads, dams, and irrigation played an important part in the development of the county. Some communities grew with the coming of the railroad, and others disappeared.

Today there are seven communities and many farms, ranches, and homes connecting them. Each one has a distinct history and a loyalty today to that history. The main economic base is agriculture, but this didn't occur without hard work, great planning, and a desire to succeed. Albion was the first seat of the newly formed county in 1879. When the Idaho State Legislature established a teacher-training school in Albion in 1893, it was already a thriving community. Albion State Normal School educated many aspiring teachers and supplied the surrounding schools with many educators for their growing populations. The college helped Albion survive when the railroad bypassed the town.

Oakley was actually a larger town than Albion by the dawn of the 20th century. Much of its growth is attributed to Latter-day Saints (LDS) pioneers settling in the town around 1879. Several of the original Victorian homes still line the streets of the town.

Three small farming and ranching communities—Almo, Malta, and Elba—that were along the stage and pioneer trail routes in the late 1800s are seen in some of the following images.

Burley was founded in 1905. The railroad was instrumental in its establishment. The earlier towns were based on stagecoach stops, but Burley rose from sagebrush as a result of businessmen, the Snake River's water, and the development of the railroad. In 1919, the county seat moved from Albion to Burley.

The Minidoka Project and the new availability of irrigation water changed the county in a very positive way. What was first seen as desert and sagebrush became rich and abundant farmland. Declo is another community that benefited from the flow of water in the canals in 1907.

Some well-known people have come from Cassia County. Edgar Rice Burroughs, author of the Tarzan series, had family here and spent summers on his brother's ranch. J. R. Simplot, an agricultural leader and businessman, was from Declo. David B. Haight, an LDS leader, was raised in Oakley. William Davis, who built the Winn-Dixie grocery chain in the Southern states, had his start in Burley. The story of "Diamondfield" Jack Davis is about the rivalry between the sheep ranchers and the cattlemen.

This book is a glimpse of some of the events, people, and places that gave Cassia County a start. It can only touch the surface of what took place here from the 1870s until the late 1930s. In the images collected here, there is a sense of determination, happiness, and optimism in the faces of the early settlers. Many have posterity who continue to live in the county, enjoying the result of their forefathers' hard work.

One

Albion

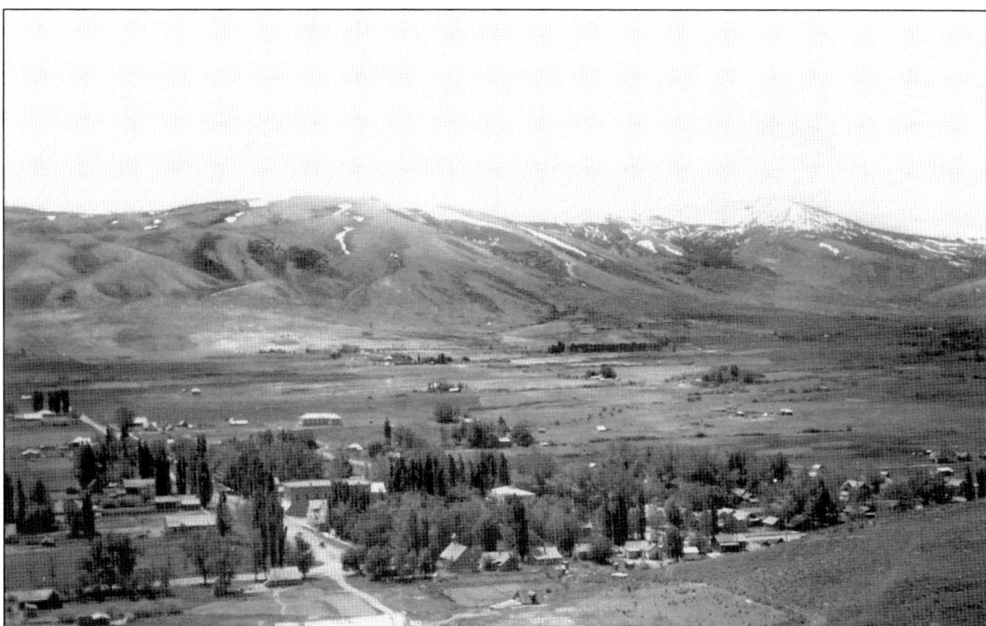

The name Albion means "mountain land high and white." When the settlers were voting for their new county seat, the town of Marsh Basin won by one vote, but some of the settlers thought the name wasn't proper enough to be a county seat, so they put names in a hat, and the town had a new name. The first two postmasters served under the name of Marsh Basin.

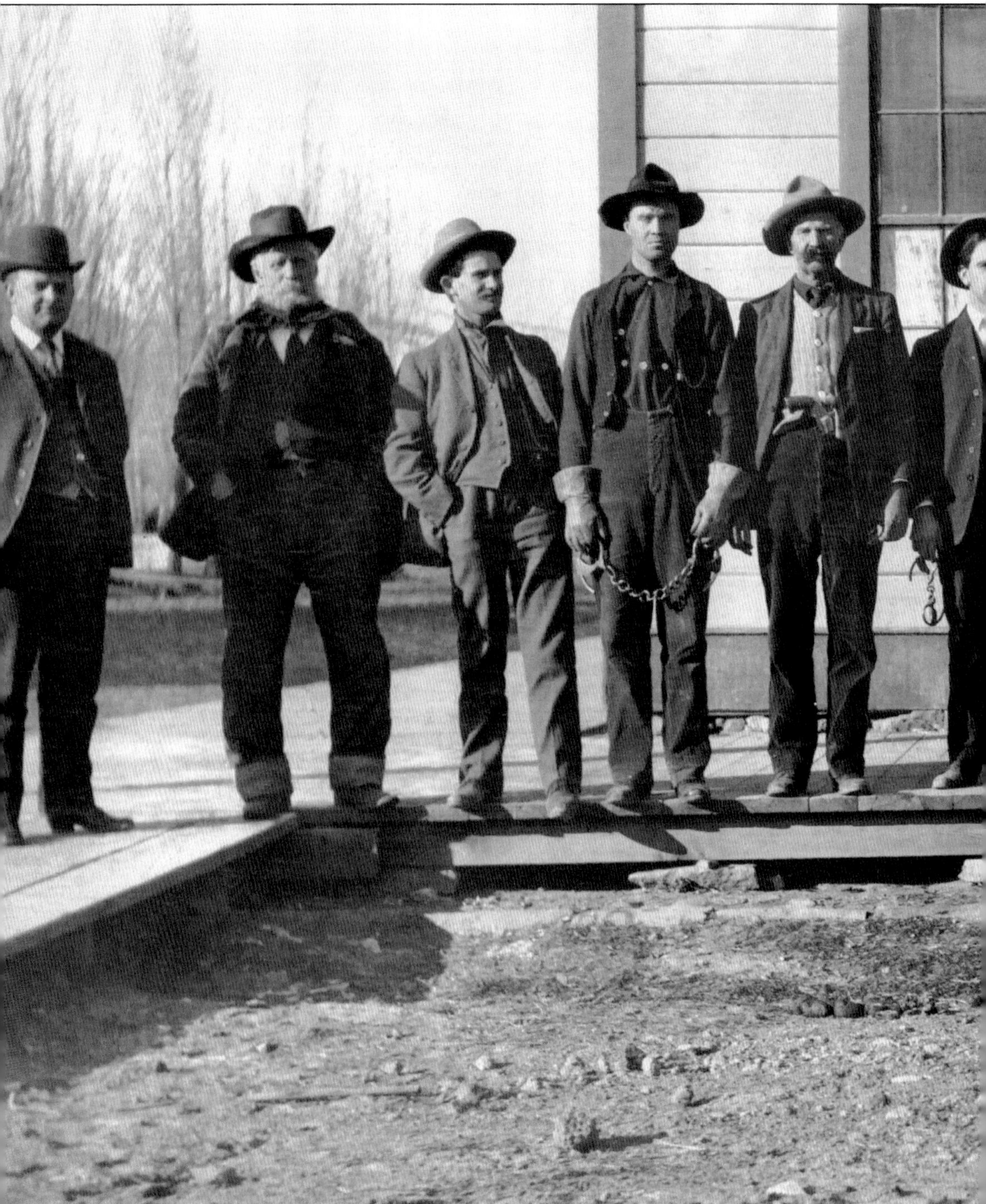

Cassia County officials and prominent citizens are standing in front of the courthouse in Albion in 1908. From left to right are B. P. Howells, attorney; John Chatburn, commissioner; Moses Smith, assessor; George Brackenbury, deputy sheriff; Val Brackenbury, sheriff; George Smith, deputy

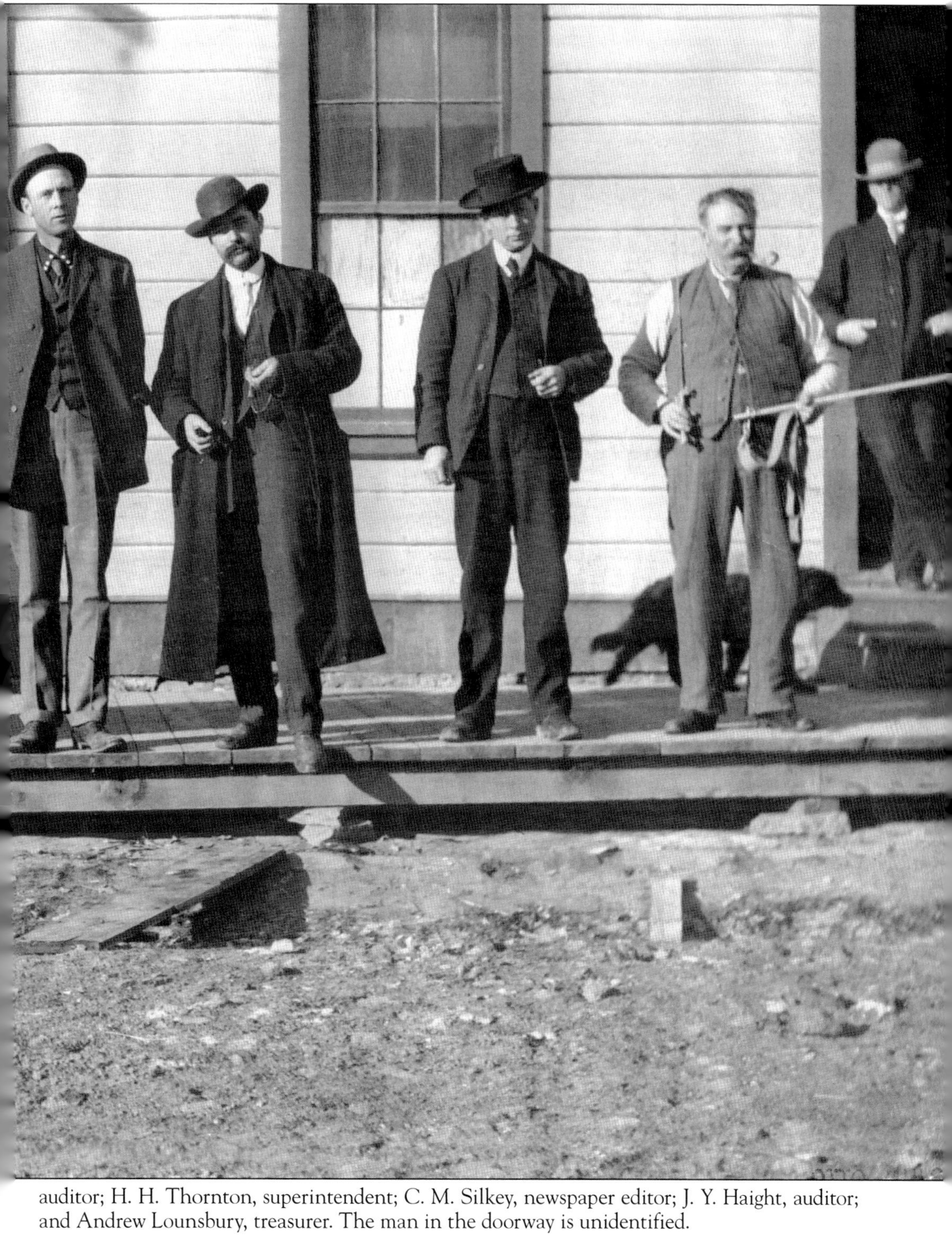

auditor; H. H. Thornton, superintendent; C. M. Silkey, newspaper editor; J. Y. Haight, auditor; and Andrew Lounsbury, treasurer. The man in the doorway is unidentified.

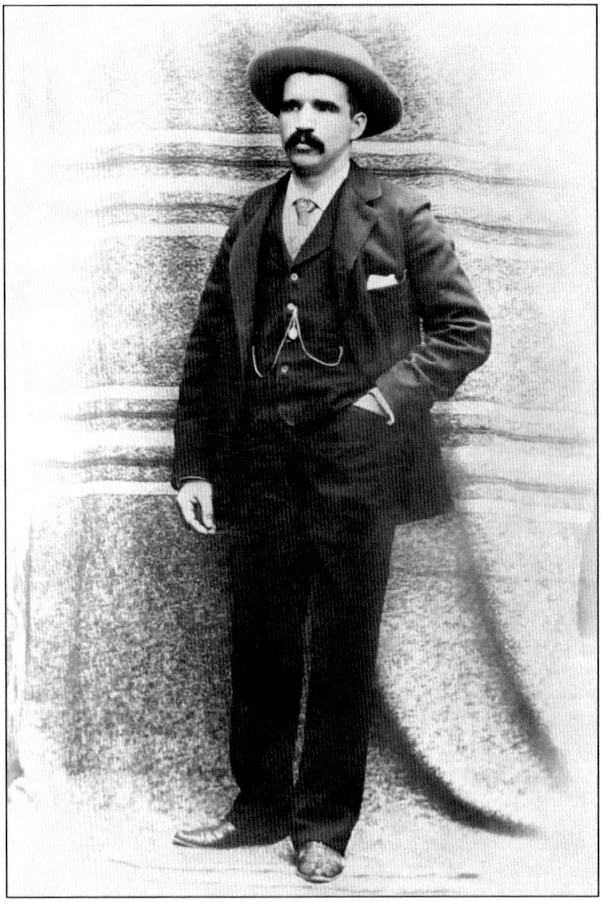

Diamondfield Jack Davis worked for the Sparks-Harrell Cattle Company in the late 1890s. Cattle and sheep were both being raised in the county, and his job was to see that the sheep didn't encroach on "cattle territory." He was accused of killing two sheepherders. The evidence was circumstantial, but he was convicted in a trial and sentenced to hang. A stay of execution was sent by a pardon board just hours before his hanging was to take place. Even though others confessed to the murder, he wasn't totally pardoned until December 1902.

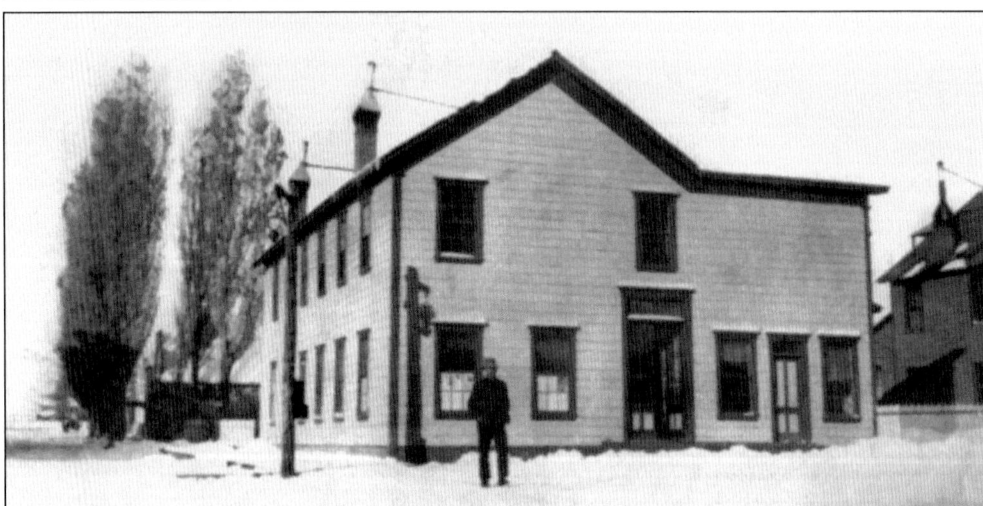

Albion was the seat from the county's beginning in 1879 until it was moved to Burley in 1919. It was here that the trial of Diamondfield Jack Davis took place. The courthouse was built by Hardy Sears in 1885 to be a hotel. Before it was completed in 1886, he sold it to the county for the courthouse.

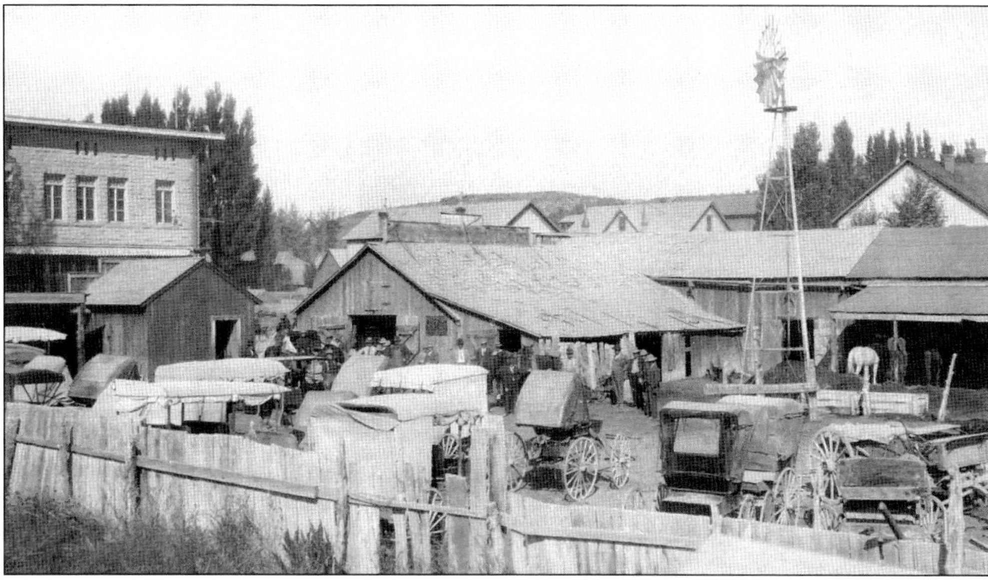

The Parks and Langley Livery Stable is seen here filled with buggies for the Diamondfield Jack trial. The attorneys who participated in the trial were William Hawley for the defense, later to become Idaho governor, and prosecutor William E. Borah, later to become a well-known U.S. Senator from Idaho. Many dignitaries traveled from Boise to witness the proceedings. Young men could rent horses and buggies here to take their dates for a drive on special evenings or Sundays. (Courtesy of Verlene Powell.)

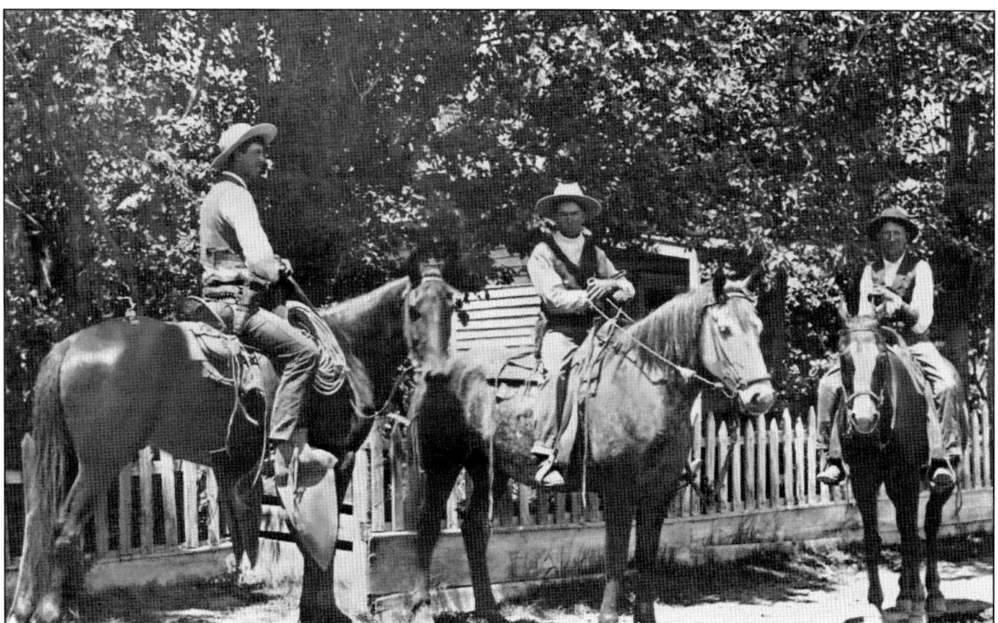

Willis Sears (center) rode horseback from the telegraph office in Minidoka to Albion to deliver the telegram that was the stay of execution for Diamondfield Jack. He made the 30-mile ride in just two and a half hours. Others in the picture are Bill Bowmen (left) and Charley Sears.

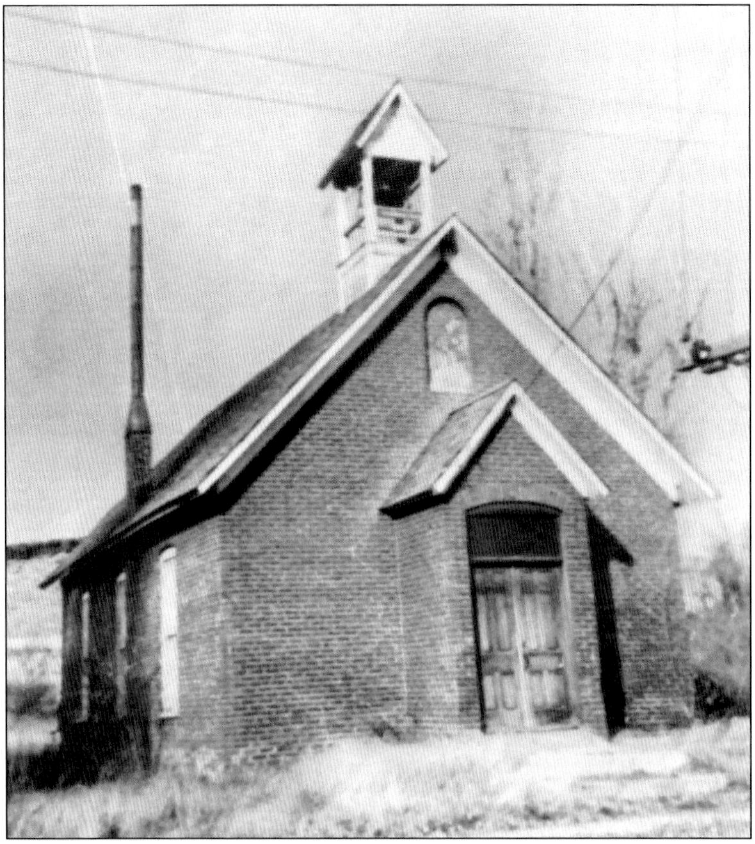

This building, constructed in 1879 as the Albion Methodist Episcopal Church, has been the meeting place for several organizations and many town meetings. The Four Leaf Clover Club (a women's club established in 1899), the Grange, and the American Legion continue to meet there. The bell in the tower is still rung on Sunday morning for the current owner, Albion Church of Christ.

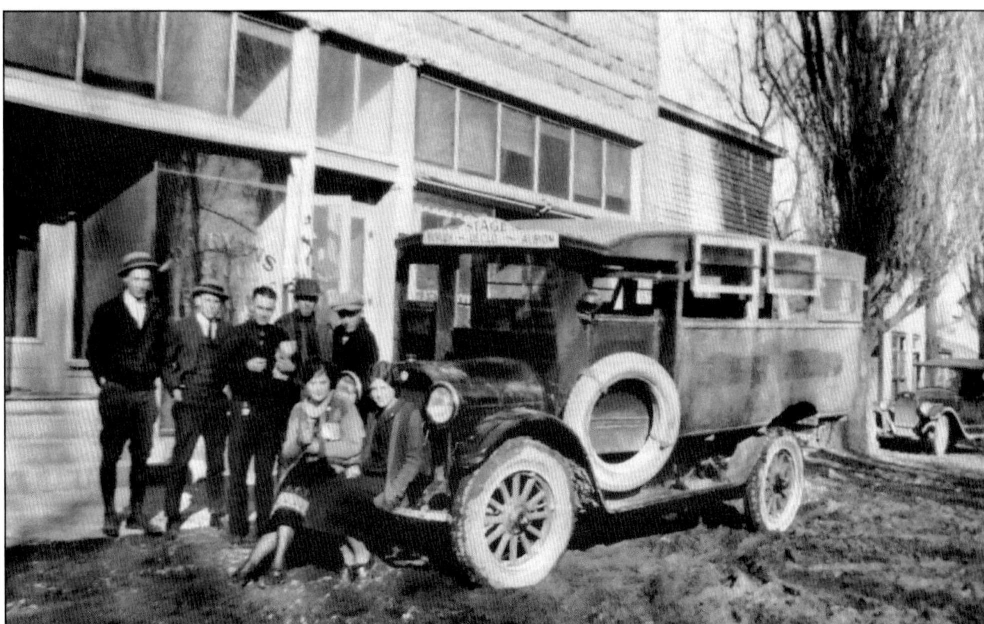

Bill Powell (fourth from left) drove a "stage truck" from Burley to Declo and Albion carrying passengers and mail. This picture was taken in Albion in front of the D. L. Evans Bank.

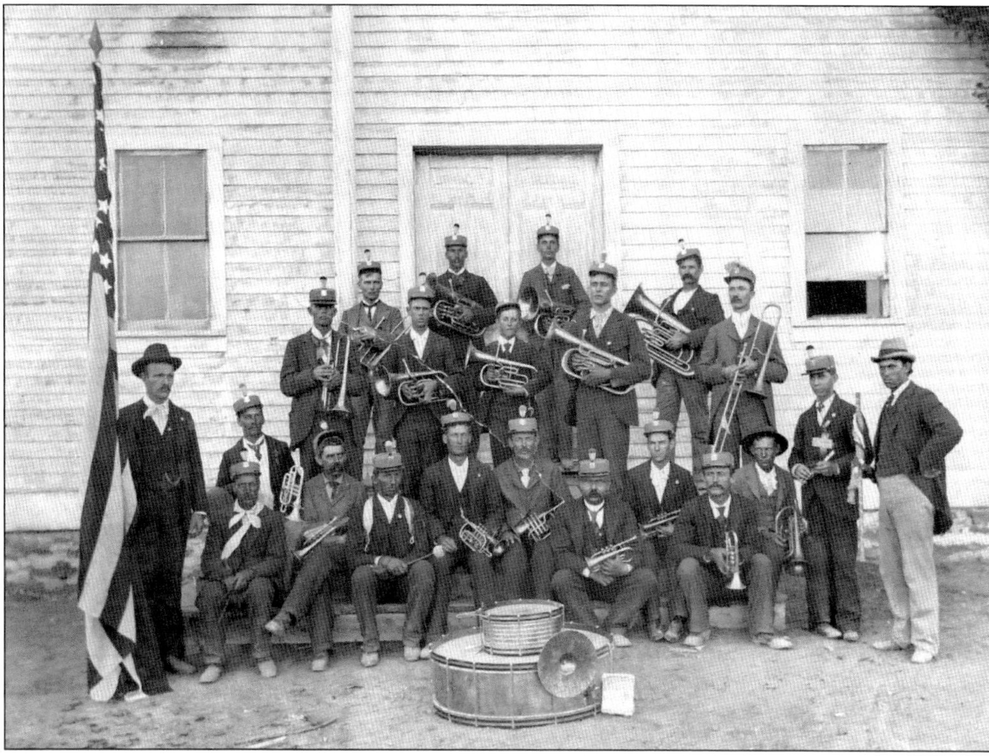

Albion celebrations were complete with the music of the county band. In 1895, this band included Bill Yeaman (with the flag). Others on the roster were, in no particular order, Frank Tramner, Ed Ramma, Milus Robison, Sam Perrins, Joe Stout, Bill Adams, William Quinn, A. S. Abbott, Frank Tremayne, Herbert DuMas, Dick Davis, Bill Hummell, George Cook, John Hansen, Matt Tremayne, John Bland, and Sam Cook. When Burley had its town site sale on May 1, 1905, a seven-piece band came from Albion for the festivities. (Courtesy of Verlene Powell.)

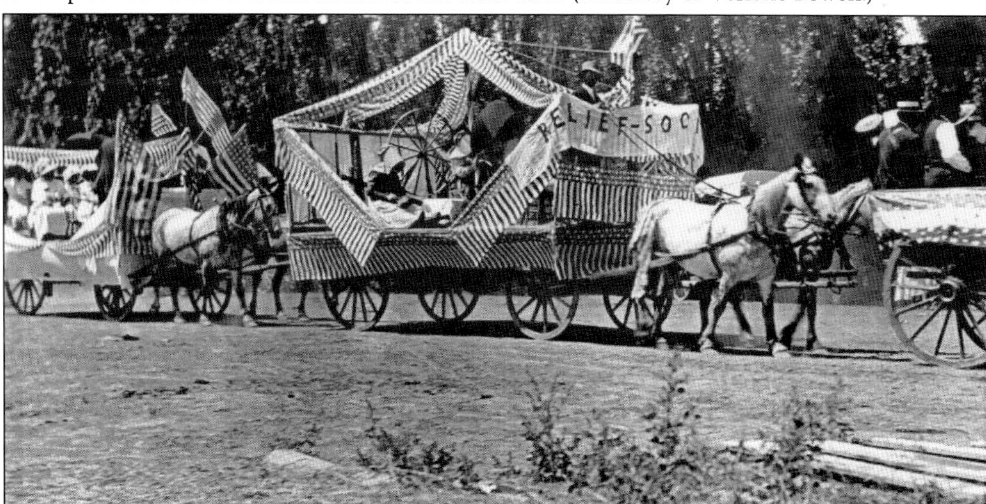

Parades have always been an important part of Cassia County celebrations. The towns with large LDS populations, such as Oakley, celebrated July 24, Pioneer Day. Albion has always celebrated the Fourth of July. This parade of 1915 was no exception. (Courtesy of Verlene Powell.)

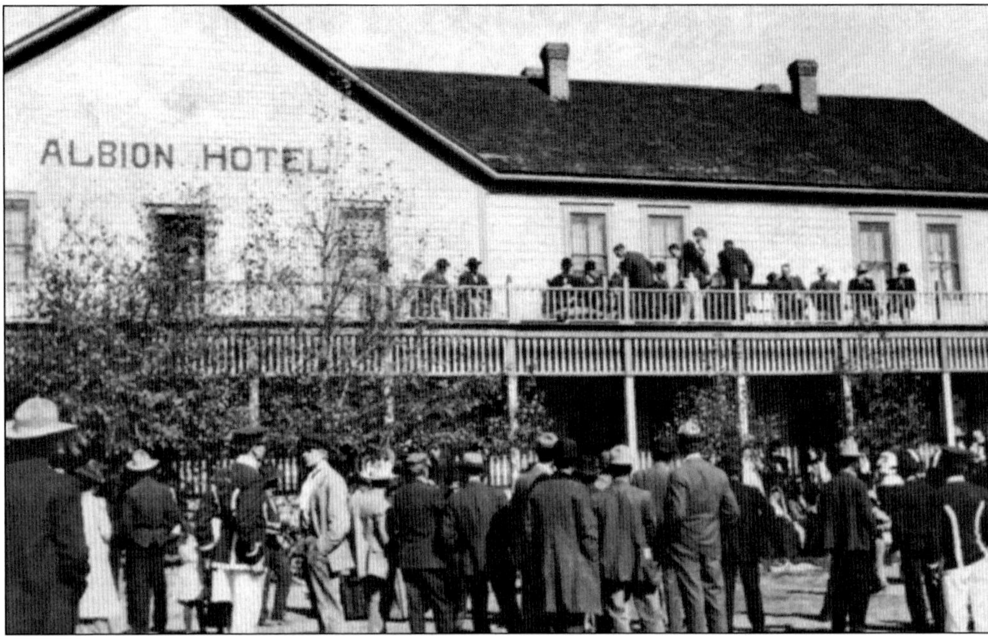

The Albion Hotel was built in the late 1880s. It was always considered a first-class establishment. Many prominent people stayed here. This is believed to be a political rally. The hotel burned down in 1914. (Courtesy of Verlene Powell.)

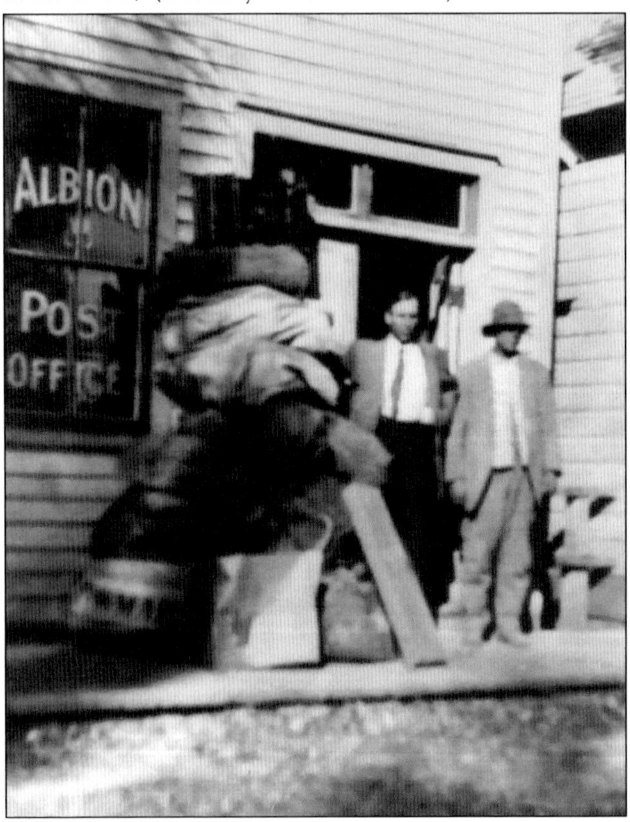

The post office had many locations through the years. Although Marsh Basin had at least two previous postmasters, the first postmaster appointed for Albion was Charles Cobb. Two mail deliveries came each day. One stage carried mail to and from Burley and one came and went to Conant and Bridge. The mail load was very heavy, in part because of the college.

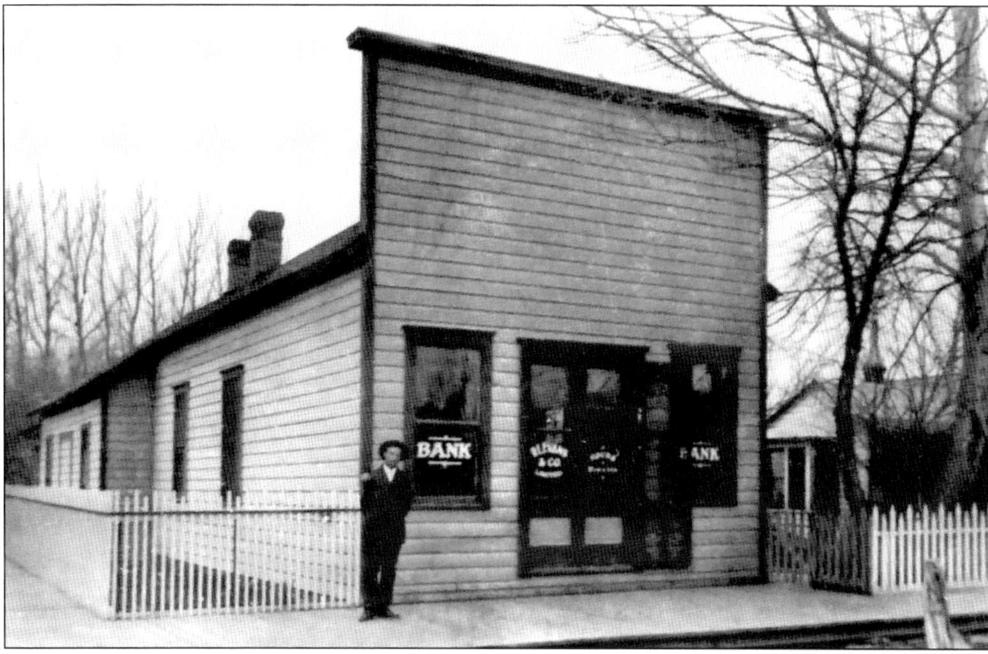

Cassia County's oldest banking institution is D. L. Evans and Company. Founded in 1904, this financial institution weathered many economic storms. It was one of two banks in the county that made it through the Great Depression. The bank helped the town of Albion through economic reverses when the county seat was moved to Burley in 1919.

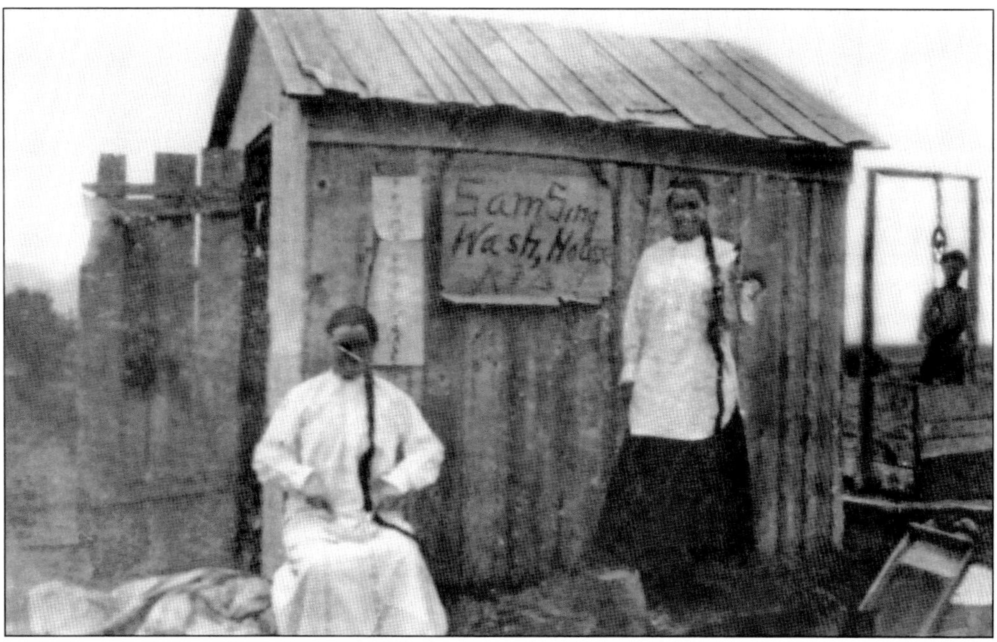

Sam Sing came to Albion with his wife, "China Mary," in the 1880s. The census listed him in 1900 as a laundryman and in 1910 as a gardener. For many years after his wife died, he would take small lotus cakes to her unmarked grave in the old Albion Cemetery.

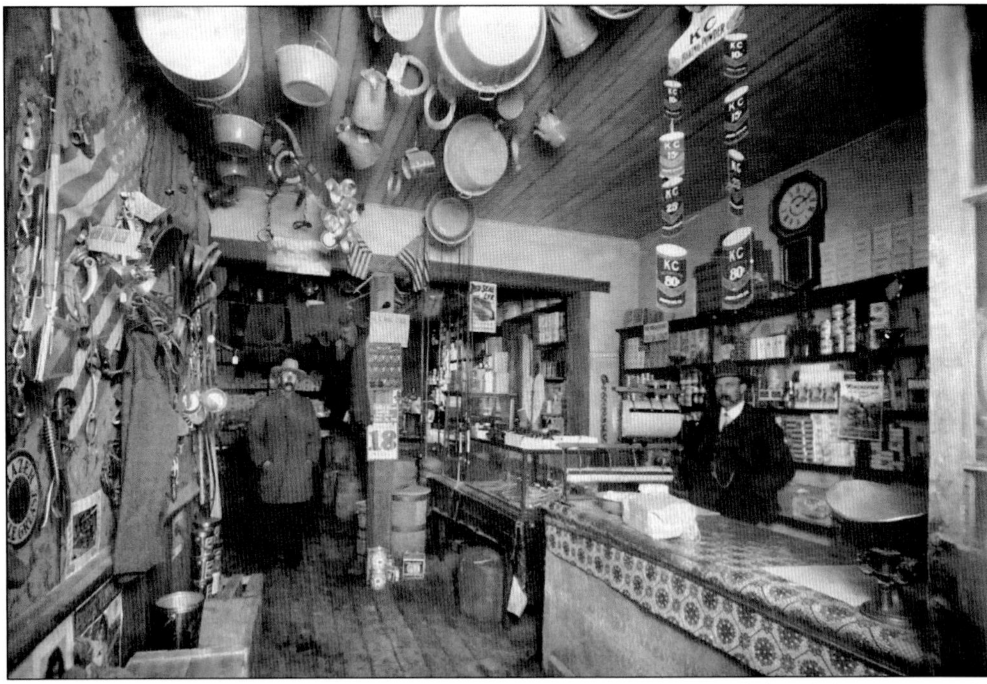

The Snodgrass general store sold just about anything. J. V. Snodgrass is behind the counter. The date on the calendar is Monday, February 18, 1907. (Courtesy of Ann Wight.)

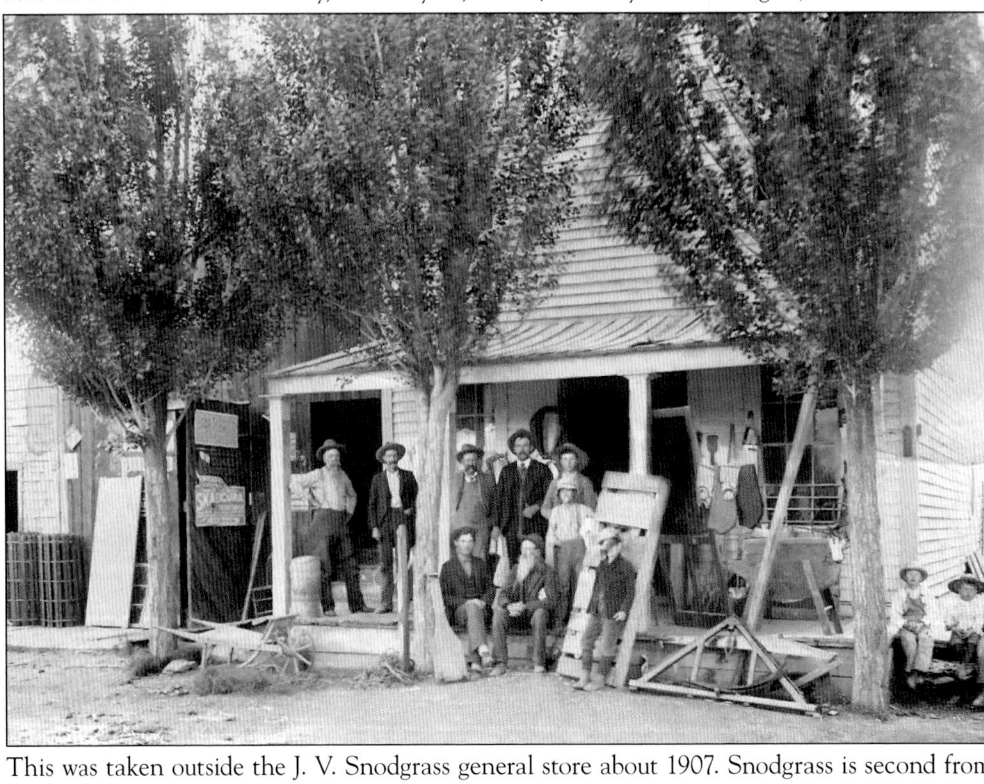

This was taken outside the J. V. Snodgrass general store about 1907. Snodgrass is second from left. (Courtesy of Ann Wight.)

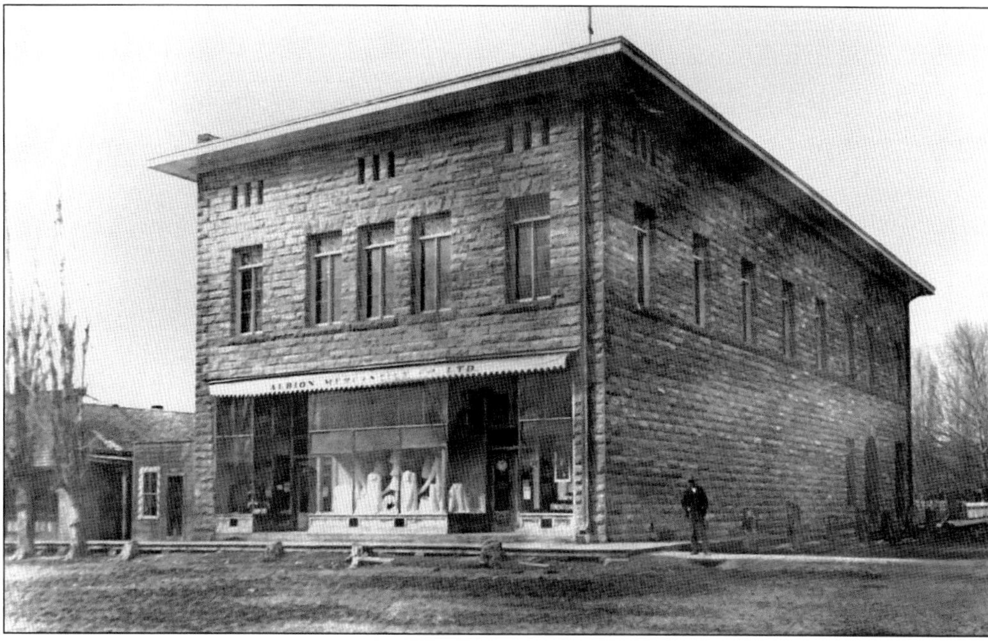

The Albion Mercantile Department Store was built around 1900. The store was advertised as "large and spacious." The upper floor was a large dance hall. The building burned down in 1926. (Both courtesy of Verlene Powell.)

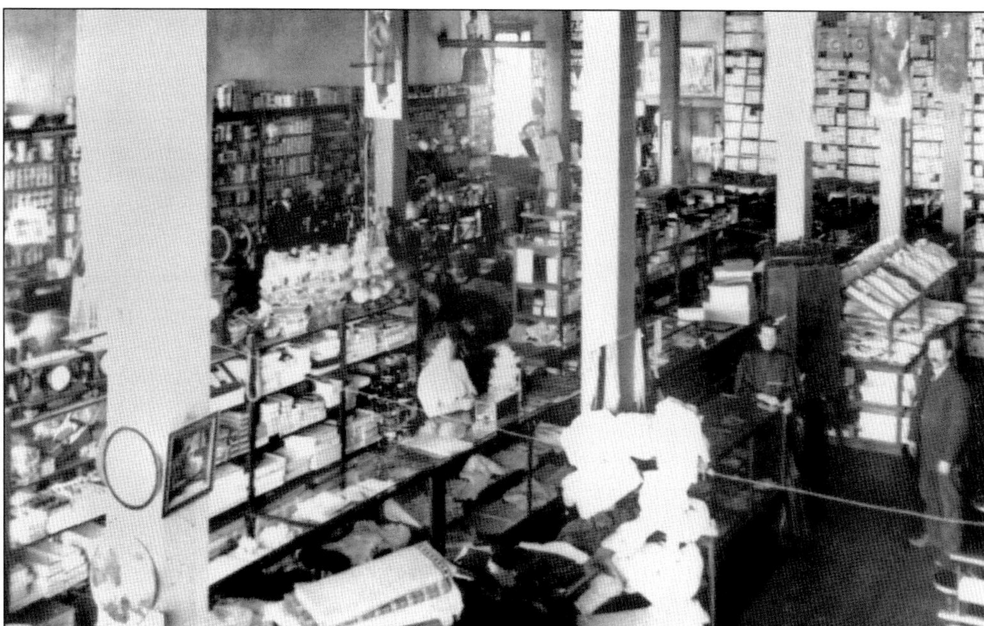

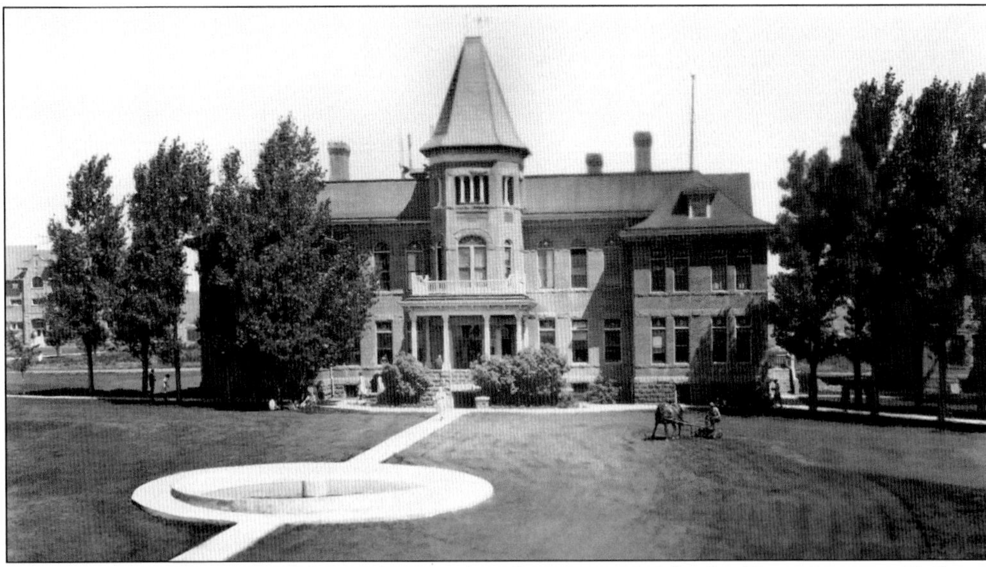

Albion State Normal School (ASNS) opened its doors in 1893. This building, Swanger Hall, was named after J. Frank Swanger, the first president of the college. It was the administrative building and was later used for classrooms until it burned down in 1947. By 1932, forty-three percent of all grade-school teachers in Idaho had graduated from ASNS. The college continued to graduate students in the teaching profession until it closed in 1951. Two of the more prominent graduates were Terrel Bell (class of 1946), who was secretary of education under Ronald Reagan, and Harold B. Lee (class of 1917), who later became president of the Church of Jesus Christ of Latter-day Saints in 1972. Notice the horse-drawn lawn mower. (Courtesy of Verlene Powell.)

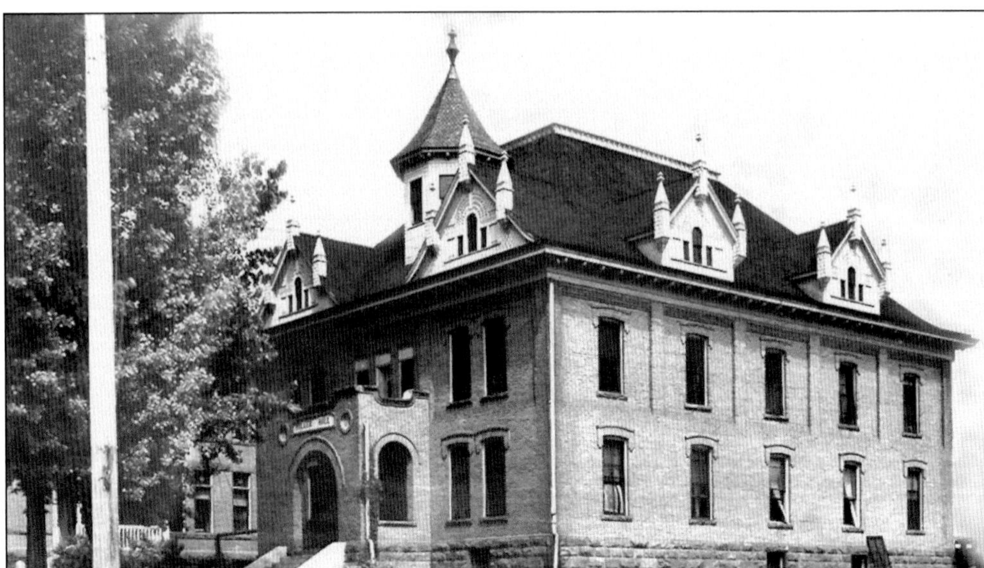

The Miller Hall on the Albion State Normal School campus was named after Josiah Miller. It was built as a ladies' dormitory and was later used as a men's dormitory. In 2008, it was restored, and it is now a conference center and bed-and-breakfast. (Courtesy of Verlene Powell.)

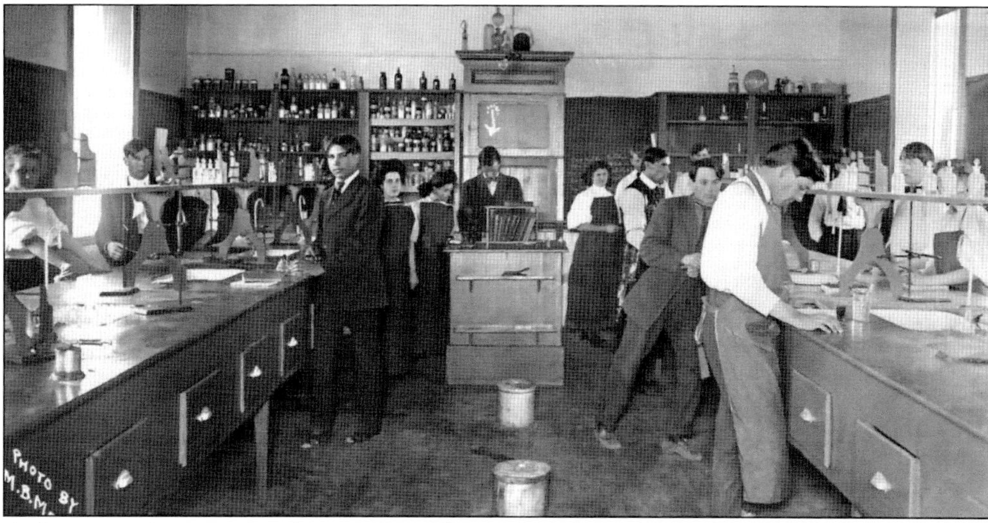

A chemistry class is pictured in 1908 at Albion State Normal School.

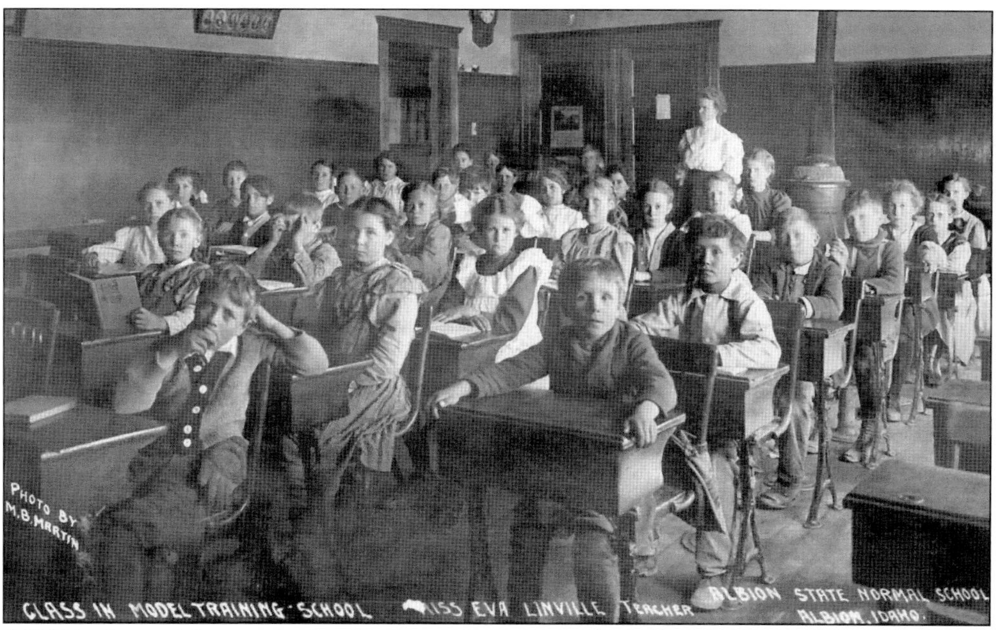

ASNS had a model training school right on the campus where the college students could student teach. The children gave the college students a real education in teaching discipline, as they had a new teacher each year.

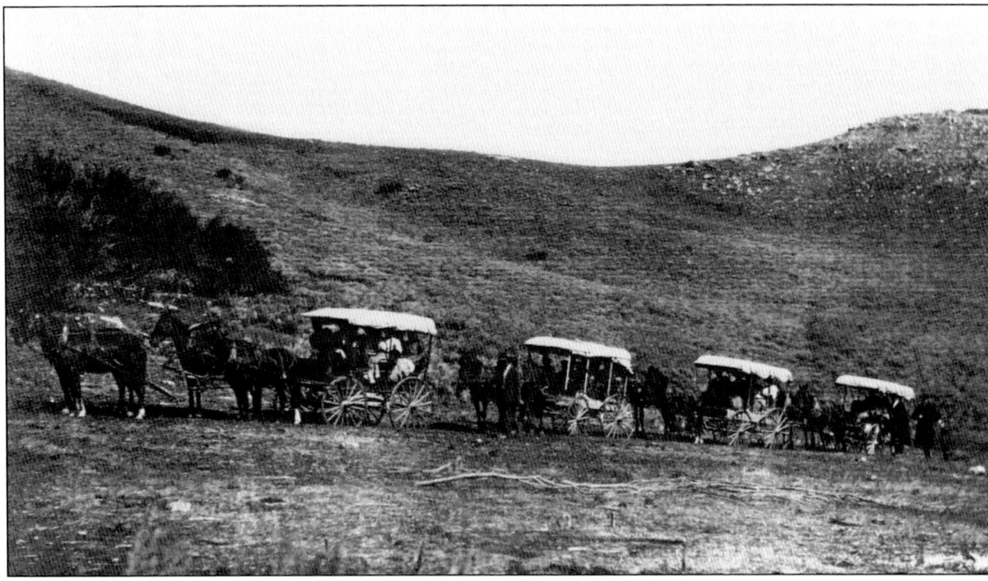

This string of buggies going to Albion was carrying Albion State Normal School students probably coming from the train depot in Burley before the school year started.

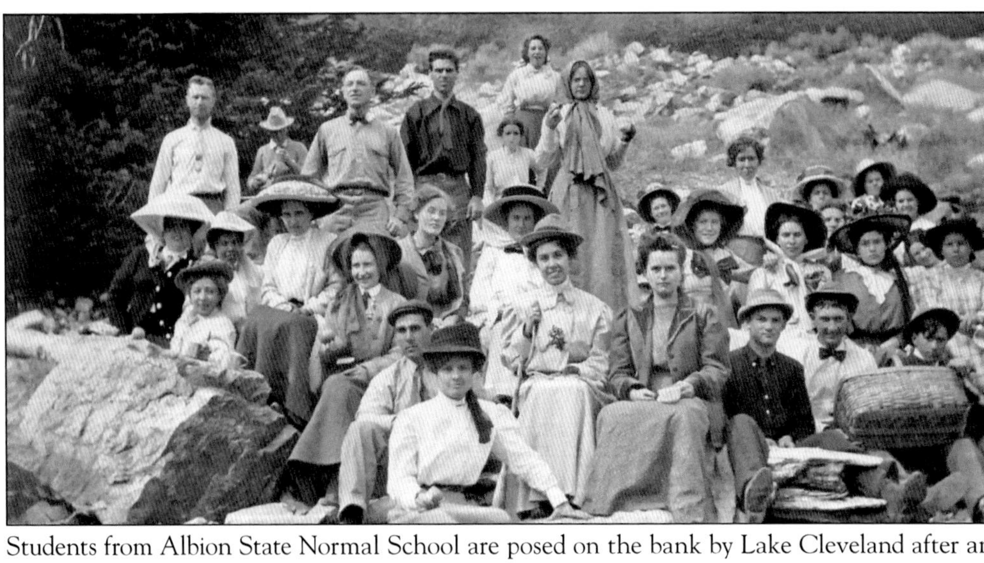

Students from Albion State Normal School are posed on the bank by Lake Cleveland after an outing in 1910.

Two

Almo

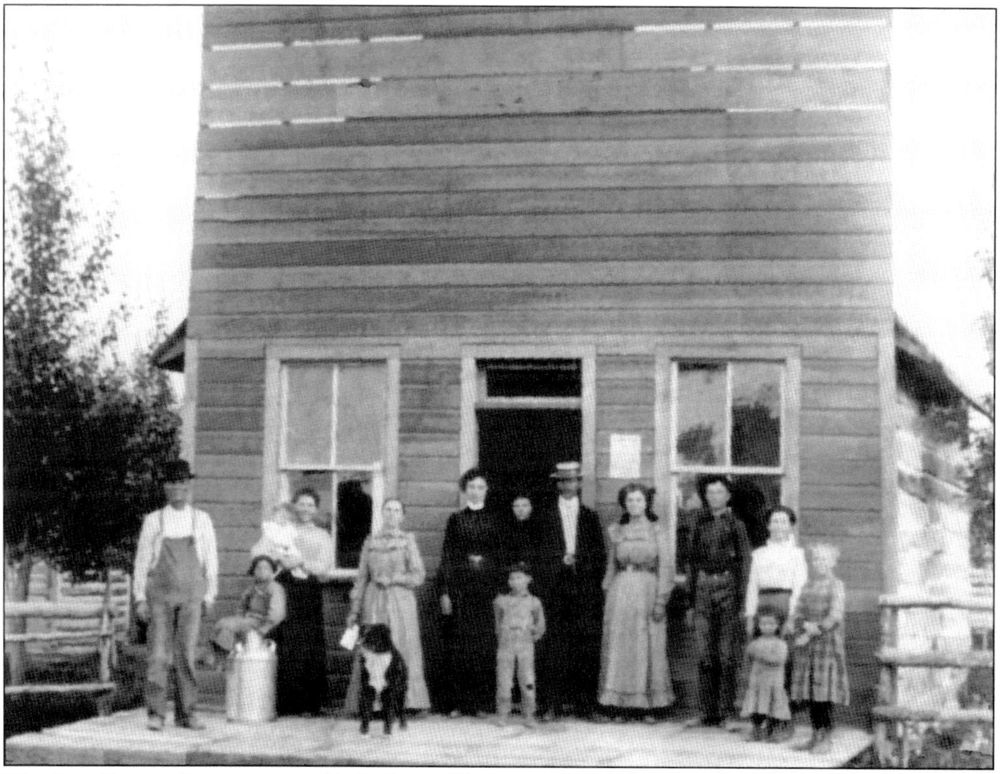

The first Eames Store was established in 1893 by brothers William and Harry Eames. Mail was delivered here. This picture shows the second Eames Store, built by Harry Eames. Pictured from left to right are Harry Eames; his wife, Julia; and their two children; Dorcas King, wife of T. O. King; Nellie King, daughter of T. O. King; two unidentified; Harold King, son of T. O. King; Charlotte Eames, daughter of Harry Eames; Ted Eames, son of Harry Eames; and three unidentified. It was located in the same place as the Tracy Store is now. (Courtesy of Phyllis Tracy.)

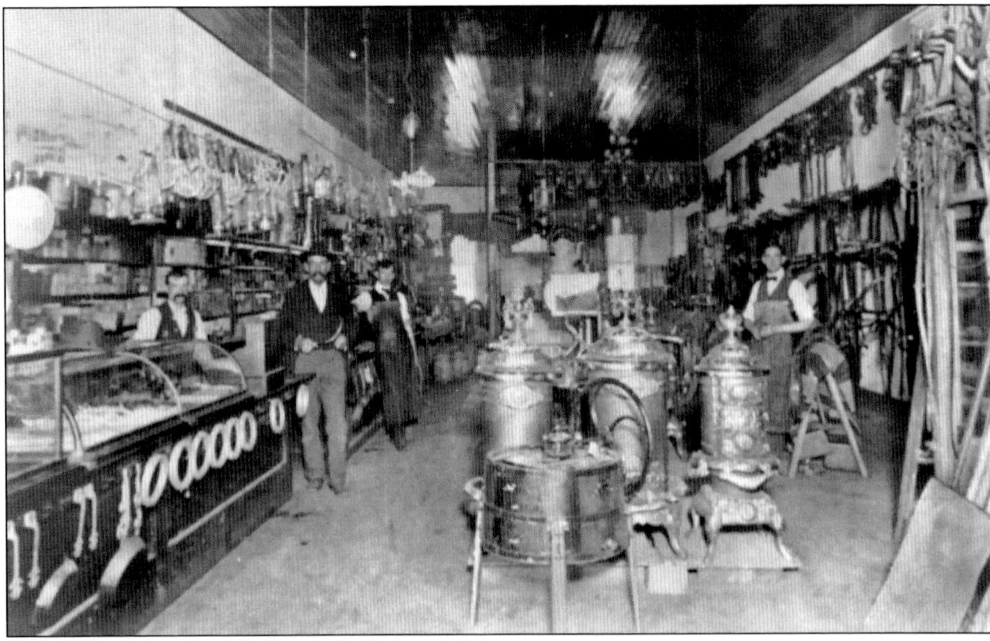

The first store in Almo was the Myron Durfee store. Freight came from the railhead in Kelton, Utah.

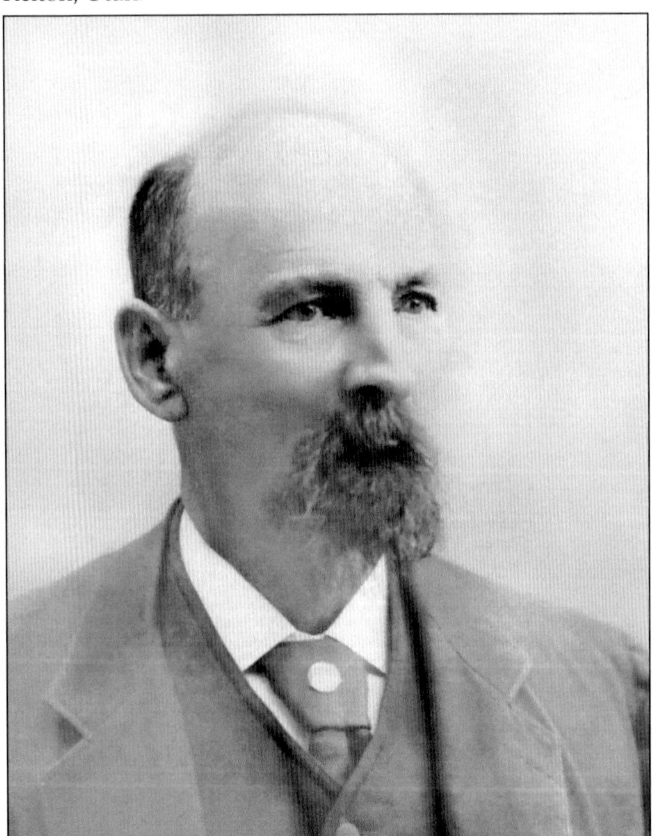

Myron Bushnell Durfee came to the Almo area with two sons and homesteaded 200 acres in the valley. He left them to tend the sheep and other livestock they had brought with them and went back to Utah for his wife and younger children. Upon his return, they built a home near the Almo Creek. (Courtesy of Jeanette Babbitt.)

Pictured in this double wedding are brides Irene Cahoon (left) and Jessie Richardson (right) and grooms Warren Richardson (left) and William Denison Cahoon. A brother and sister married another sister and brother. (Courtesy of Jeanette Babbitt.)

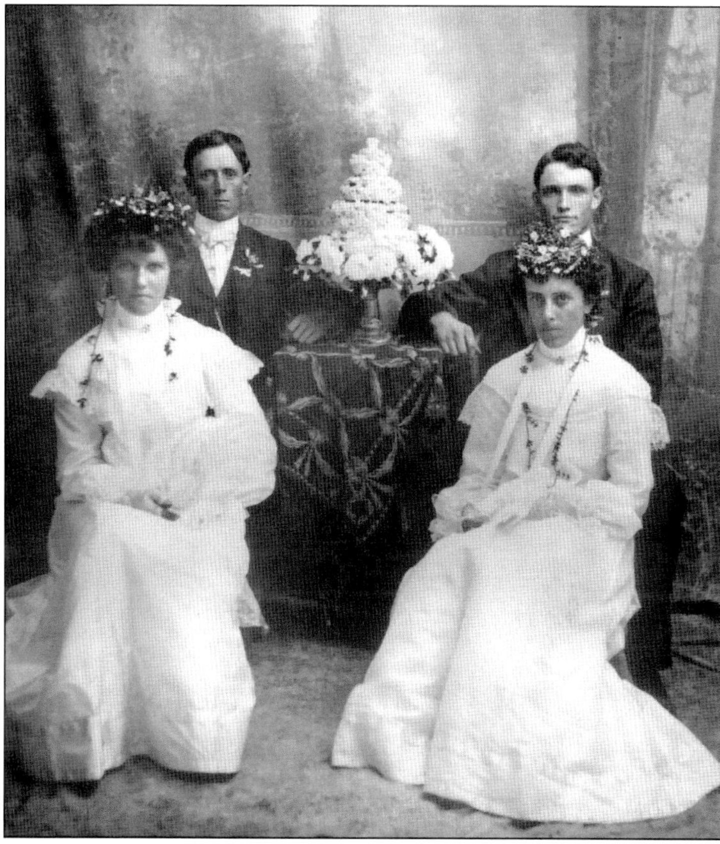

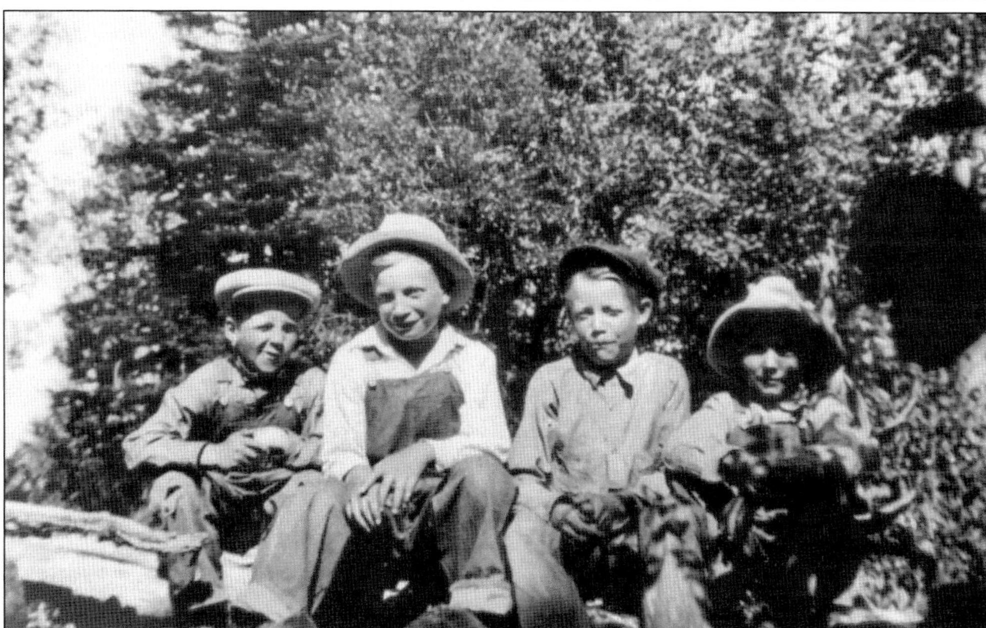

These four boys were neighbors. Pictured are, from left to right, Neil Durfee, Joey Wake, Ivan Durfee, and Cleon Durfee. (Courtesy of Jeanette Babbitt.)

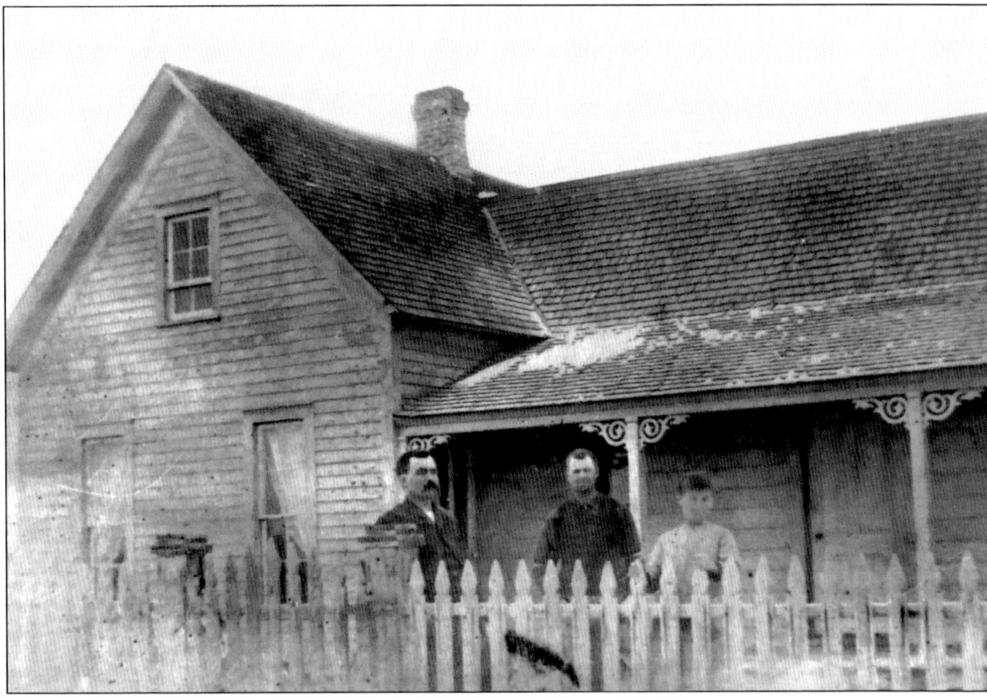

Jacob Paden owned a sawmill in the canyon above Almo in the 1880s. He built the first shingled home in town, complete with gingerbread trim and a picket fence. (Courtesy of Jeanette Babbitt.)

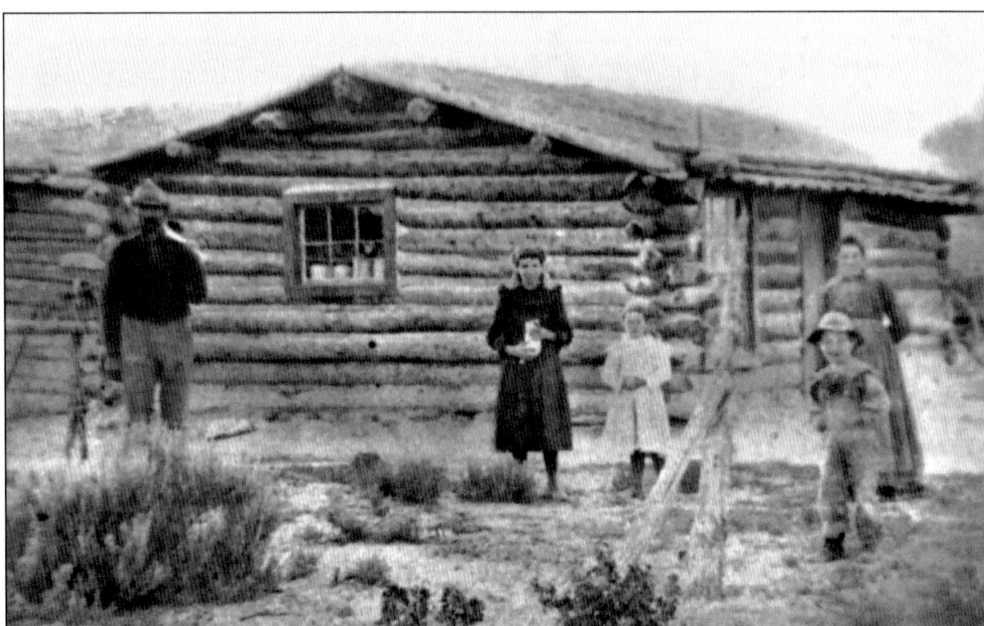

As the settlers came to the Almo valley, this was the most common type of home they built. This home was built by Thomas Owen King. (Courtesy of Jeanette Babbitt.)

Thomas Owen King was a pony express rider in 1860. A silver knife was issued by the Pony Express Company. A pistol was usually issued, but the U.S. government had run out of them. Although the company advertised for 16-year-old orphans, he was able to get the job at 20 years old. (Courtesy of Phyllis Tracy.)

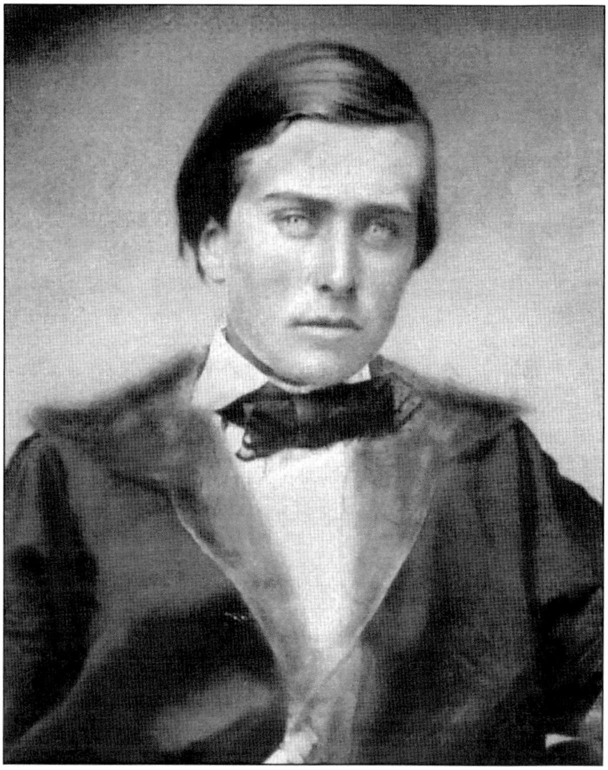

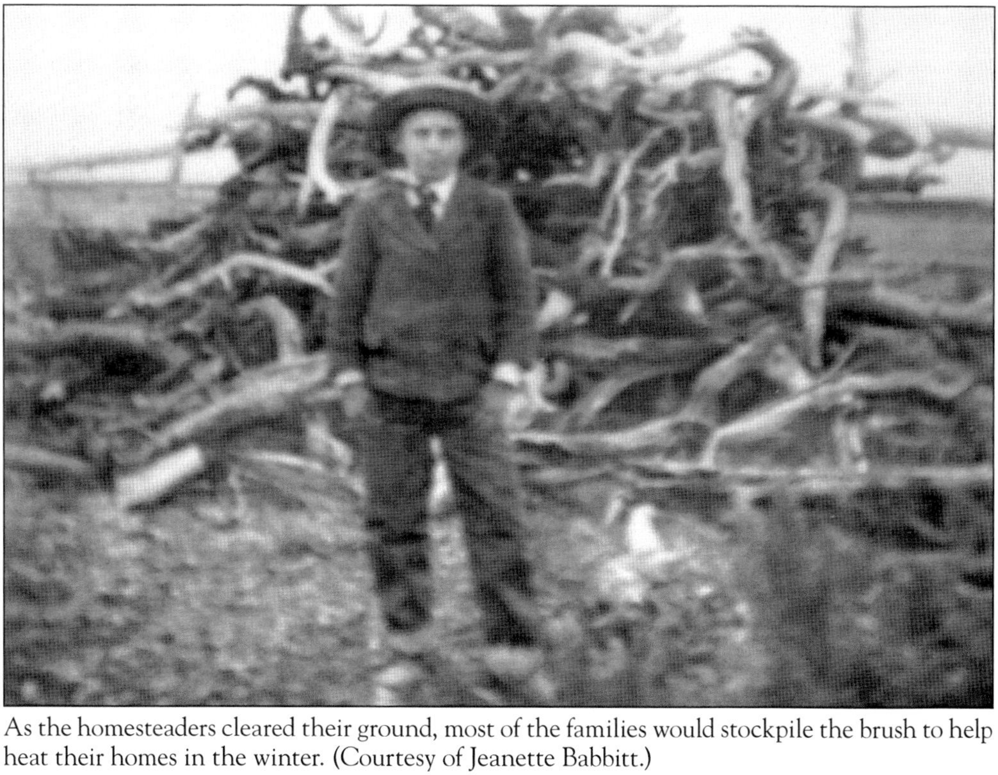

As the homesteaders cleared their ground, most of the families would stockpile the brush to help heat their homes in the winter. (Courtesy of Jeanette Babbitt.)

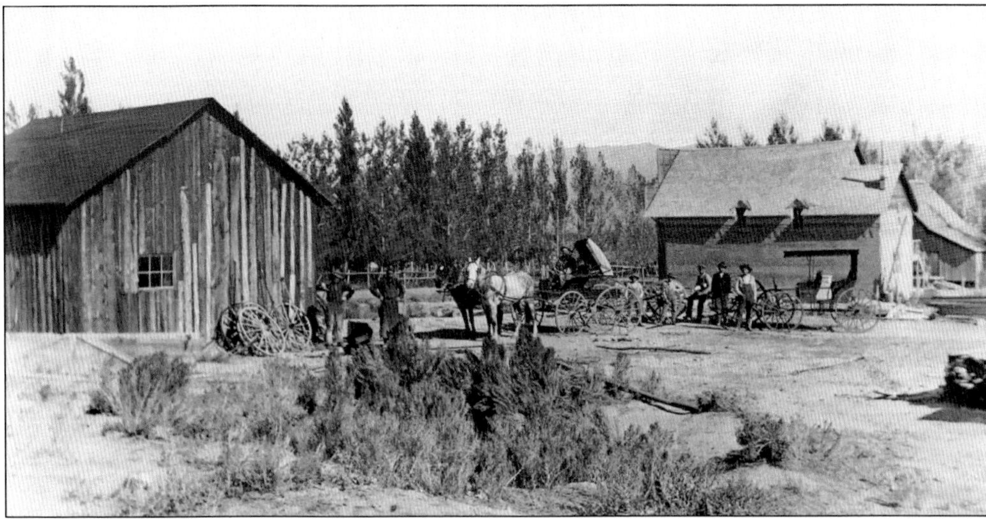

This image was taken in 1894 of the blacksmith shop on the left and the Eames-Tracy Store on the right. The blacksmith was Wid Fryer from Deweyville. He stayed for two years. His helper, Arthur Green, ran the bellows and was paid 25¢ a day. Pictured from left to right are Arthur Green, Wid Fryer, Jess Jones in buggy, Louis Eames, George Eames, Walter Bruesh, Dennie Durfee, and Chris Green. (Courtesy of Phyllis Tracy.)

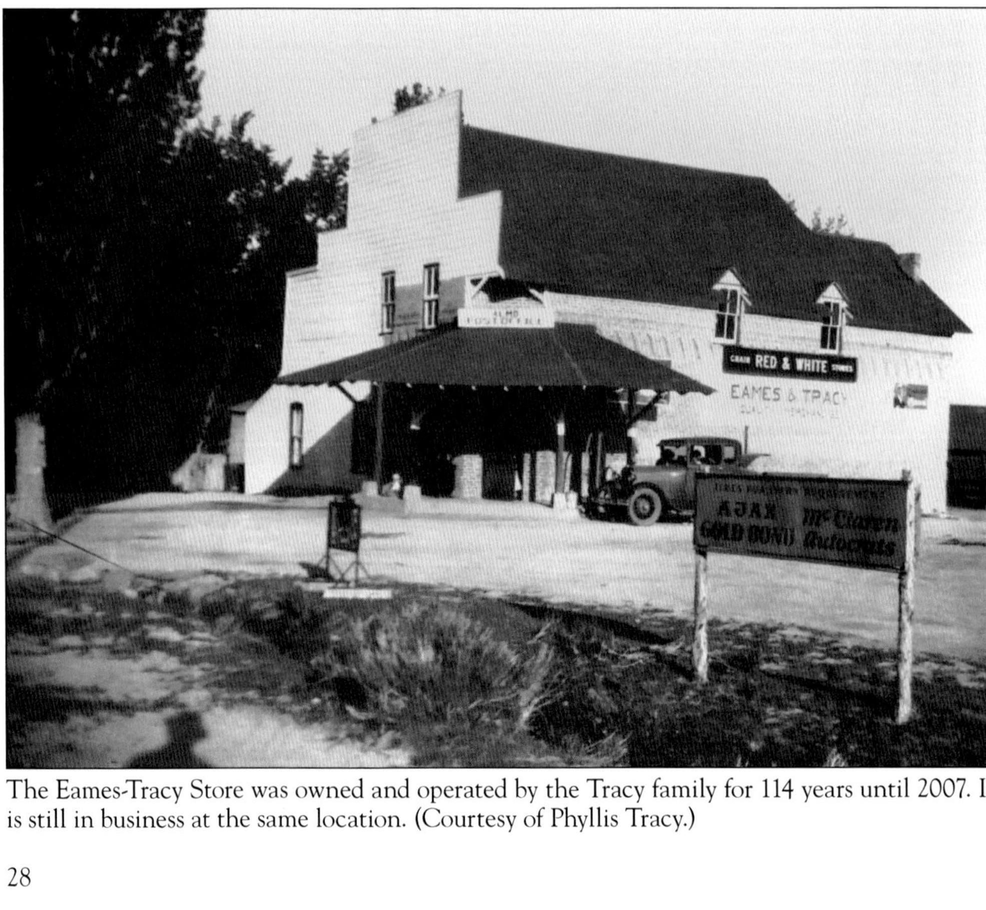

The Eames-Tracy Store was owned and operated by the Tracy family for 114 years until 2007. It is still in business at the same location. (Courtesy of Phyllis Tracy.)

The Almo LDS Church was built in 1902 by mostly volunteer labor.

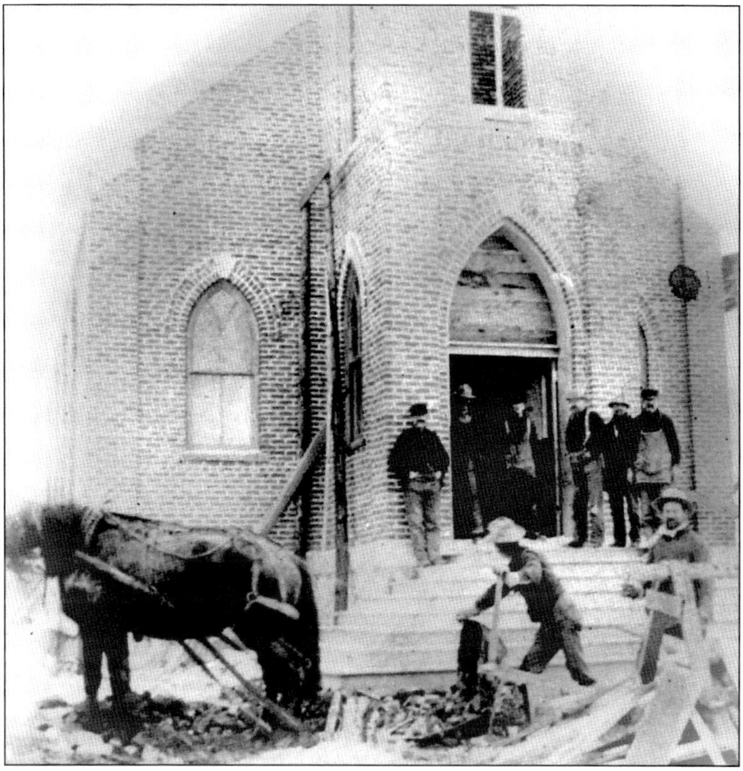

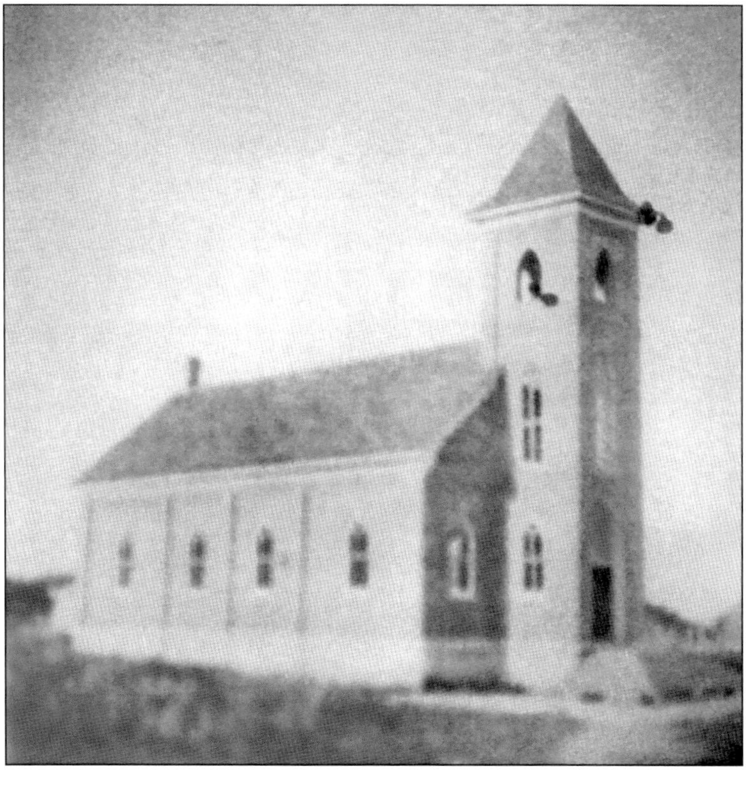

When it was finished in 1902, the Almo LDS Church became the community gathering spot for all residents.

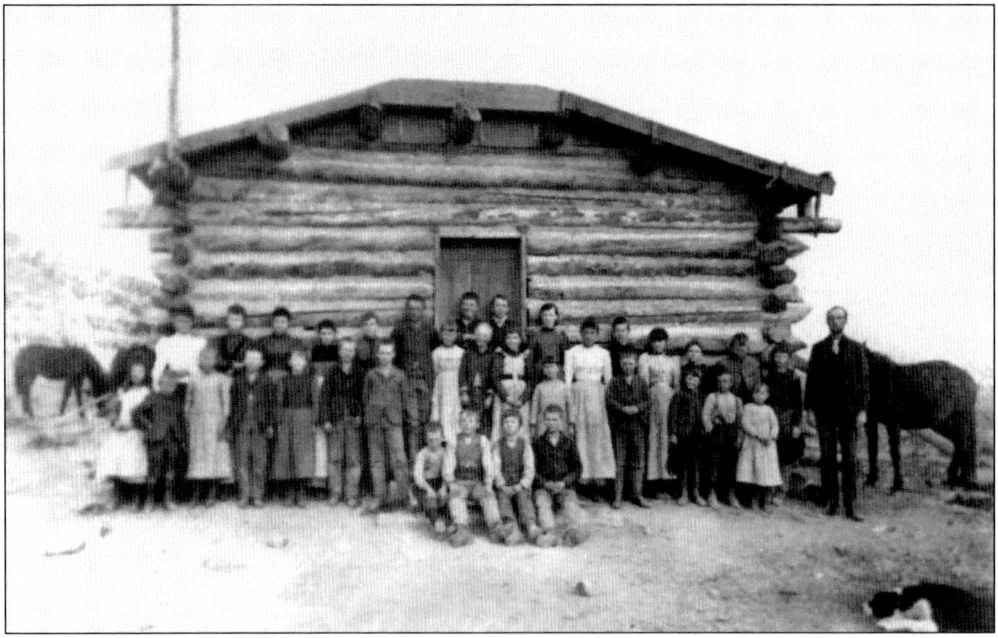

The Cove School was the first school in the community of Almo. This picture was taken in 1896.

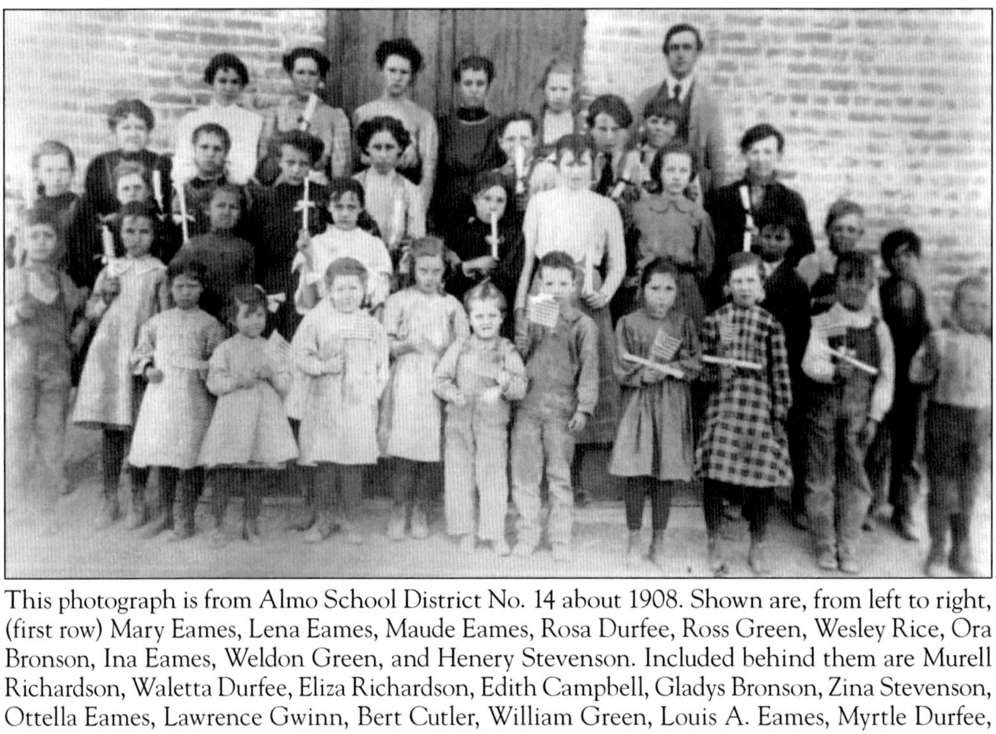

This photograph is from Almo School District No. 14 about 1908. Shown are, from left to right, (first row) Mary Eames, Lena Eames, Maude Eames, Rosa Durfee, Ross Green, Wesley Rice, Ora Bronson, Ina Eames, Weldon Green, and Henery Stevenson. Included behind them are Murell Richardson, Waletta Durfee, Eliza Richardson, Edith Campbell, Gladys Bronson, Zina Stevenson, Ottella Eames, Lawrence Gwinn, Bert Cutler, William Green, Louis A. Eames, Myrtle Durfee, Viola Eames, Ellen Cutler, and Mary Ann ?. The rest are unidentified.

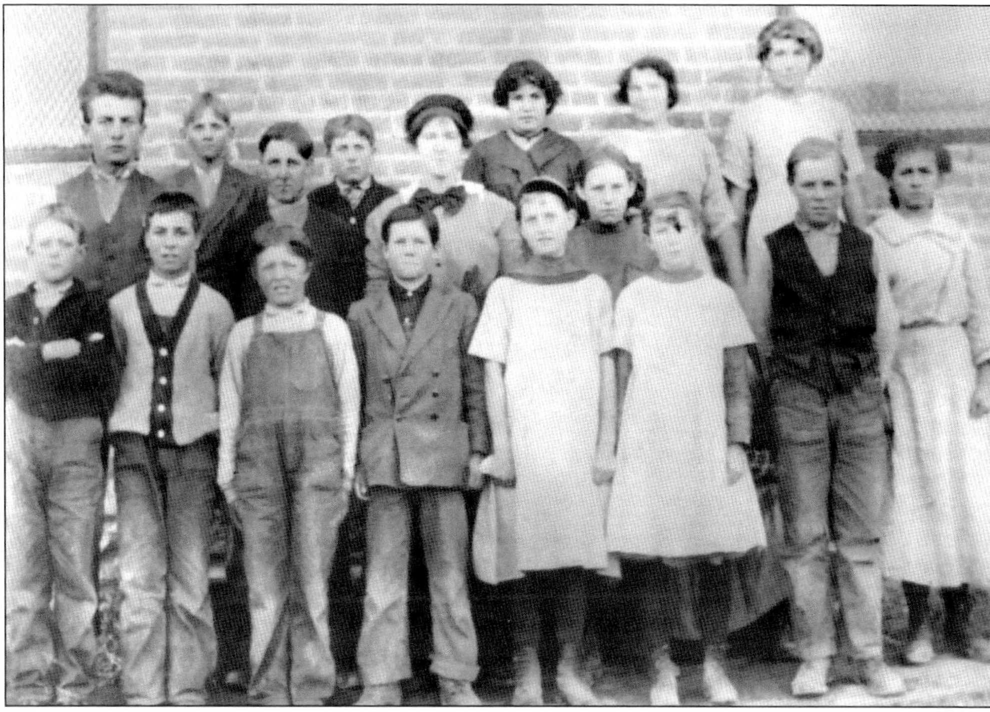

Pictured here are Almo School children in 1912.

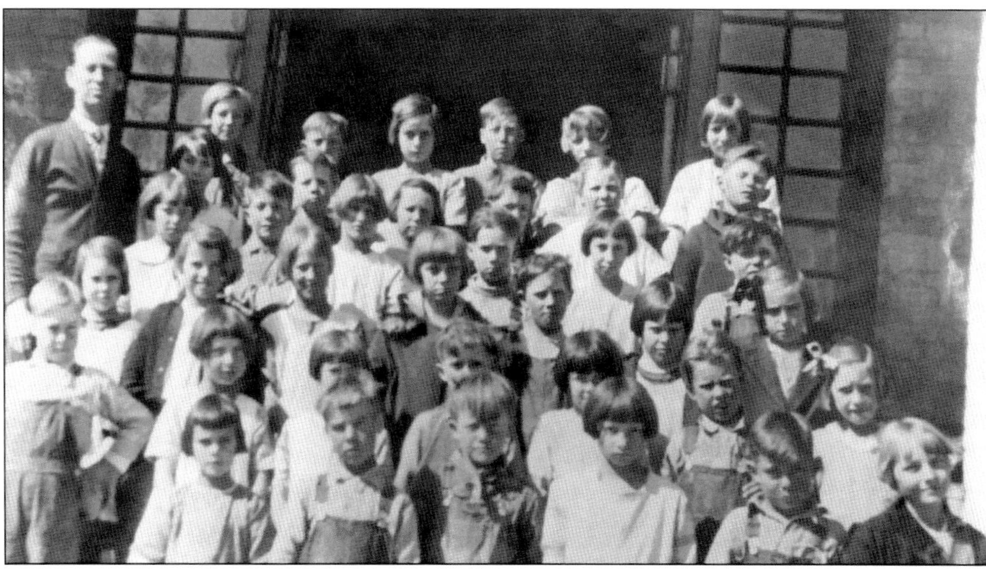

At the Almo School in 1925 are, from left to right, (first row) Chloe Taylor, Ovis Durfee, Ivan Durfee, June Bateman, Chad Jones, and Zoa Durfee; (second row) Orin Durfee, Edith Ward, Edris Ward, Darwin Eames, Delia Sheridan, Calvin Lowe, and Mary Bruesch; (third row) La Fawn Jones, Meryle Horne, Norma Hansen, Leatha Cahoon, Merlyn Horne, Ruth Jones, and Lois Bruesch; (fourth row) Elva Durfee, Keith Jones, Edith Taylor, Alfred Ward, Dixie Belnap, and Asael Thompson; (fifth row) Lucy Bateman, Joseph Barrett, Naomi Durfee, Nathaniel Wake, Louise Lloyd, and Dwayne Ward; (sixth row) teacher Norman Steele, Erica Lowe, Rodney Eames, Hazel Ward, Jessie Lloyd, Fern Durfee, and Marjorie Taylor.

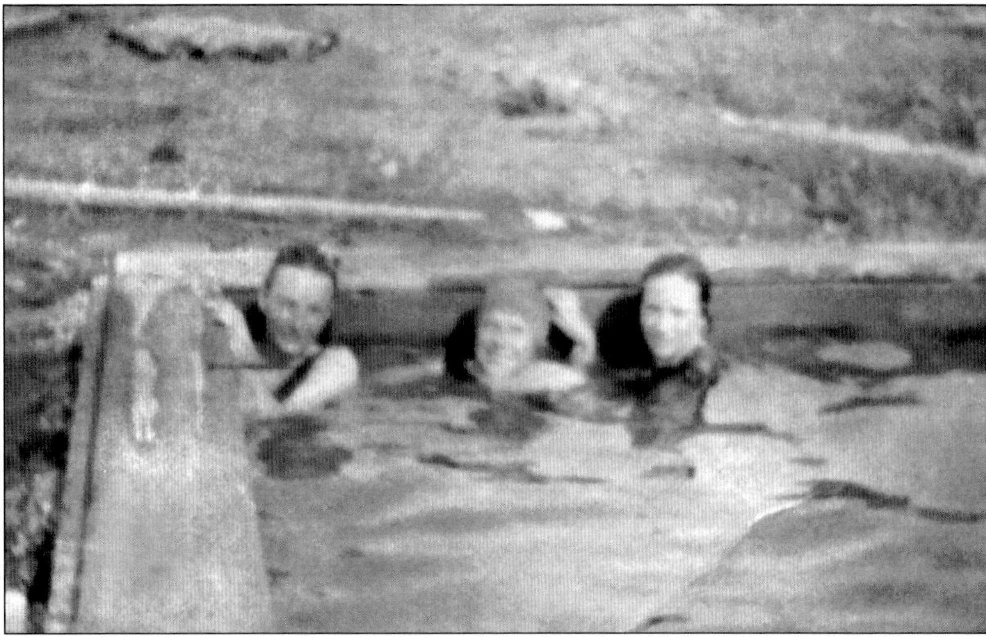

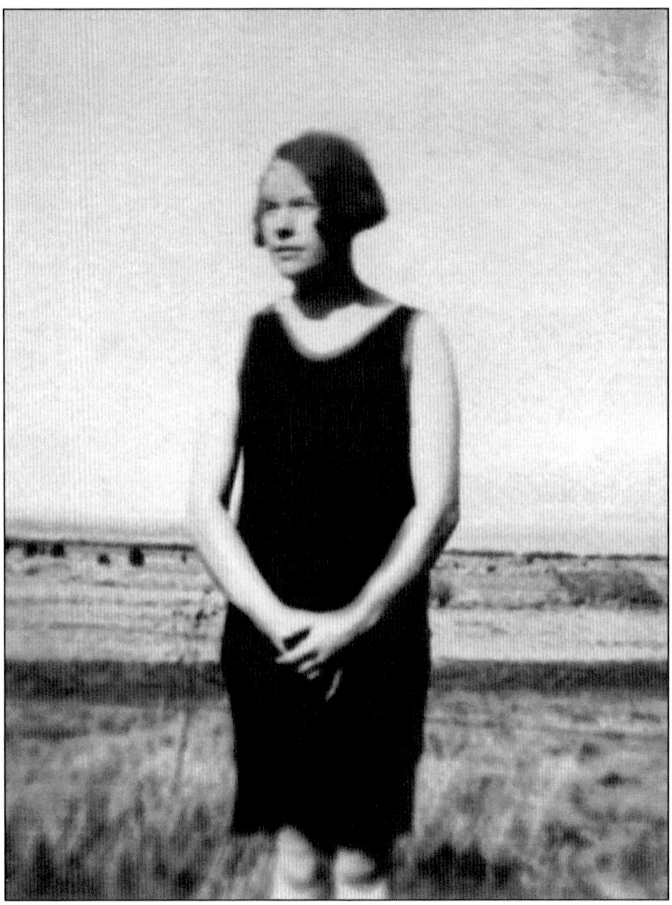

Journal entries from pioneers who traveled through the valley told of marshes that were quite likely created by warm springs. Henry Miller and Rosa Durfee developed a natural spring of warm water into a swimming resort in the early 1900s. The unidentified swimsuit model is wearing her modest black swimsuit.

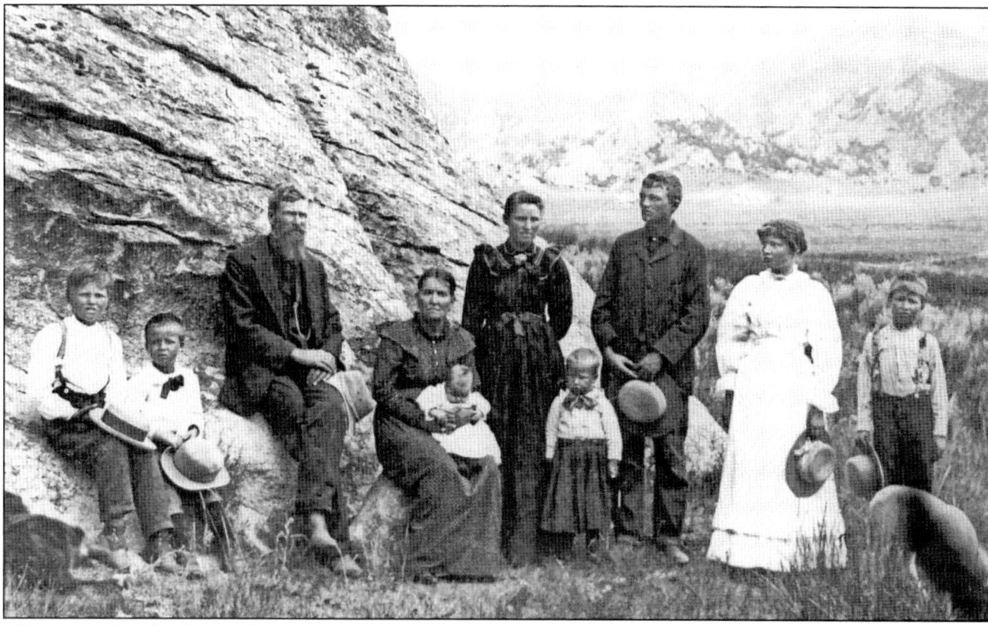

The Ben Brackenbury family of Almo lived just a short distance from the City of Rocks. This was a popular location for a family outing.

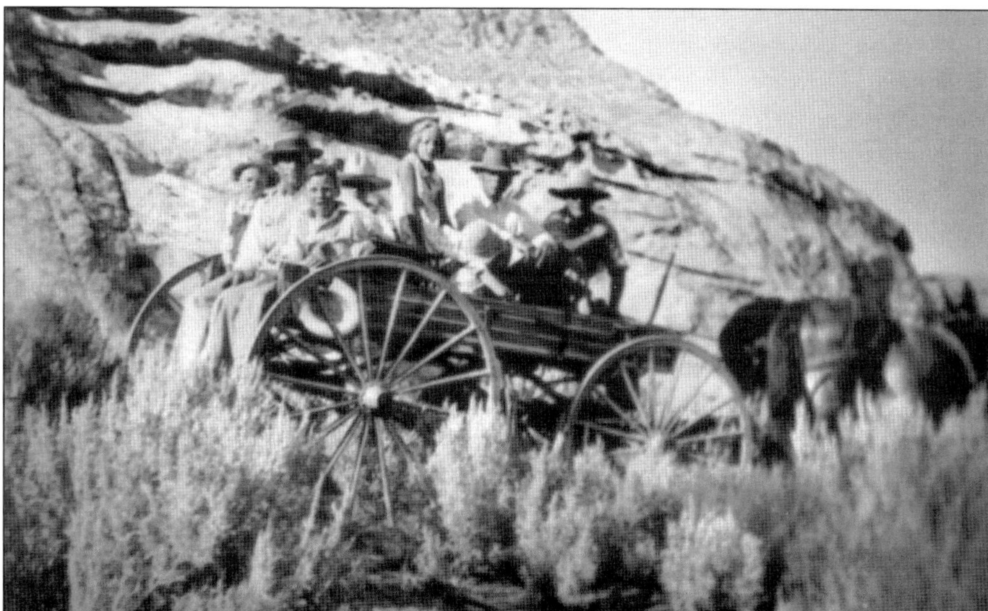

During the 1920 drought, area cattle ranchers sold all the cattle they could and sent them to the railroad in Oakley, then bought about 2,000 head of sheep. They formed a company they called the Thumb and Bum Company. The ranchers would send their children to help herd the sheep. Orin Durfee was the main sheepherder; when he was low on supplies, someone would come with provisions, and Durfee would in turn fix a great Dutch oven dinner. This went on into the 1950s. This is an early picture of a group that came to join Durfee. Pictured from left to right are Wayne Durfee, Ivan Leo Durfee, Ivan Durfee Jr., Mary Ann Durfee, Fern Durfee, Gene Durfee, and Keturah Durfee.

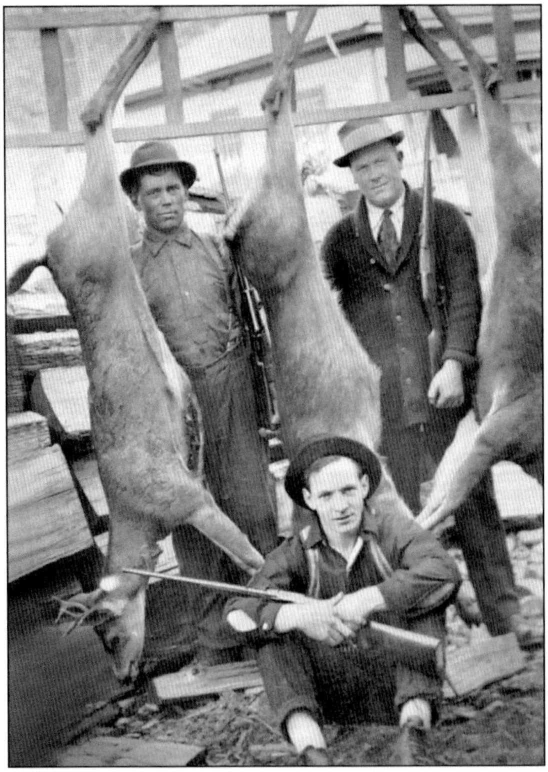

Game was plentiful in the mountains around Almo. People would pay the local men to take them to good hunting spots.

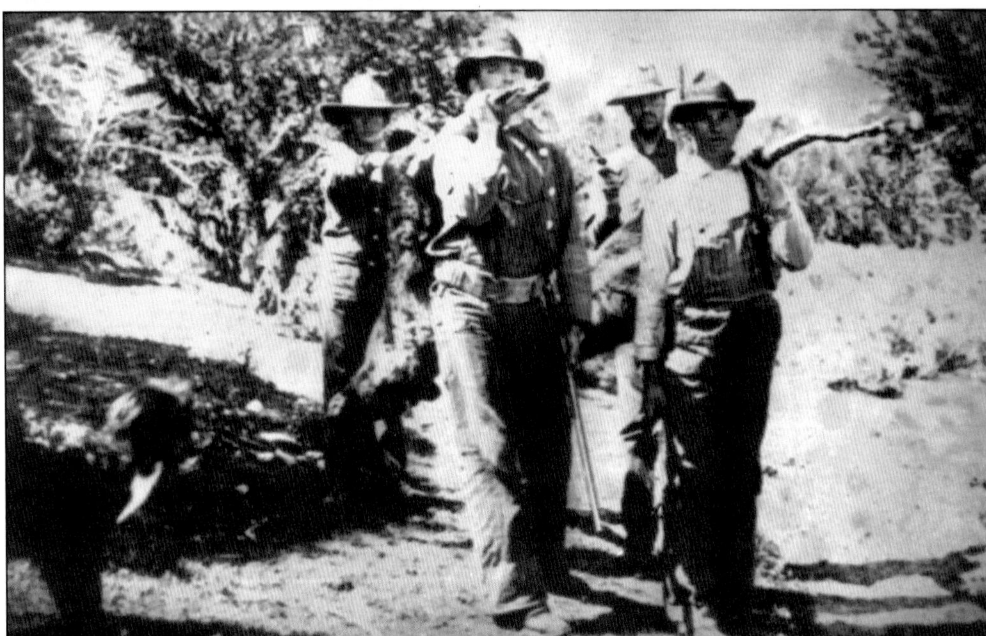

During the early 1900s, ranchers were reporting that a black bear had been sighted and was coming in from the mountains and killing livestock. These men went looking for him and brought home the evidence of their successful hunt. From left to right are, in front, Billy Cahoon and Pate Cahoon, and in back, George Brackenbury and Gordon Edwards. (Courtesy of Jeanette Babbitt.)

Three

BURLEY

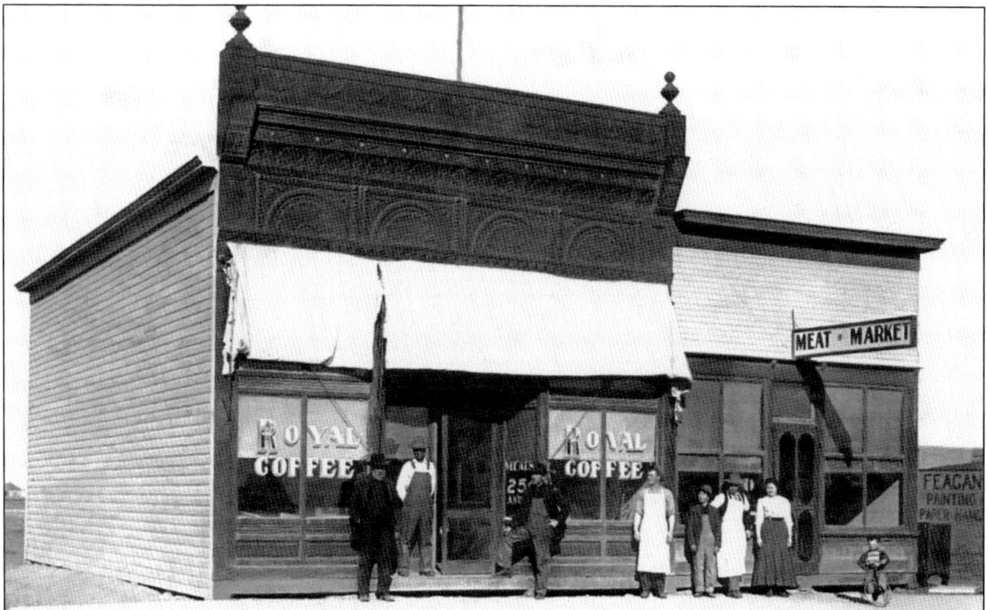

When the town sites went on sale in the new town of Commerce, Francis Marion Cummins, prominent land owner and businessman of Oakley, purchased three business lots on North Overland Avenue. He and his son Cliff owned and operated a restaurant and meat market. They advertised a full meal for 25¢. It was later decided to rename the town after David Burley, a passenger agent for the Oregon Short Line Railroad. Charles Haight, the first postmaster, had his Burley Mercantile and post office in this same location just south of the railroad depot. (Courtesy of Jamie Larsen.)

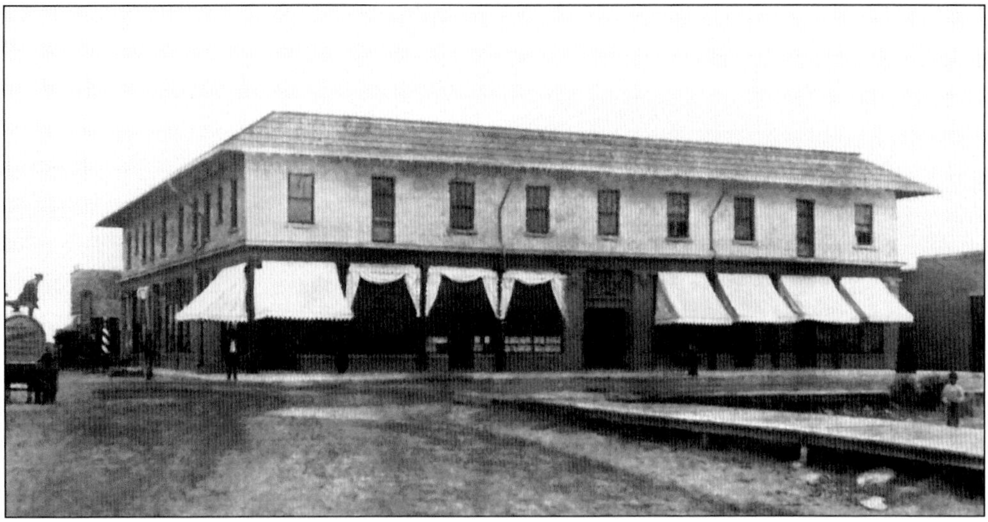

The Burley Hotel stood on the northwest corner of Overland Avenue and Main Street until it burned on January 31, 1913. The Bank of Commerce was in this building at the time. It reopened just a few days later in another location with business as usual. Notice the wooden sidewalks.

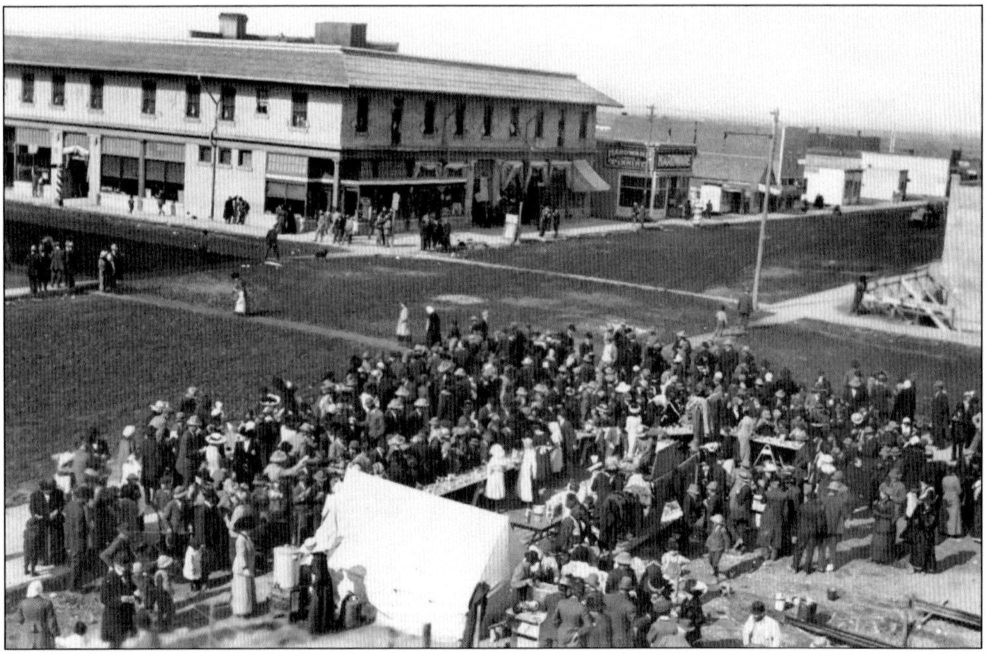

In 1912, the town of Burley was aggressively campaigning to be the seat of Cassia County. They invited the town of Oakley to a dinner, held on the corner of Main Street and Overland Avenue, to persuade the Oakley residents to vote for Burley. Oakley residents came to the dinner, but the loyalty to Albion was too strong, and they didn't support Burley. In 1919, Burley did become the county seat.

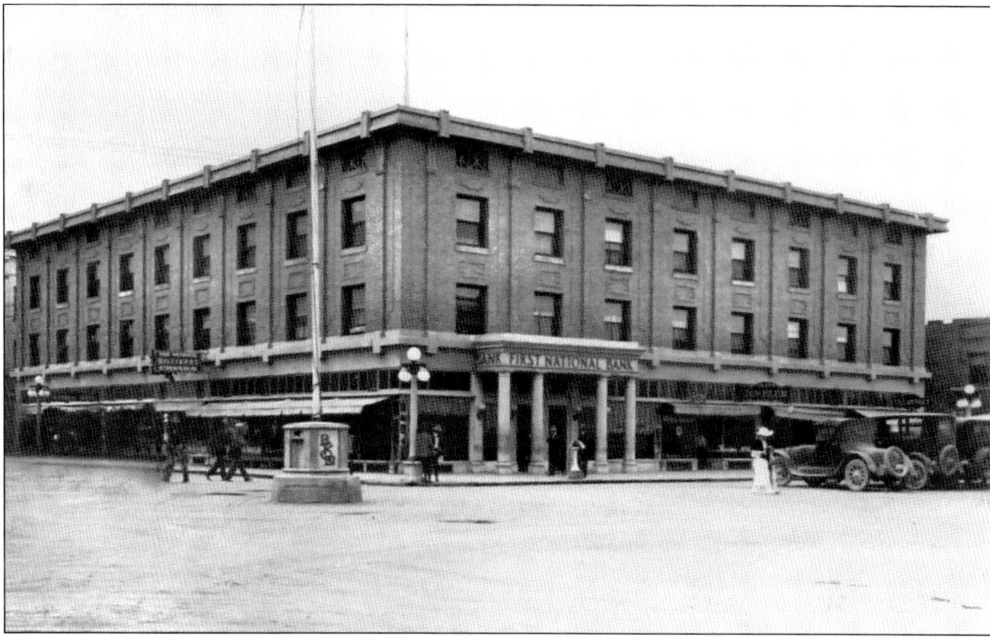

After the Hotel Burley burned in 1913, the National Hotel, pictured here, was built on the same site. It was completed in 1916. It was larger and grander and soon became the gathering place for many local as well as national conventions. The First National Bank and later the Cassia National Bank was on the first floor. There were many other businesses, such as a barbershop and coffee shop on the ground floor. This landmark hotel was torn down in 1973.

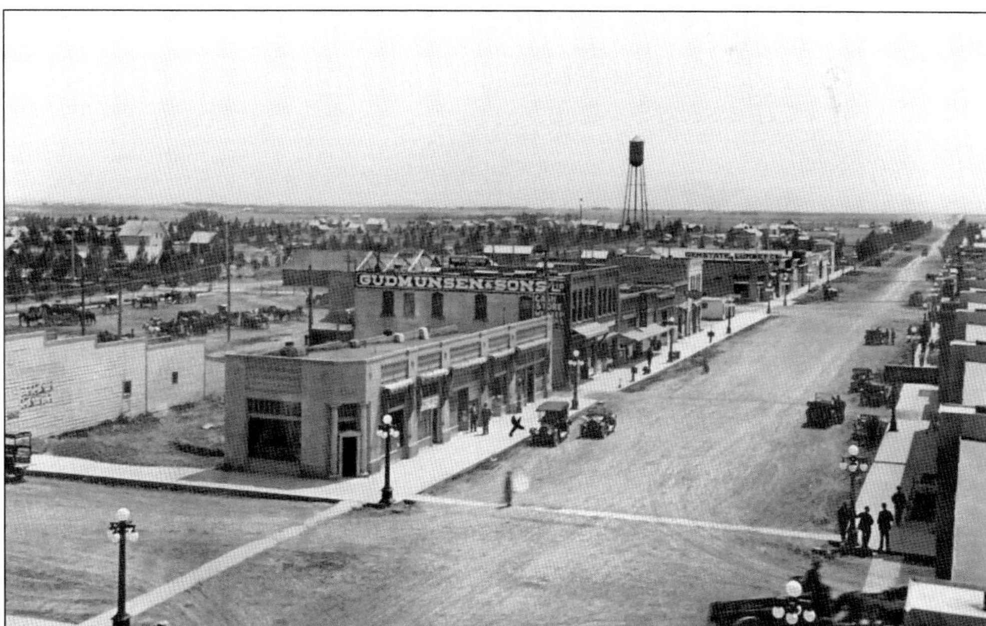

This view of Overland Avenue looking south from the Burley Hotel shows the growth of the town in just a few short years.

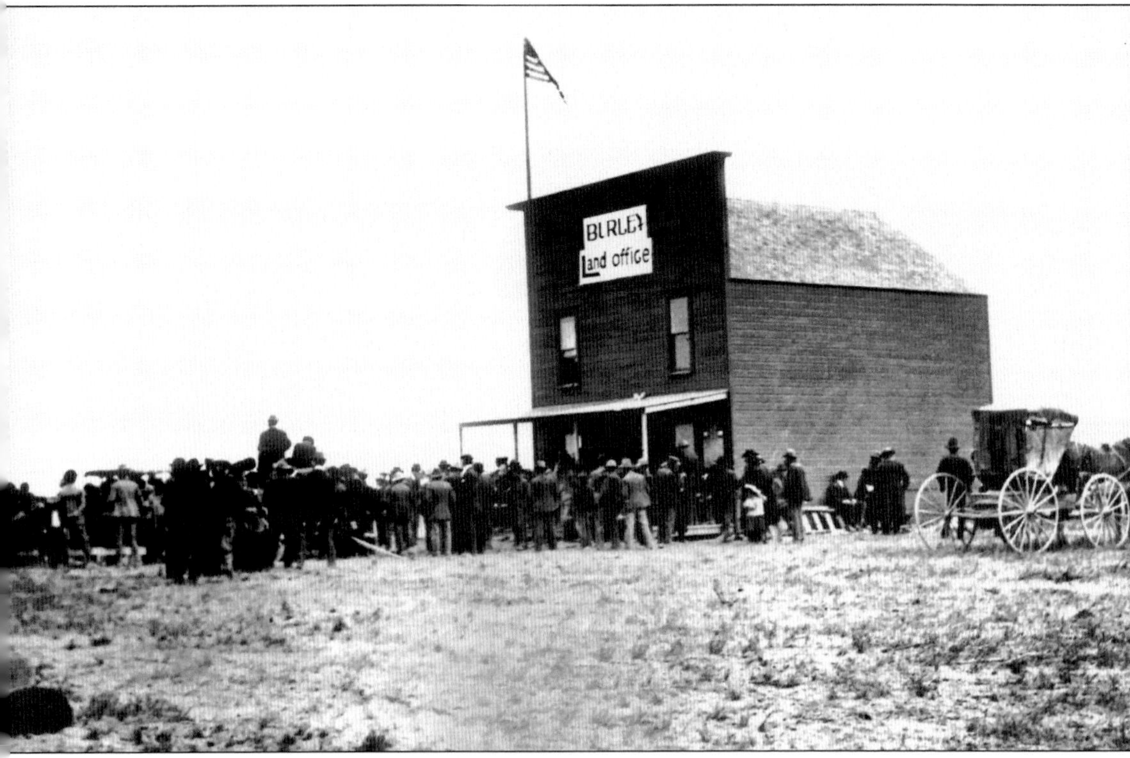

Land sales for the city of Burley began on May 1, 1905. I. B. Perrine and Josiah E. Miller, along with William T. Jack of Oakley, W. L. Burton of Milner, and S. H. Hayes of Boise organized a town site company to develop the land on the south side of the Snake River. Miller's wife, Isabella, owned much of the property that was sold to the town site company and then surveyed and divided into business and residential lots. The town was named for David E. Burley, a passenger agent for the Oregon Short Line, a part of the Union Pacific Railroad, who actually never lived in the town.

Col. J. E. Miller was a prominent leader in Cassia County from the late 1880s until his death in 1921. A Civil War soldier, he is considered Burley's founding father and was Burley's first mayor. Miller gave property to the City of Burley for a cemetery, parks, and schools. As a member of the state legislature, he was instrumental in getting the teachers' college located in Albion and even deeded some of is property to the state for this institution.

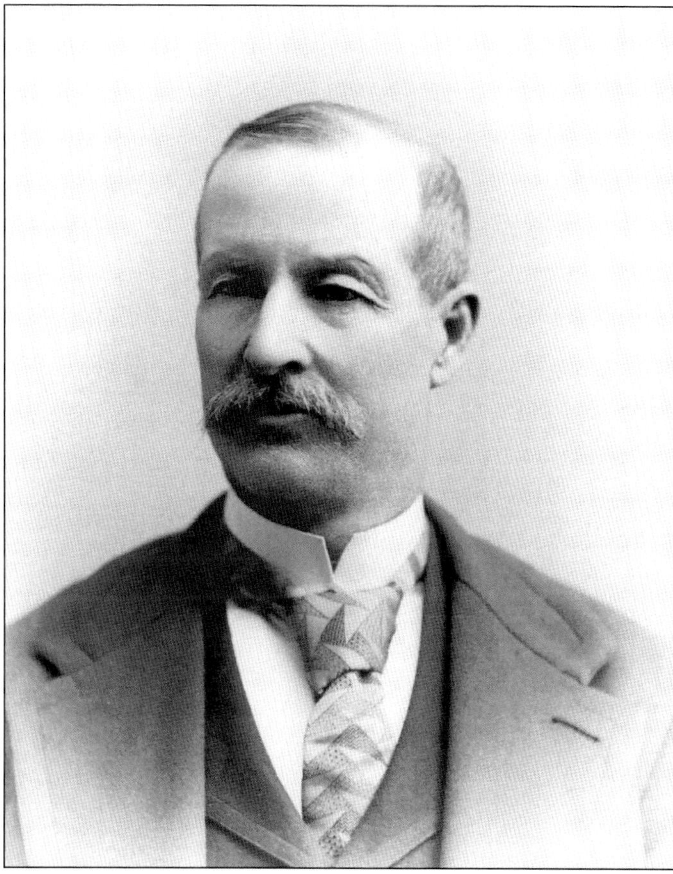

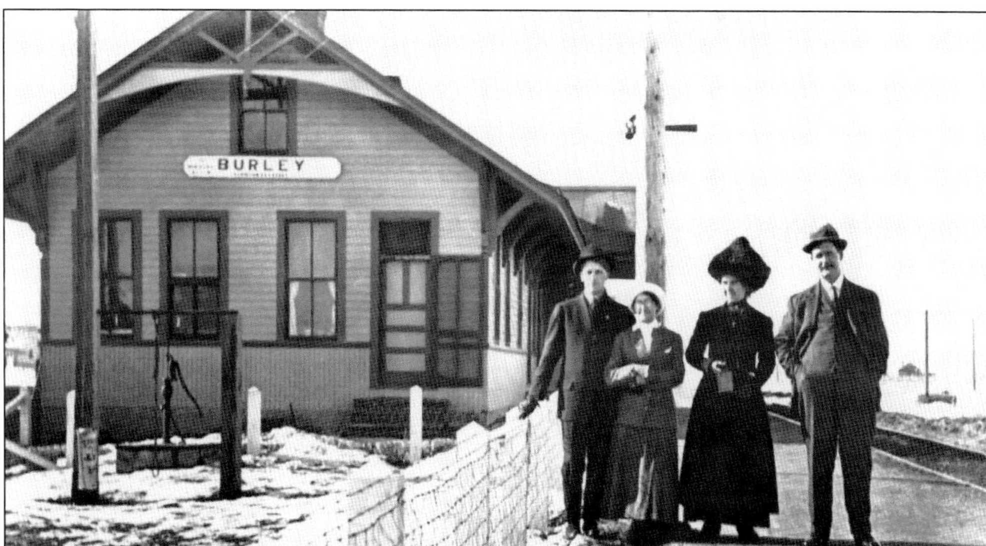

The railroad arrived in the three-week-old town of Burley on May 24, 1905. By its first anniversary, Burley had a nice passenger and freight depot. The train bridge near Heyburn was the first one to cross the Snake River connecting Cassia and Minidoka Counties.

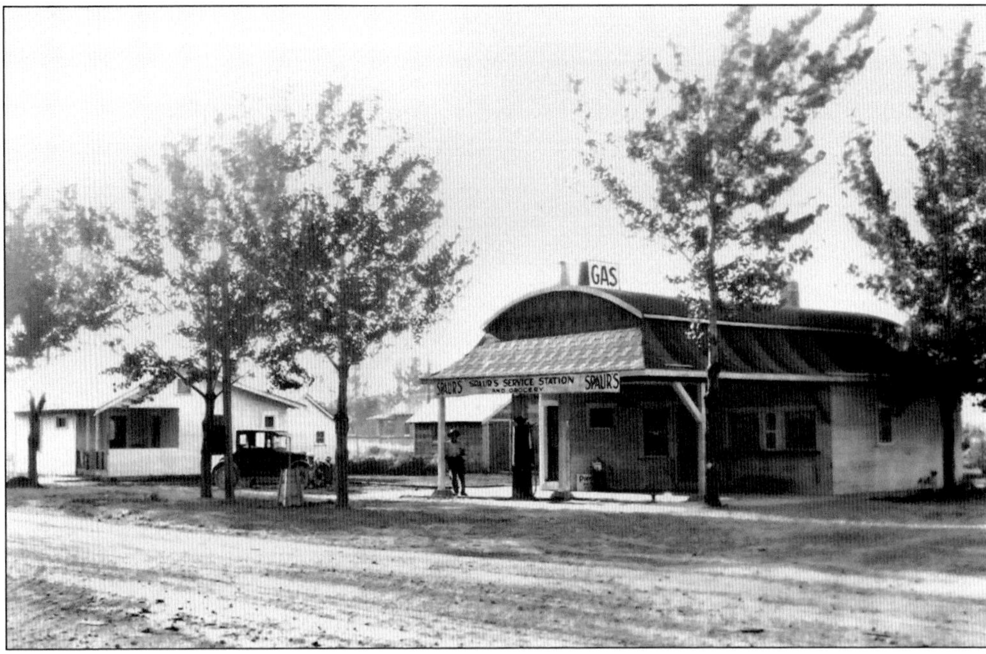

Spaurs Grocery and service station was located on Sixteenth Street. It was a convenient neighborhood business for many years as Burley expanded south of the downtown business district.

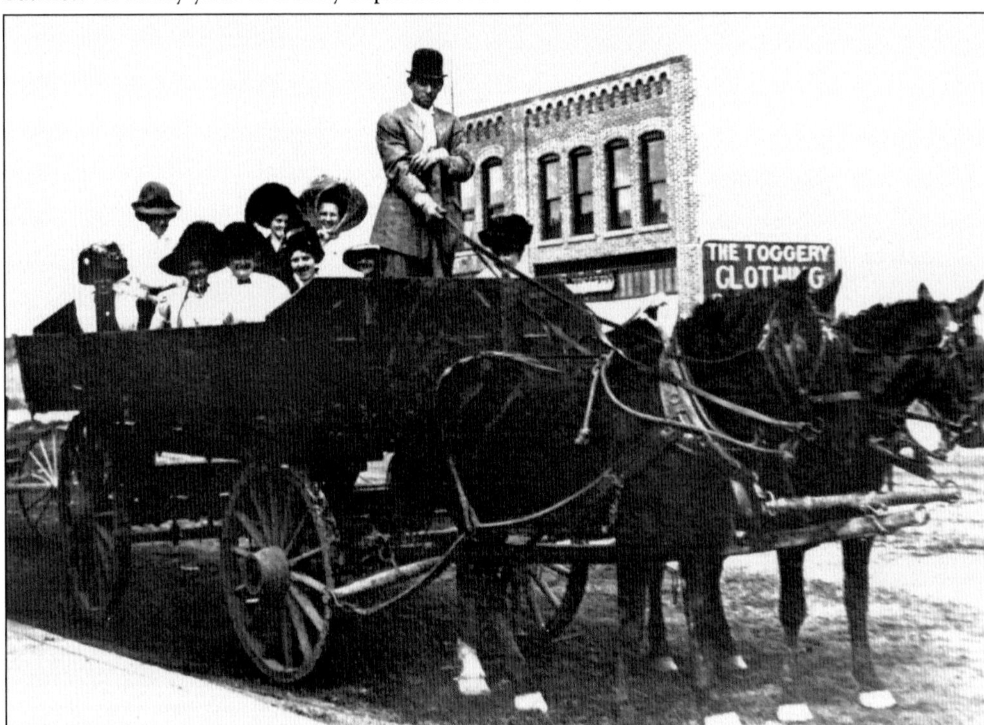

These Burley matrons were off for a social afternoon at Mrs. Amey's house in the country. Included in the picture are Mrs. Amey, Mrs. C. W. Kaar, Ethel Minter, Mildred Rich, Mildred Anderson, Nelle Oberholtzer, and Ida Dickey. The driver is unidentified.

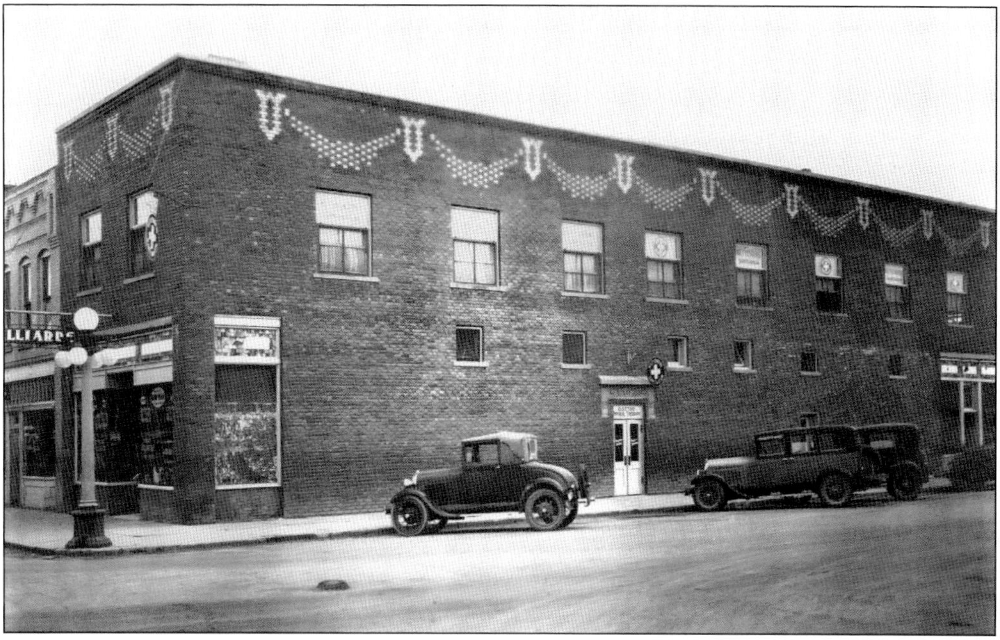

The Chadwick building was built in 1917. The ground floor was a pool hall and cigar store. Upstairs was the Kettering Sanitarium. The patients were treated here with electroshock therapy.

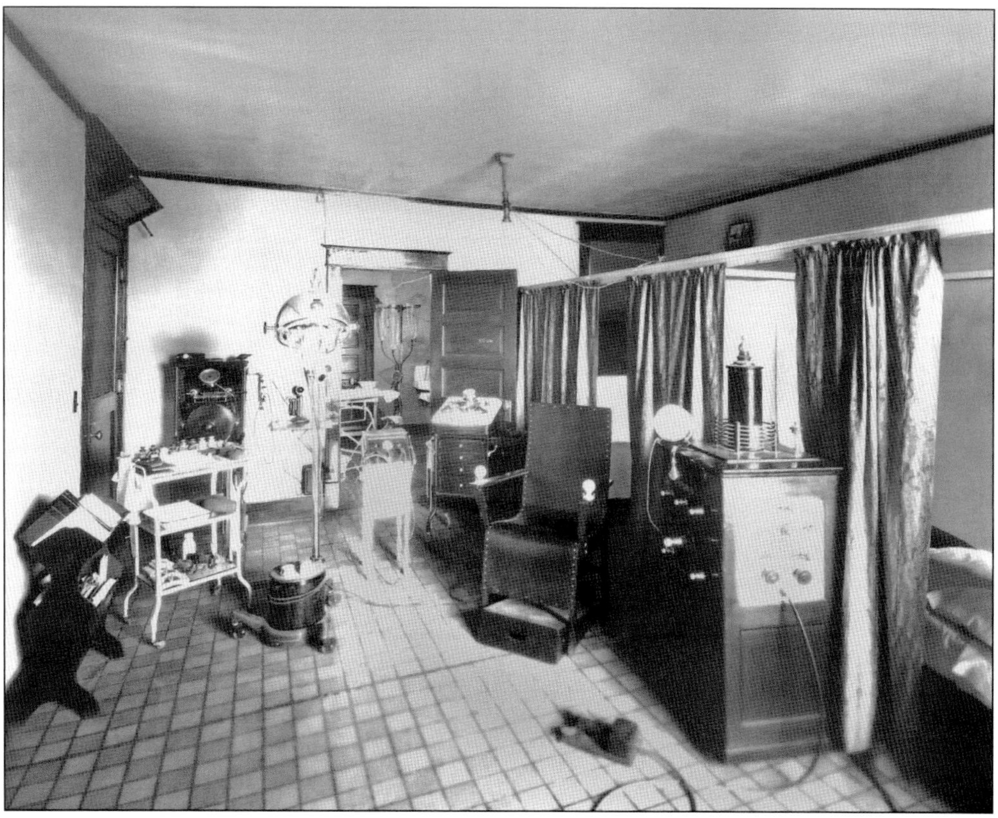

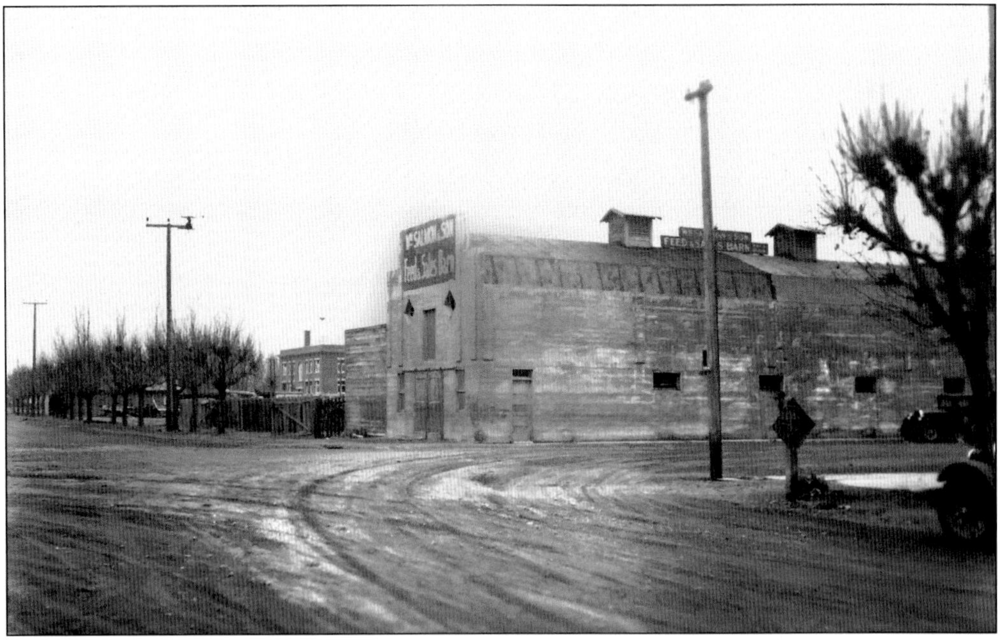

This was one of the more prominent livery stables in Burley. The William Salmon and Son Feed and Sales Barn was located on Albion Avenue and Thirteenth Street. This picture was taken about 1917. The close proximity to the courthouse and other downtown businesses made it a convenient place for the farmers when they came to town.

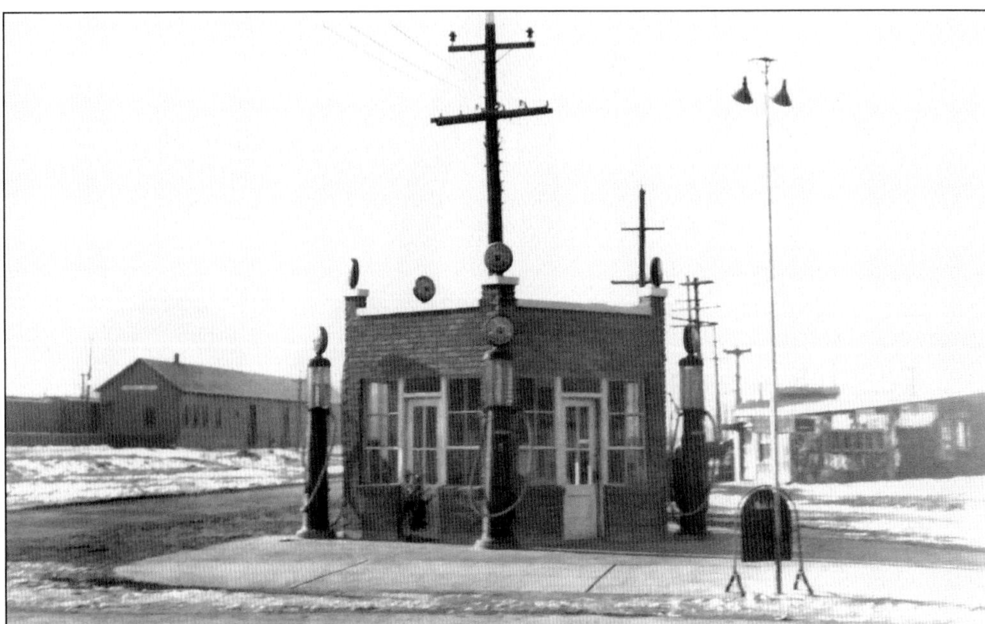

As automobiles became the norm, service stations popped up on every available corner. This one was located on Overland Avenue next to the railroad. The old depot is on the left in the background.

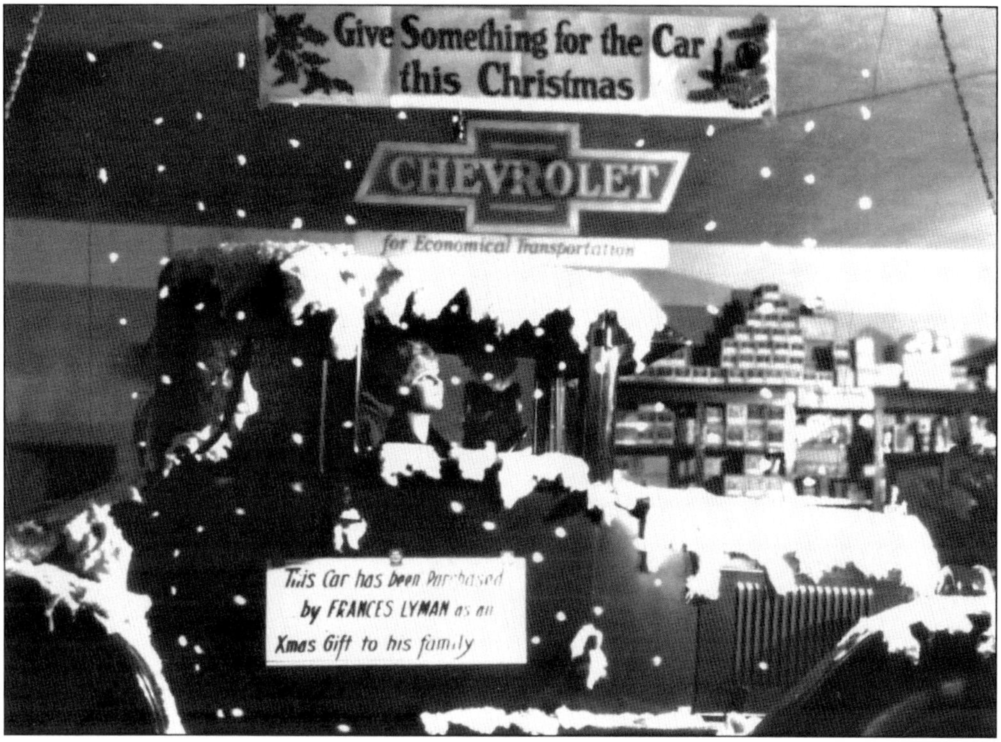

Purchases such as this car were signs of the prosperity the residents of Burley must have felt as they experienced the changes that were taking place in the early 1900s.

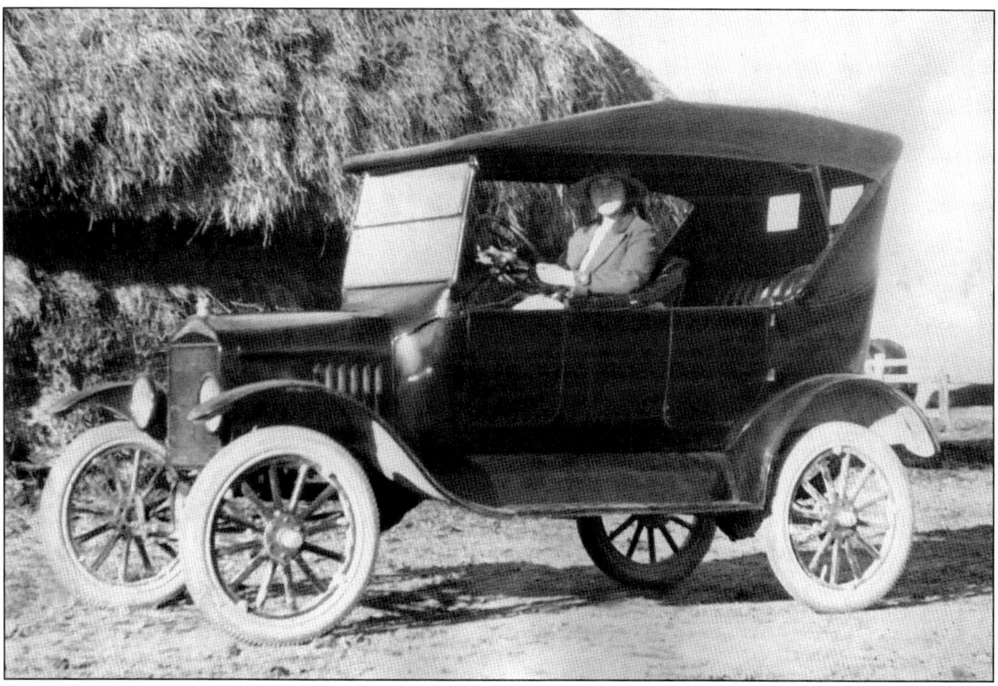

Eunice Congleton, pictured about 1921, was one of the first ladies in Burley to own her own car. She taught school for 45 years, and her husband farmed south of Burley.

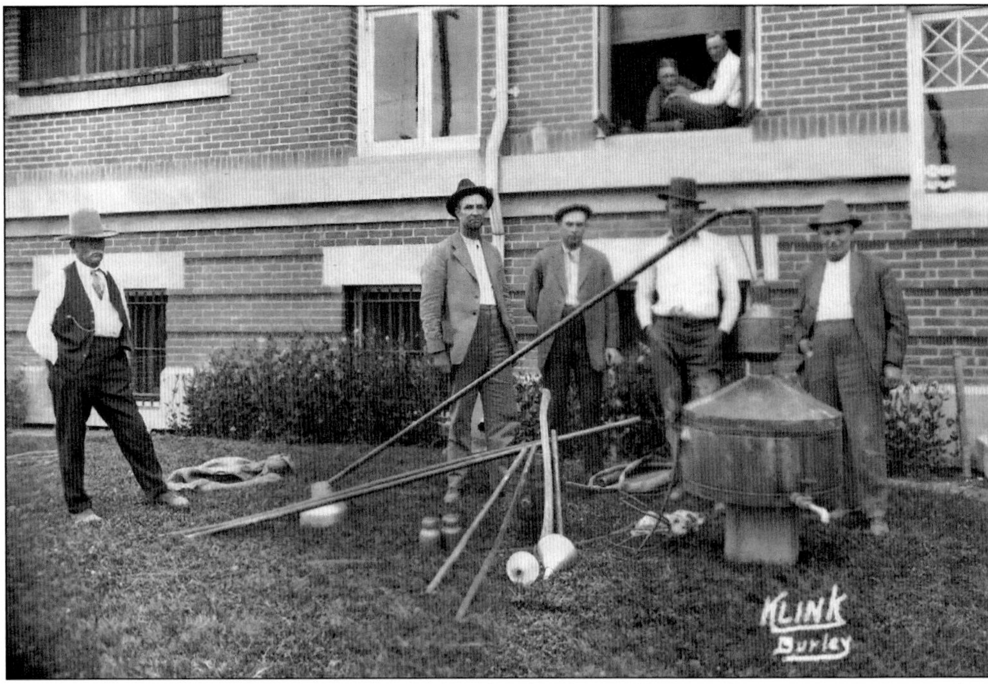

Because of a law passed in 1909, it was already illegal to sell alcohol in Cassia County when national Prohibition went into effect in the 1920s. Law enforcement officers are shown here with some of the moonshine and whiskey stills they confiscated. The contents were poured out. Then they had the problem of disposing of all the equipment.

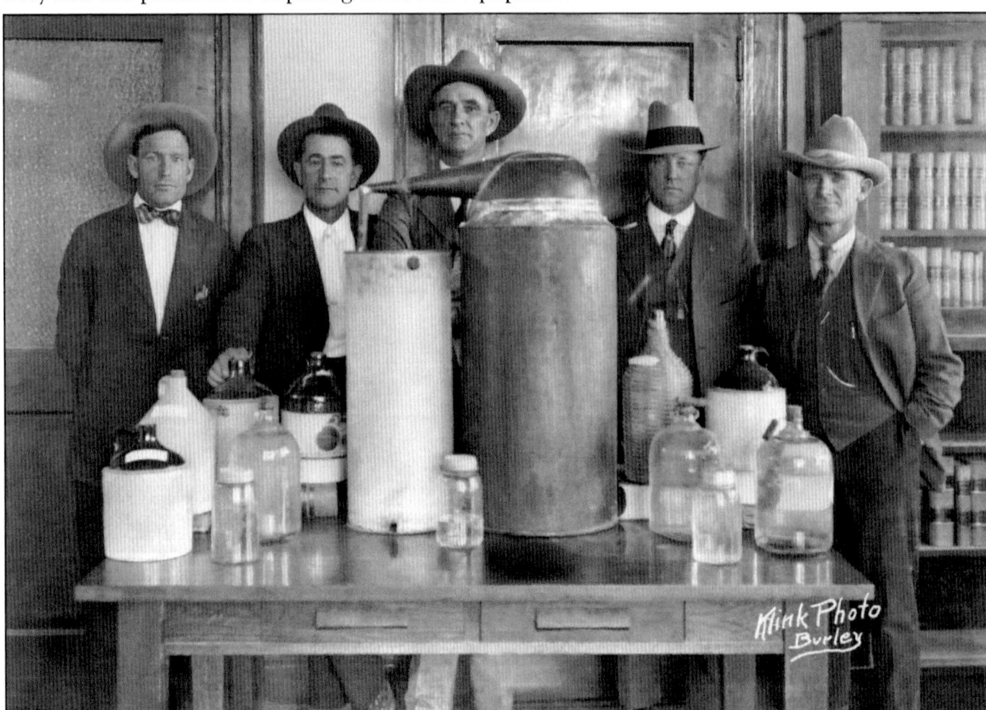

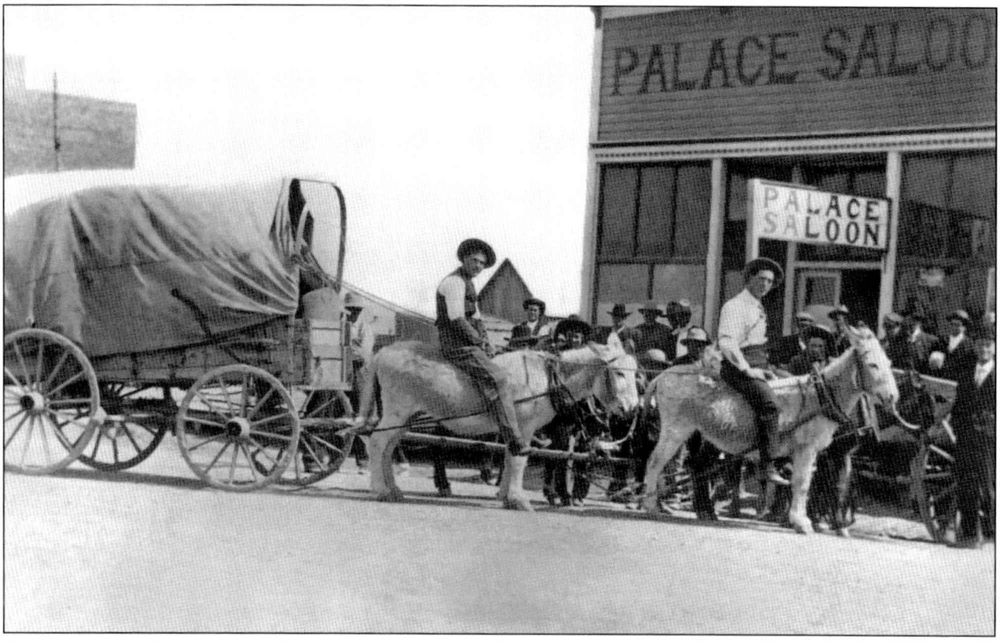

This scene in front of the Palace Saloon was taken in the early 1900s.

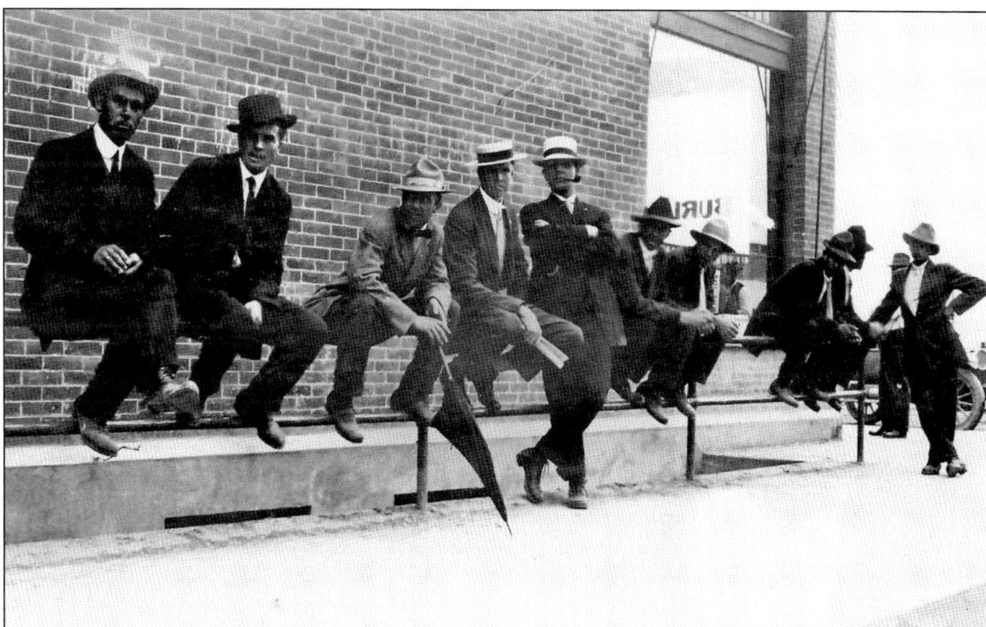

The corner of Main Street and Overland Avenue was a favorite meeting place where men could meet friends and hear the latest news in the early days. It was known as the "loafing corner."

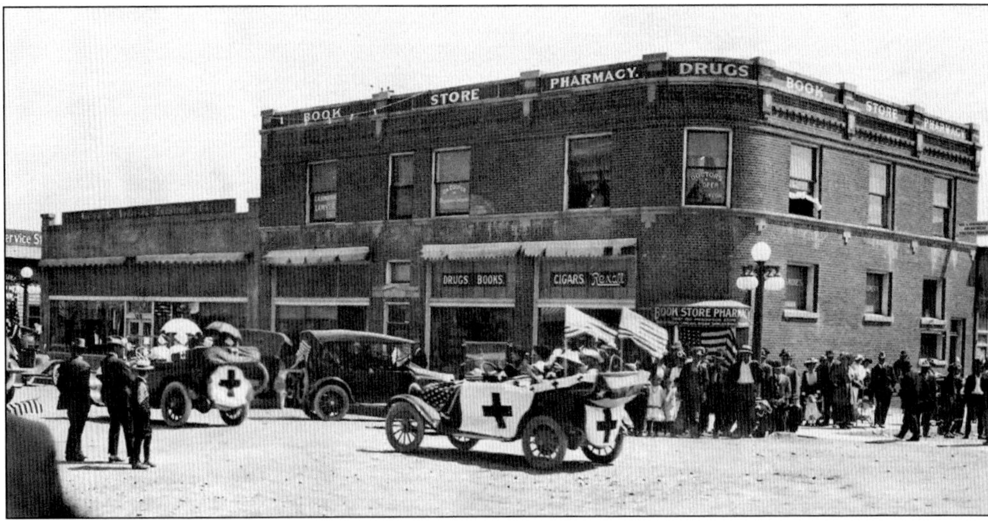

During World War I, the Red Cross held parades to encourage support and raise money for the war effort. This picture shows the Book Store Pharmacy on the northeast corner of Overland Avenue and Main Street.

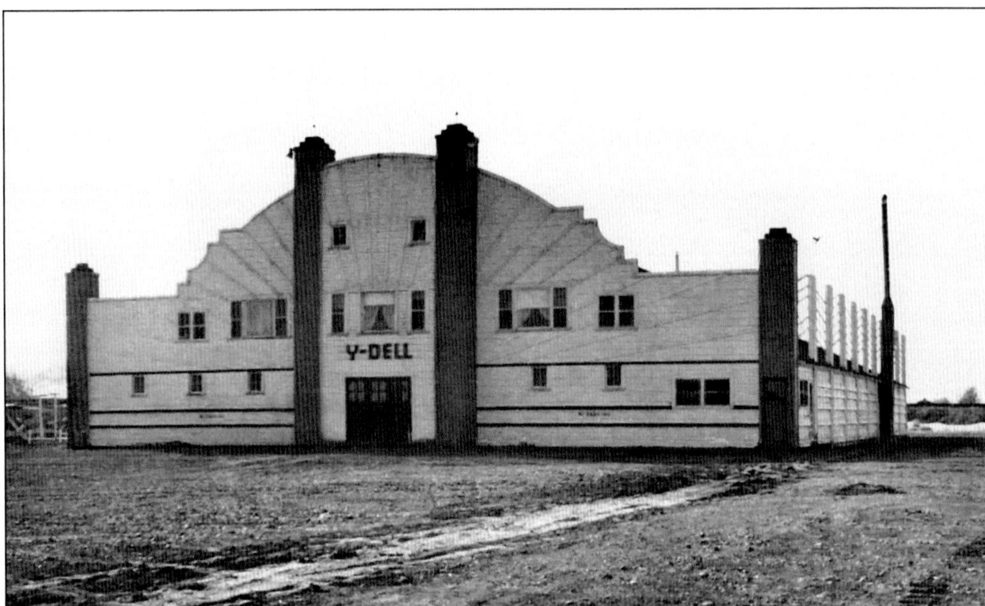

The Y-Dell Ballroom opened in 1937, bringing in the finest dance bands to Burley. People came from all around southern Idaho to see some of the biggest names, such as Lawrence Welk, Sammy Kay, the Ink Spots, Alvino Ray, and many others. The Y-Dell got its name because of the location at the intersection of Highways 30 and 81 and the owner, Dell Holland. (Courtesy of Martell Holland.)

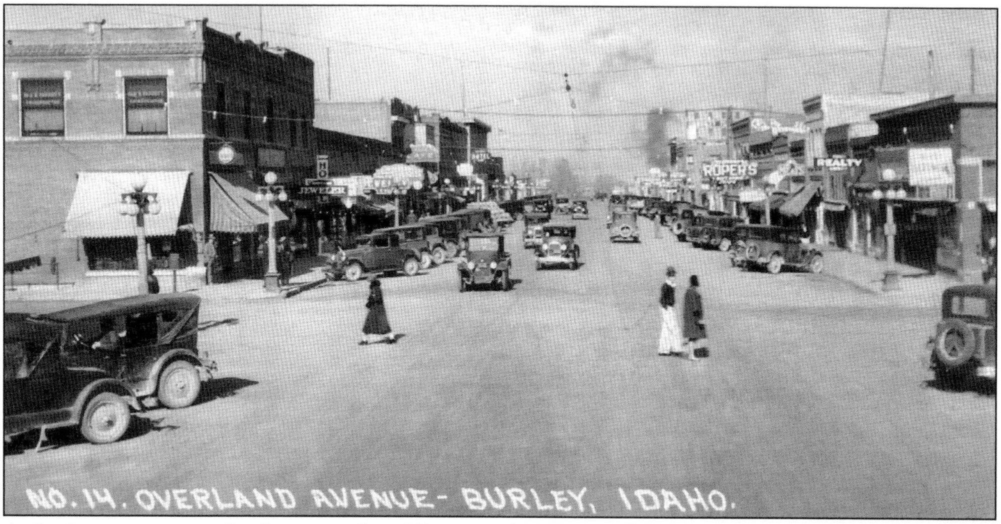

A Burley street scene looking north at Thirteenth Street is shown here about 1920. It shows the activity of the downtown area and businesses such as Aikman's Grocery, Roper's, King's, and Burley Realty and Abstract.

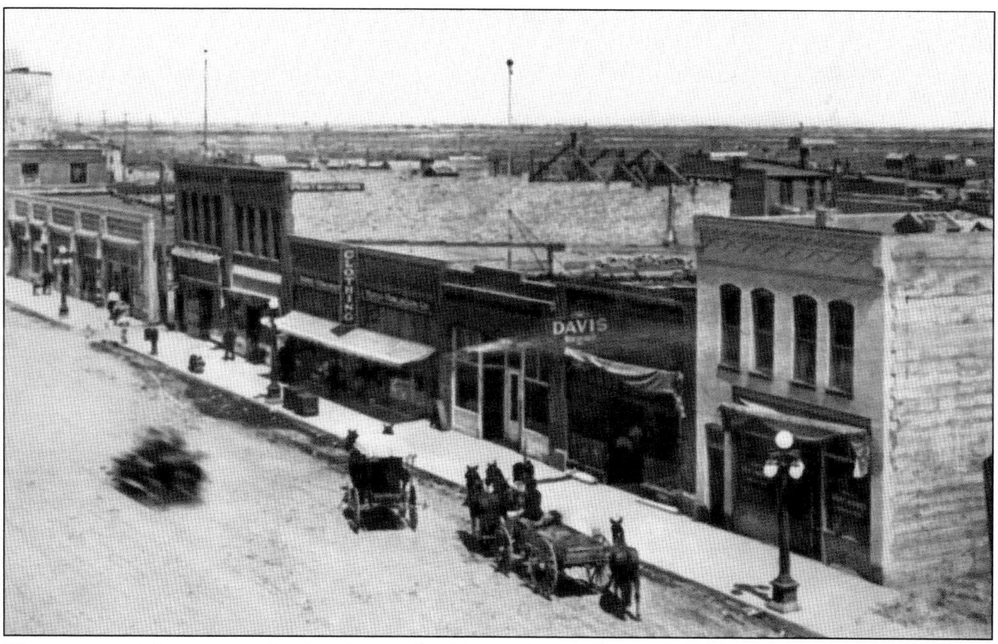

This scene of downtown Burley shows the Davis General Mercantile in the early 1920s. A son of W. M. Davis, William Davis, went to Florida and bought a small group of stores. He was quite successful and built it into what is now known as the Winn-Dixie food stores.

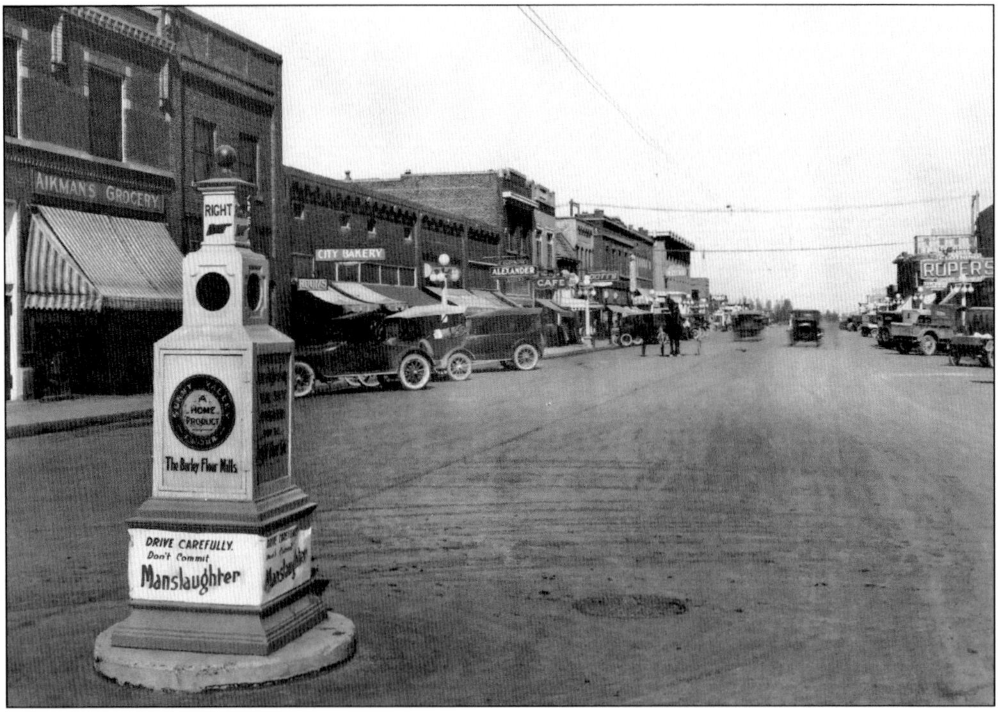

Many of the main intersections in Burley had reminders for people to drive safely as the community adapted to motorized vehicles. The sign says "Drive carefully, don't commit manslaughter."

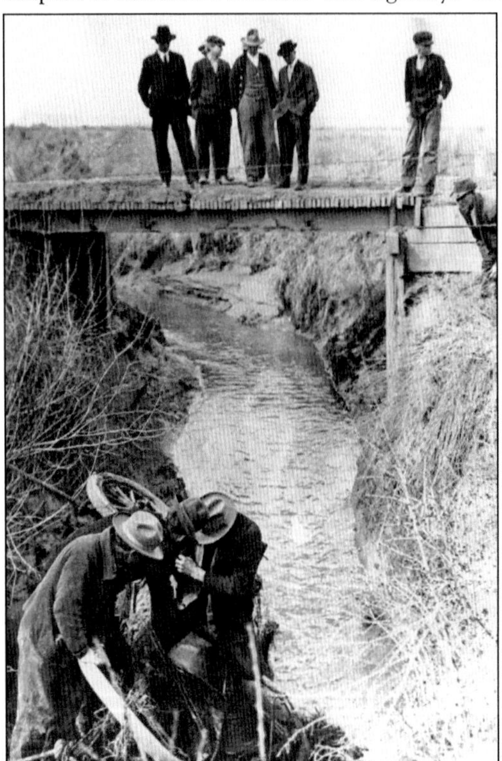

Burley came close to being a town without any attorneys when this car plunged over the bridge on Overland Avenue and into Goose Creek in 1914. The group was returning at night from a district court session in Albion. The survivors were T. Bailey Lee, W. E. Abraham, S. T. Lowe, and T. J. Keogh. John Youmans, the driver, lost his life when he was pinned underneath.

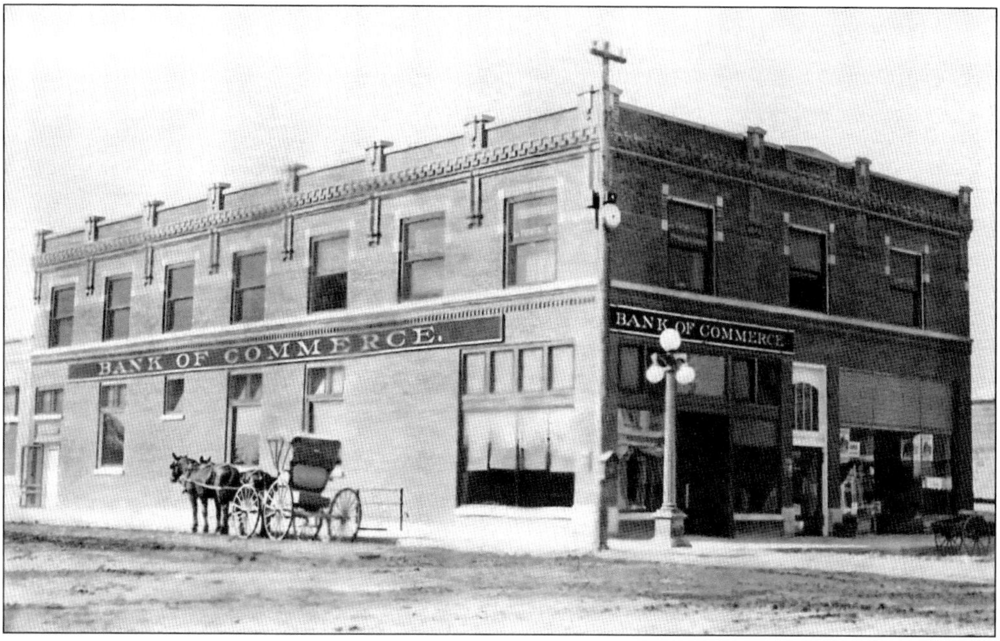

The Bank of Commerce was organized in 1909 by C. M. Oberholtzer. It moved into the Rich Building on September 1, 1913, eight months after its first location in the Hotel Burley was destroyed by fire. The interior of the bank (below) shows Oberholtzer on the far left.

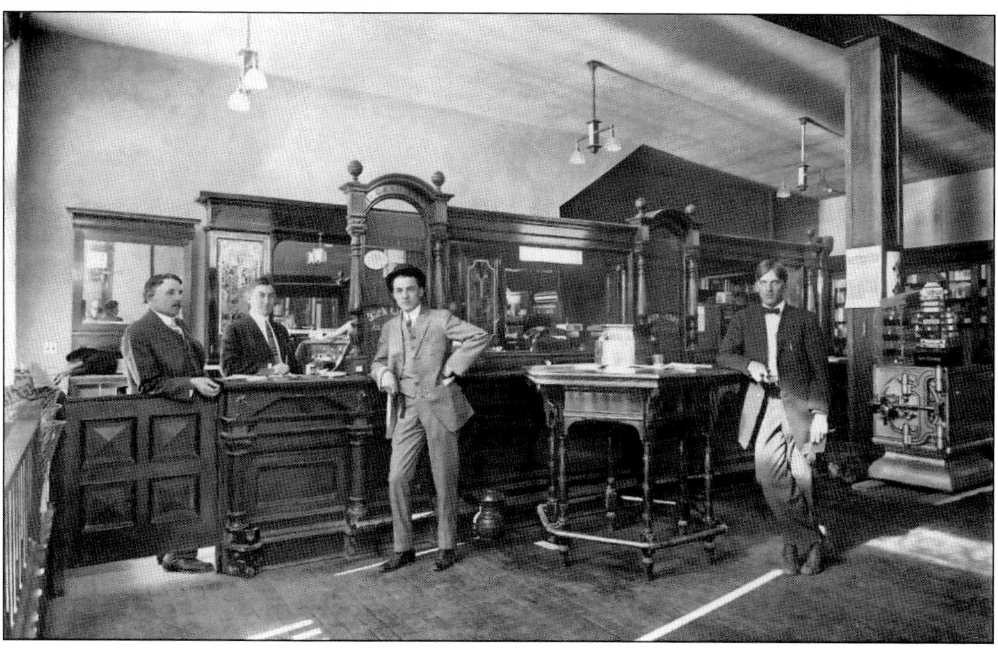

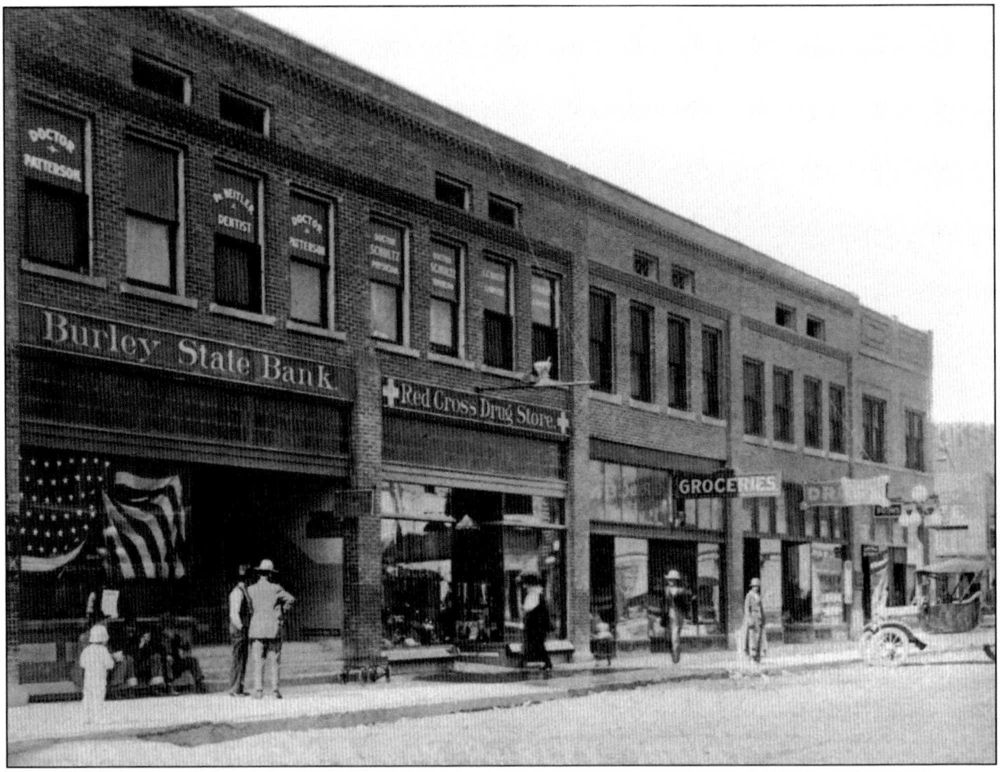

This picture was taken from the southwest corner of Main Street and Overland Avenue looking west.

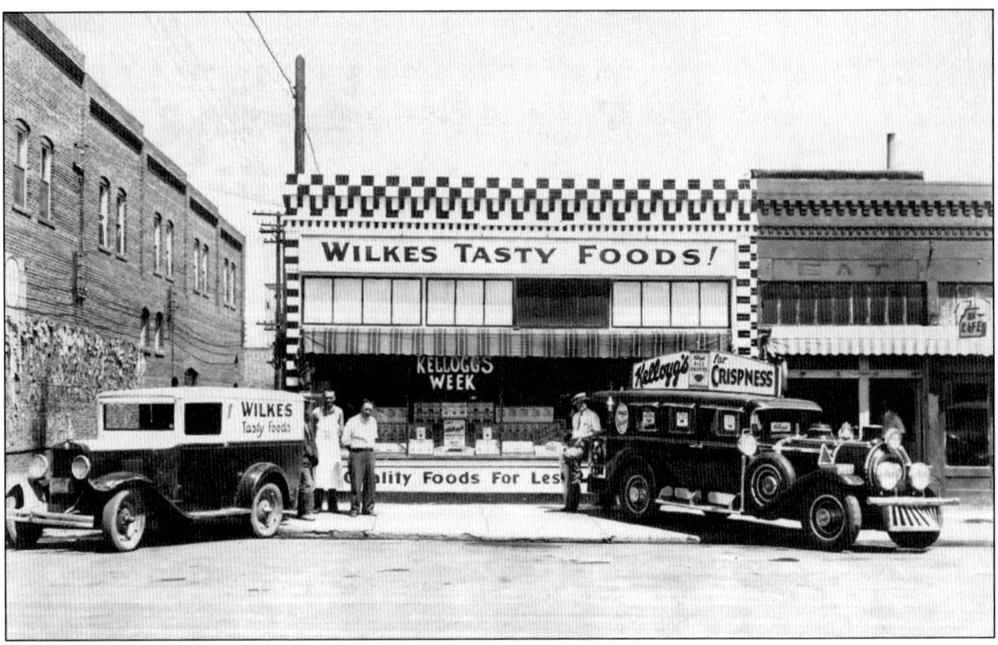

The Wilkes Grocery was on East Main Street. The car in front was probably touring the country as an advertising method for the cereal company.

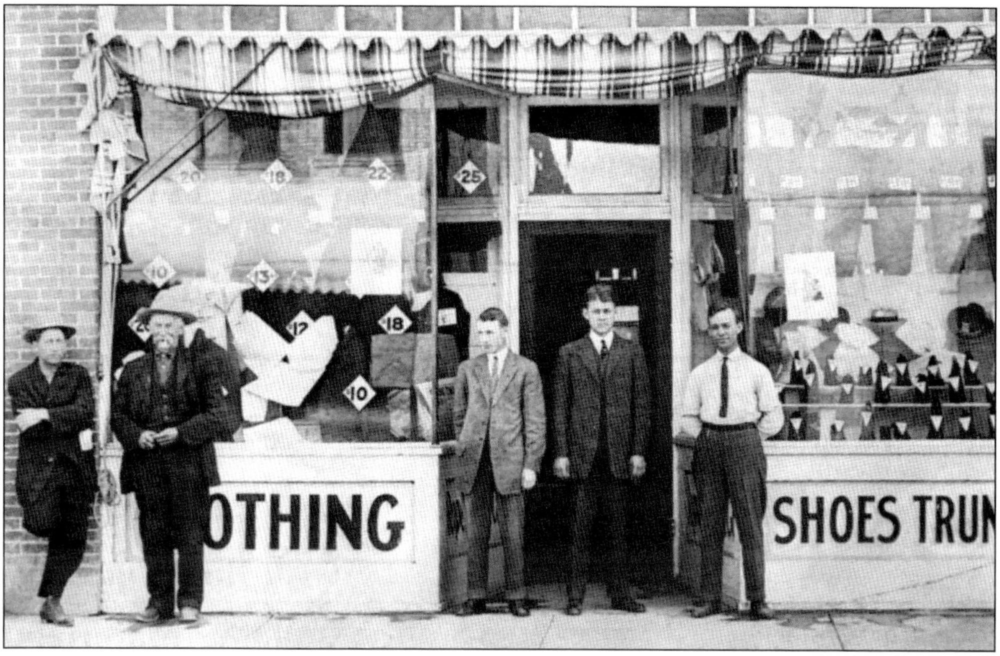

This was taken in front of the first Roper's clothing store. Pictured from left to right are Jack Gaskill, Frank Bedke, employees Lott McCurry and Noel Groshong, and owner William Roper. The business was a popular store that expanded beyond Burley until the family closed the doors in 1999.

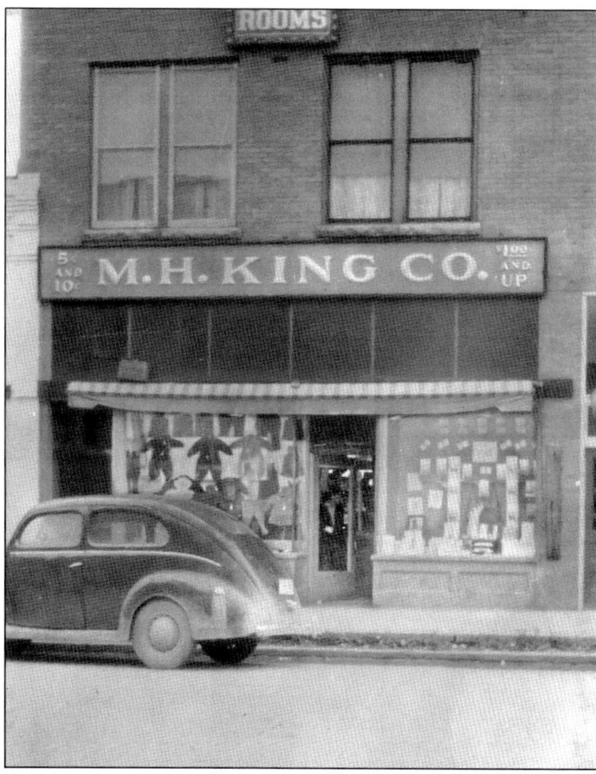

M. H. King opened his first store in 1915. Shown here is its second location. King's Variety Store went on to open stores in three surrounding states and is still growing today.

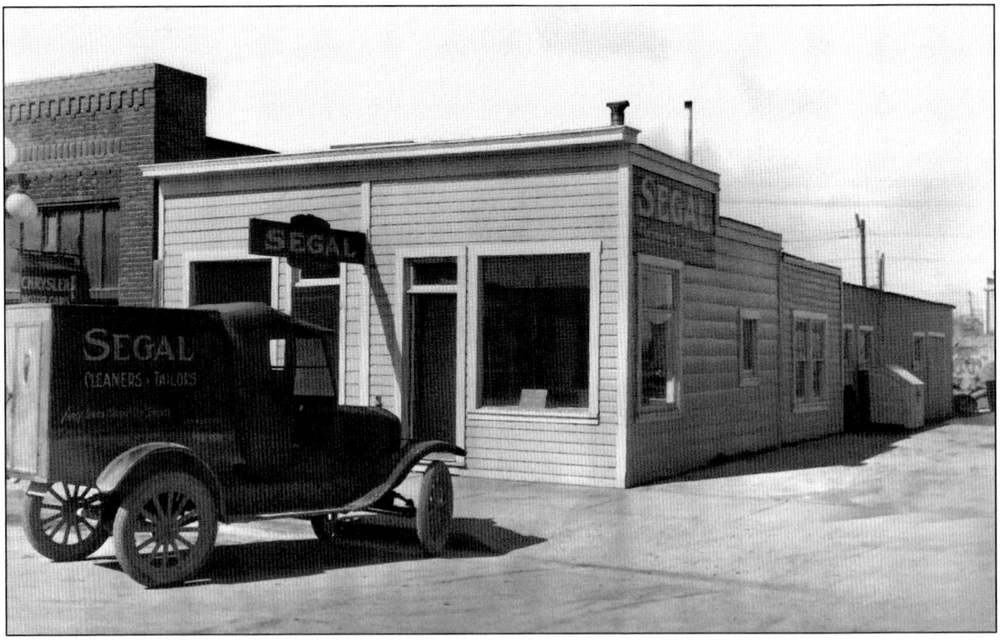

Louis Segal's Cleaners and Tailors was on Overland north of Main Street. He would take a man's measurements for a new suit and send them off to be custom made. His family was one of the three Jewish families to settle in the Burley area.

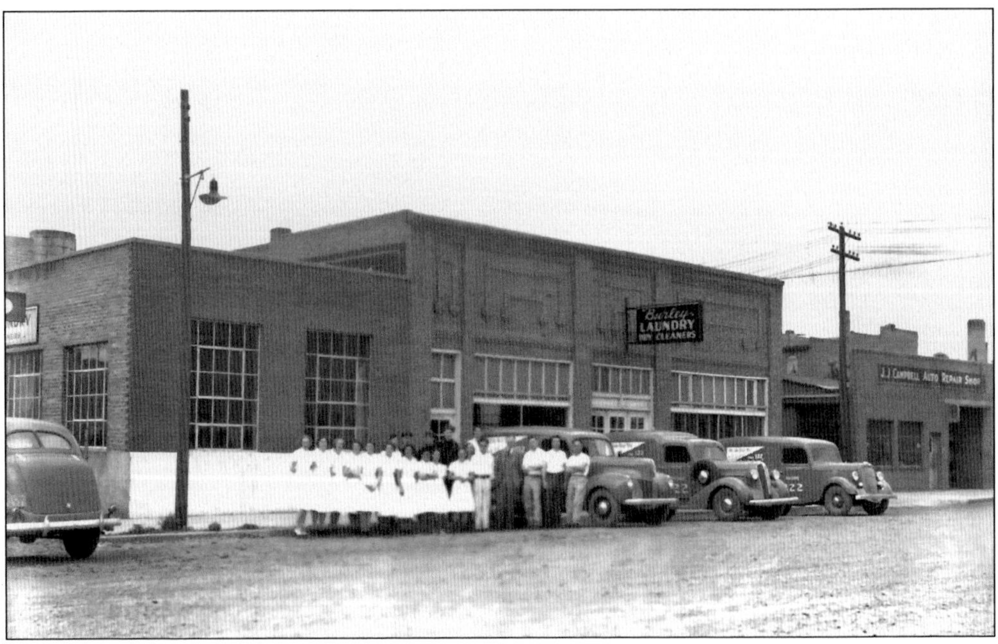

Burley Laundry was located on Albion Avenue.

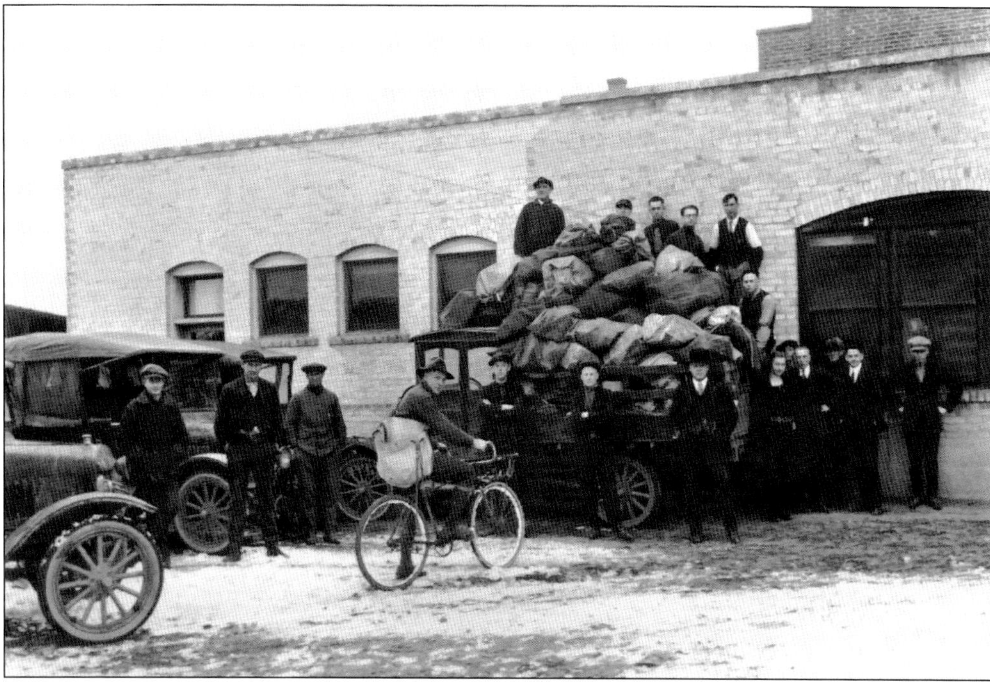

During the winter, mail delivery was difficult, but it was an important connection with the families and friends that so many early settlers had left behind in many parts of the world. This location was on Oakley Avenue.

Mary Stones Stephens was a community nurse from 1919 to 1935. She lived in the View area south of Burley. During the outbreak of flu in 1919, the View Church was turned into a hospital, and she was the nurse. The following spring, she worked with patients who contracted whooping cough and smallpox. In 1928 and 1929, she nursed people through the typhoid fever epidemic. At one time, she had four women in her home ready to give birth. Three babies were born within 35 minutes, and the fourth was born just a few hours later. (Courtesy of Pati Christensen.)

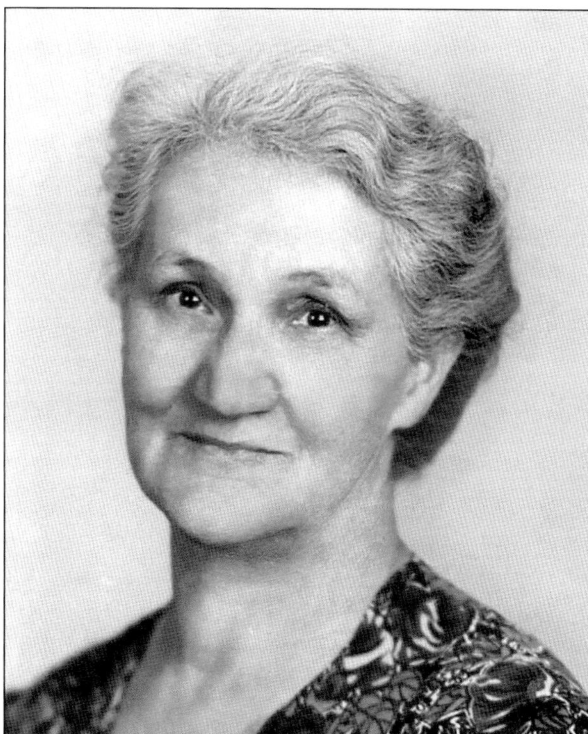

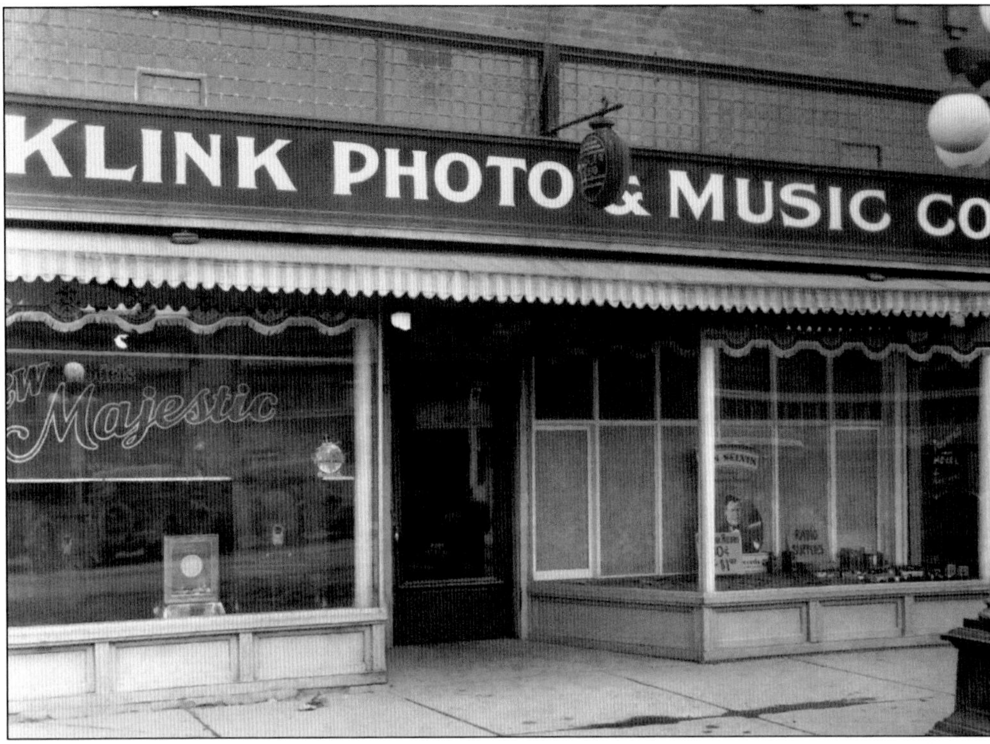

The Klink family started in business on Overland Avenue in 1919 with a photograph and music store. Many early Burley photographs are attributed to George Klink. His brother, Albert, had a flower shop that operated under the family name.

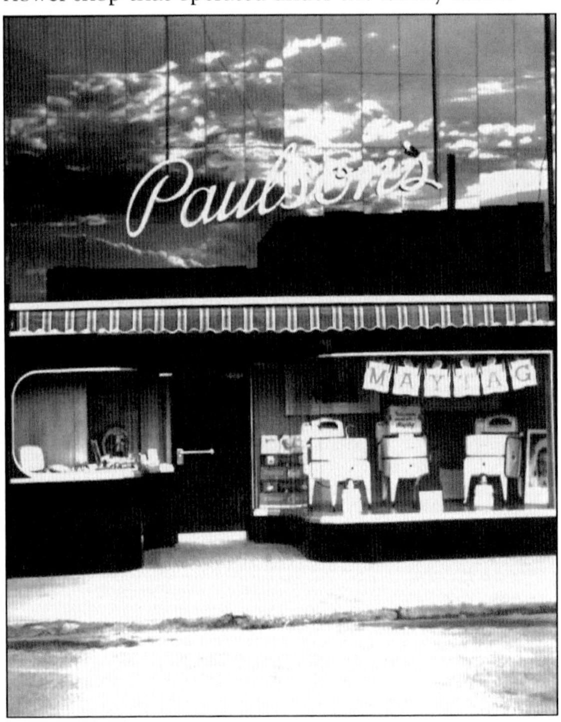

Gus Paulson and his brother, Otto, had a jewelry store on Overland Avenue. They expanded by carrying radios as they became popular. Otto, an amateur photographer, is also credited for taking many of the early Burley photographs.

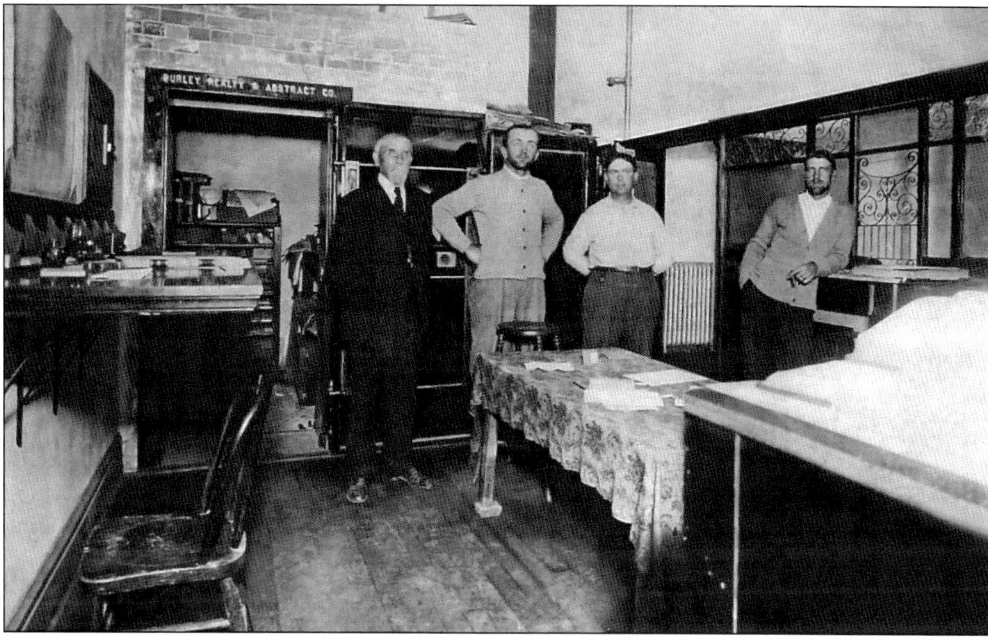

J. C. Gaskill opened Burley Realty and Abstract in 1905. S. H. Kunau joined him in the early 1920s. They operated their business as Burley Realty and Abstract and Cassia County Abstract. The employees pictured here are unidentified.

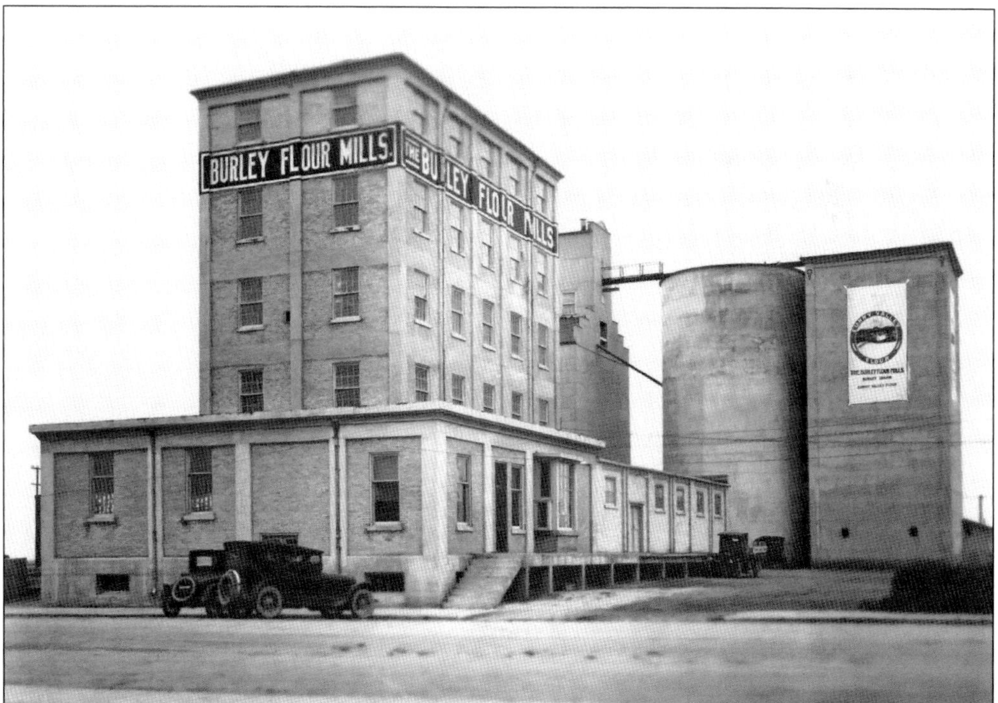

The Burley Flour Mills, started in 1909, was Burley's first industry and Idaho's largest flour mill at the time. The first manager of the mill was Clarence C. "Pop" Baker. It was in business for 61 years.

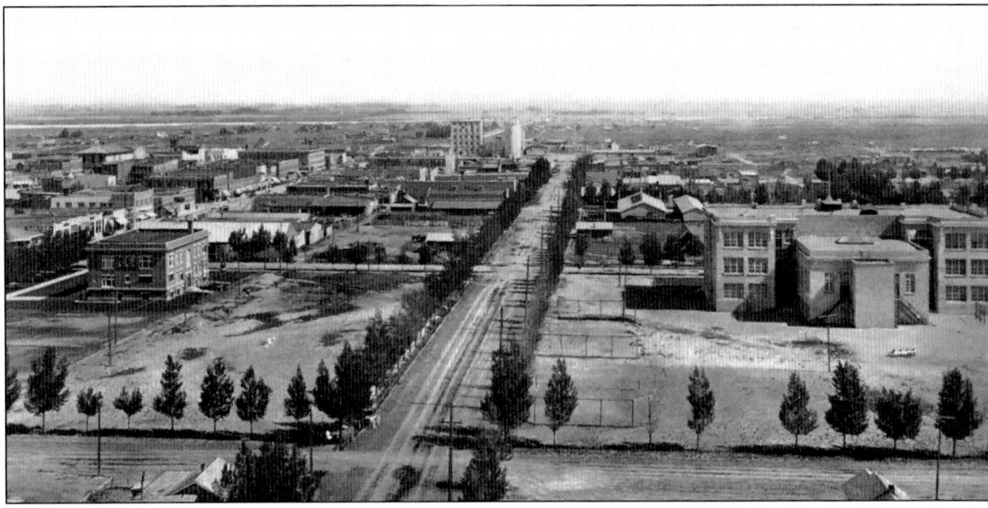

The water tower was the site of this panoramic view of Burley toward the Snake River. In the center of the picture is Albion Avenue. The large building on the left is the city hall, and the bigger building on the right is the Burley High School.

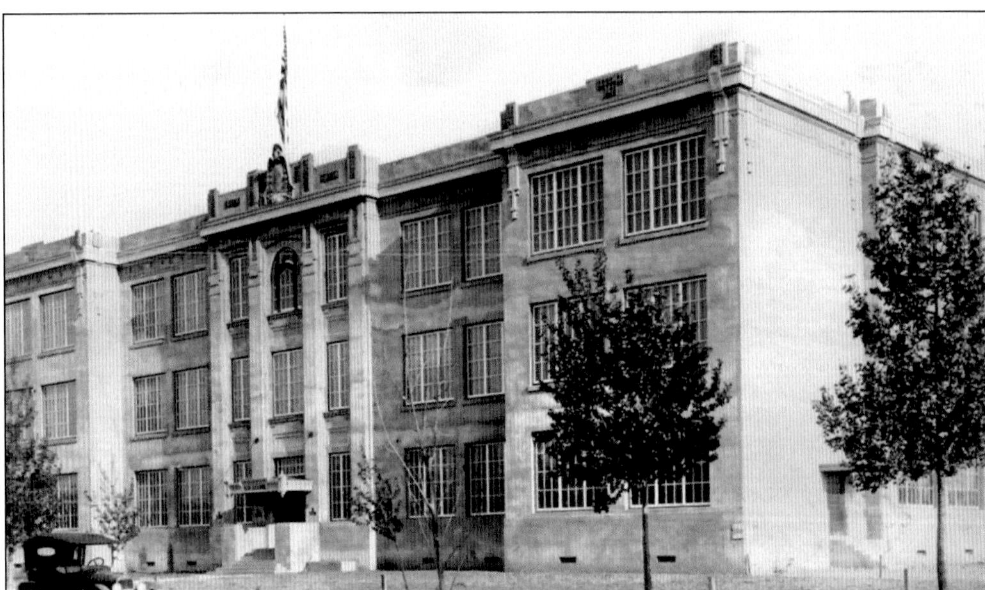

Burley High School was built in 1915. It was located downtown behind the city hall. It served as the high school until 1955, when a new school was built. It was then used as the junior high school until it burned in 1973. The football team would practice on the grounds by Burley City Hall.

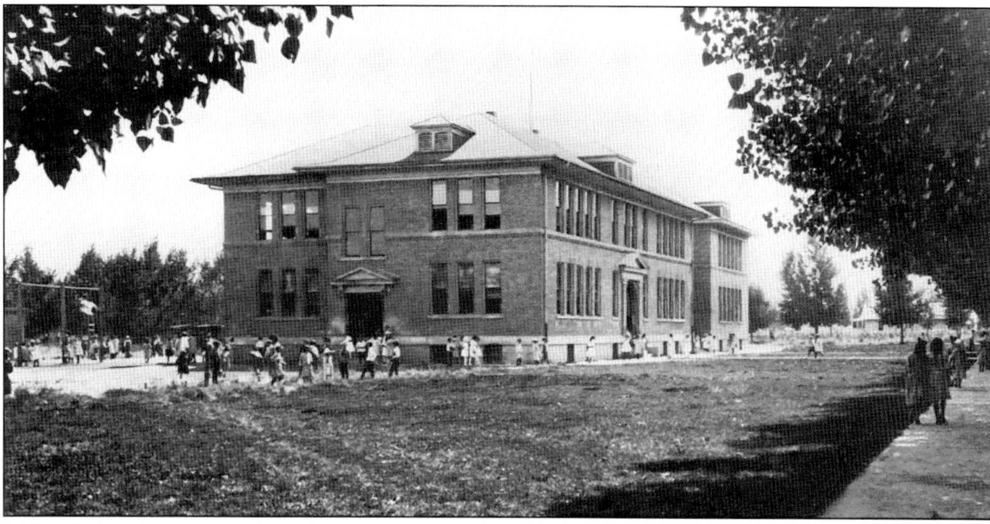

Miller School was one of the first buildings in Burley that was built for the purpose of education. It was named after Josiah E. Miller. It was constructed about 1914 at a cost of $15,000. The upper floor was added later at a cost of $3,500 and was used as the high school for a time with the elementary grades below.

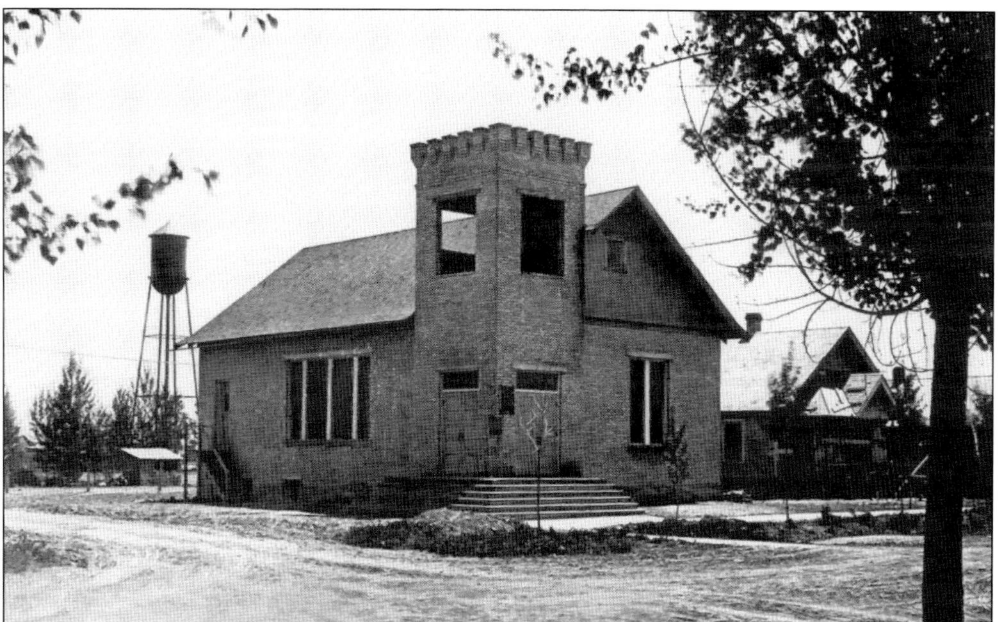

The First Presbyterian Church of Burley was organized in 1906. The town site company presented the church with its first plot of ground, which the church later traded for this more suitable location on Oakley Avenue.

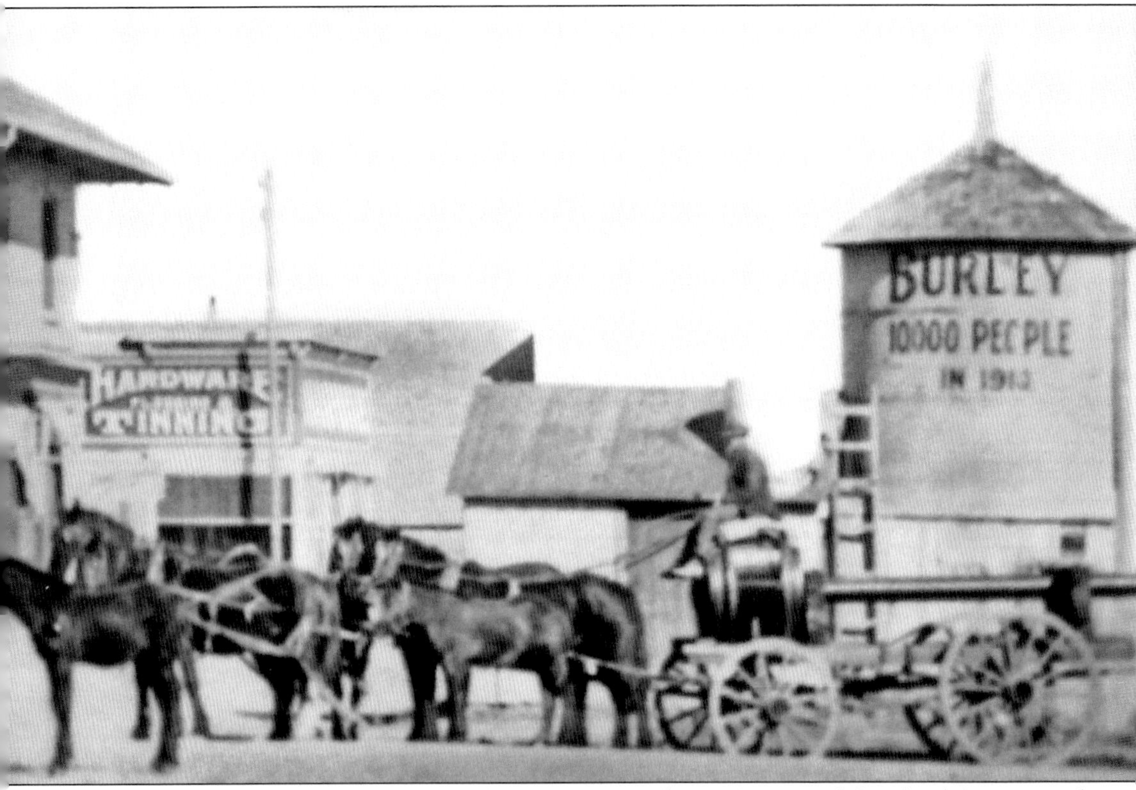

A city well was dug at the center of the intersection of Main Street and Overland Avenue, and a huge tank was erected over the well. The words "Burley, 10,000 people in 1910" was painted on it in bold letters. This is a goal Burley is still trying to reach. This tank stood for a few years until a water tower was built a few blocks south on Albion Avenue. (Courtesy of Dick and Ilene Fuqua.)

Four

Declo

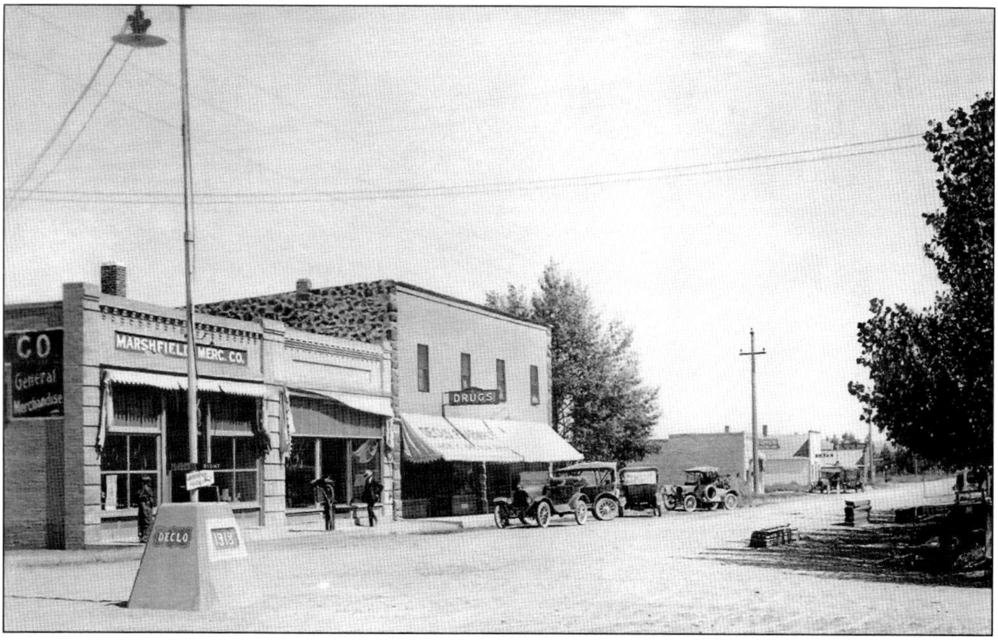

The flagpole at the center of the main intersection of Declo was the gathering spot for many. Some brides remember being "chivareed" and of being tied to the pole. When Lar Gillett built his grocery store in 1914, the town was still being called Marshfield. He carried a small supply of stamps, envelopes, and postcards for the convenience of his customers. When the town got its own post office in 1917, he became the first postmaster, and mail was picked up in his store.

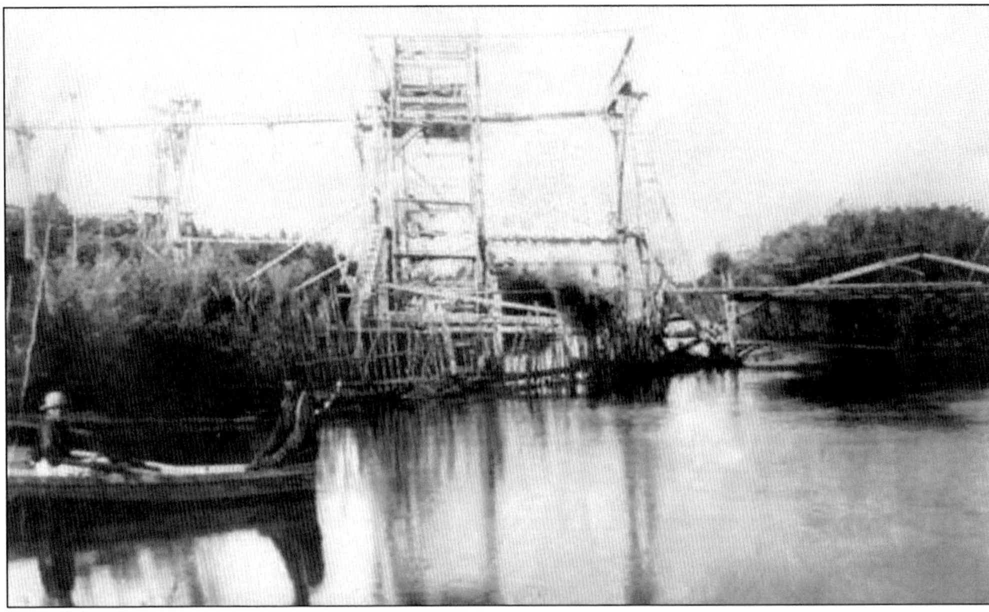

Before the Minidoka Dam was built, Peter August Peterson, a Swedish immigrant, built a waterwheel to pull water from the Snake River. The water was used to irrigate his farm, located about two miles north of present-day Declo.

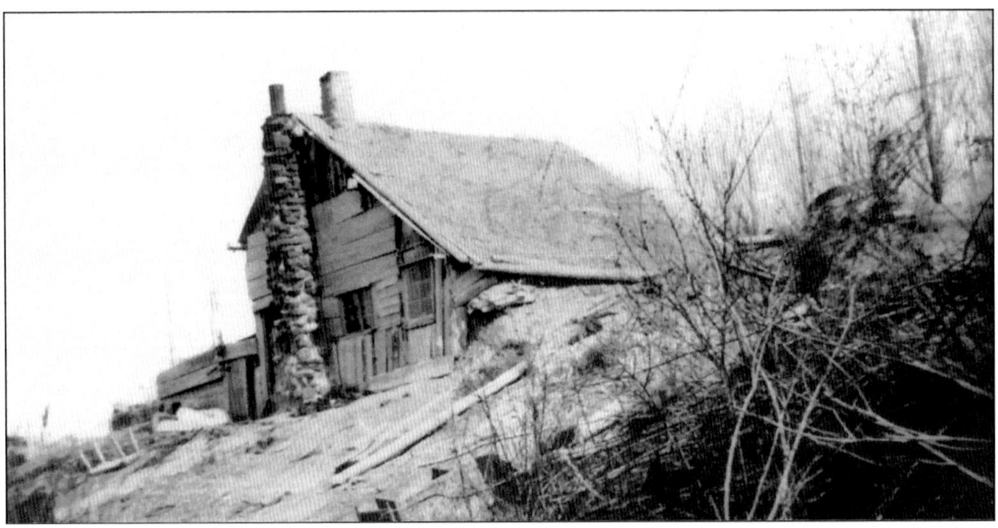

Peter August Peterson's dugout home near the Marshfield Ferry was built when the family settled here in 1894. When it became time for Peter and Emma Sophia Peterson's children to attend school, she asked the state for a teacher but was told there had to be a minimum of 10 children to qualify for a school. Some of their children were too old for school, so they brought a Rasmussen child home to live with them. This gave them 10 children between themselves and their neighbors. They only had to "borrow" the child for one year, as more families moved in.

The first school building in Marshfield was built in 1908.

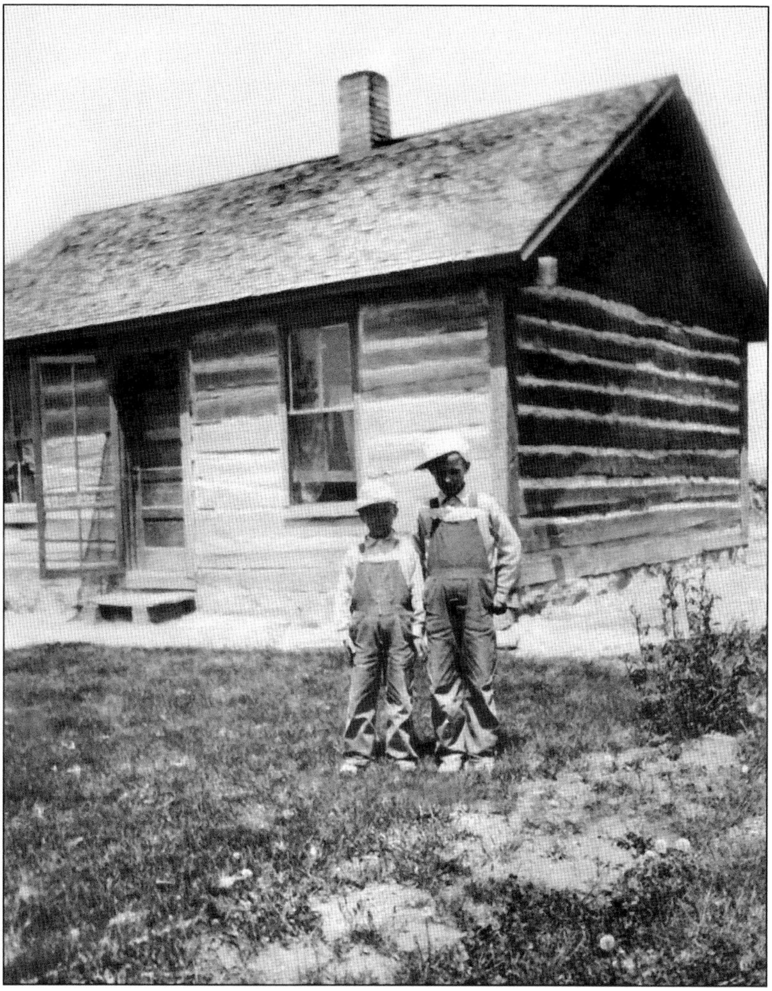

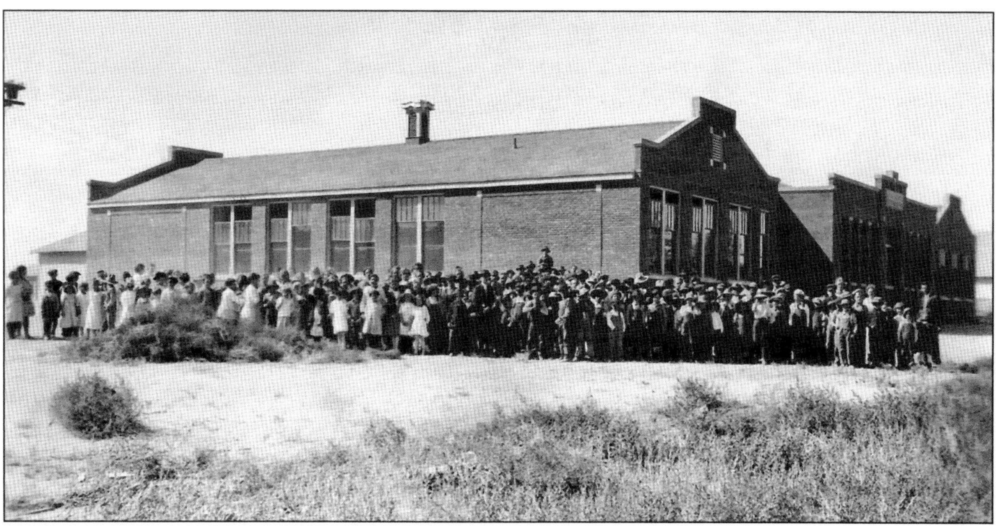

By 1920, this building had been built for the Declo students.

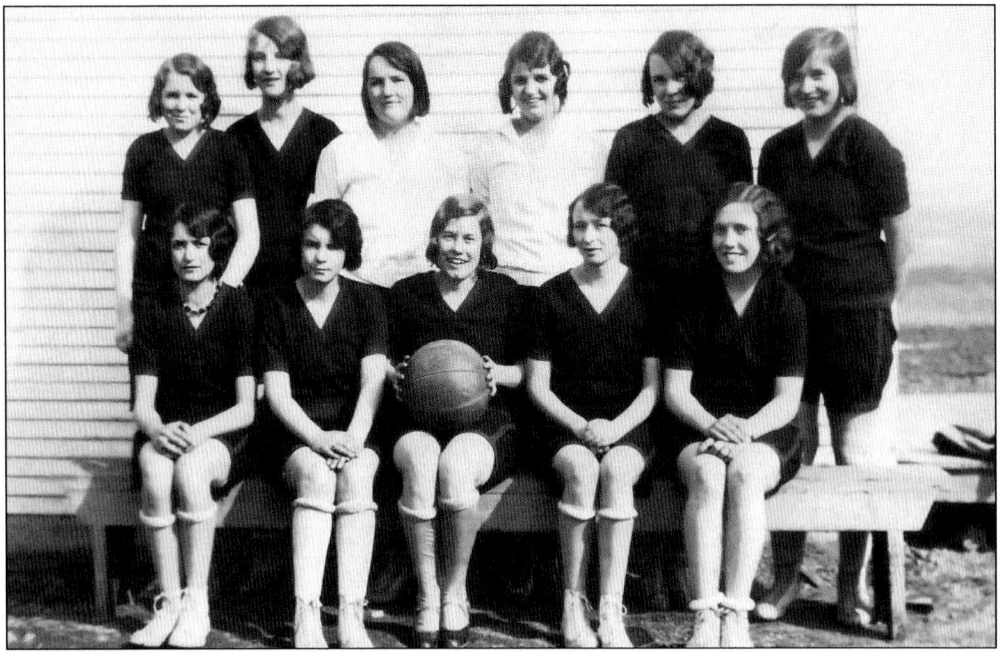

The women's basketball team of Declo in 1930 included, from left to right, (first row) Dorothy T., May H., Velma Williams, Norma Sidwell, and Fern V.; (second row) Wanda ?, Gladys H., Beulah Gummerson, Eva N., Mildred Finley, and LeOre C. Girls would roll their stockings down, much to the dismay of their mothers. (Courtesy of Leah Beck.)

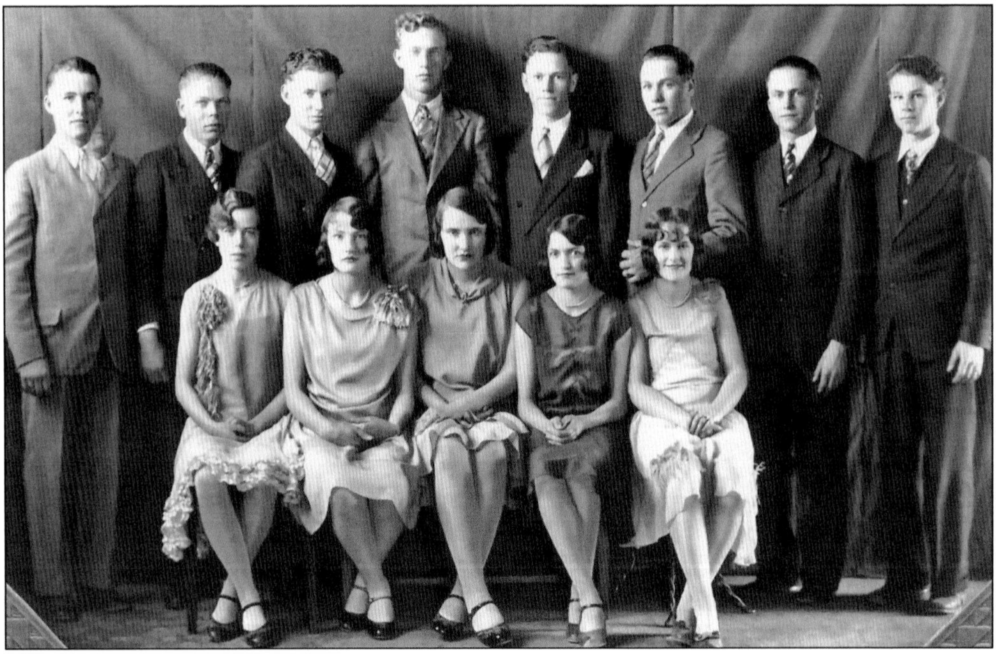

This is the Declo High School class of 1929. The alphabetical listing includes Jack Anderson, Joe Ballard, Devon Clark, Blaine Curtis, Mary Darrington, Clifford Darrington, Helen Herbold, Thelma Jibson, Carl Osterhout, Jasper Richardson, Leona Stutz, Dorothy Tennant, and Eugene Wilcox. (Courtesy of Leah Beck.)

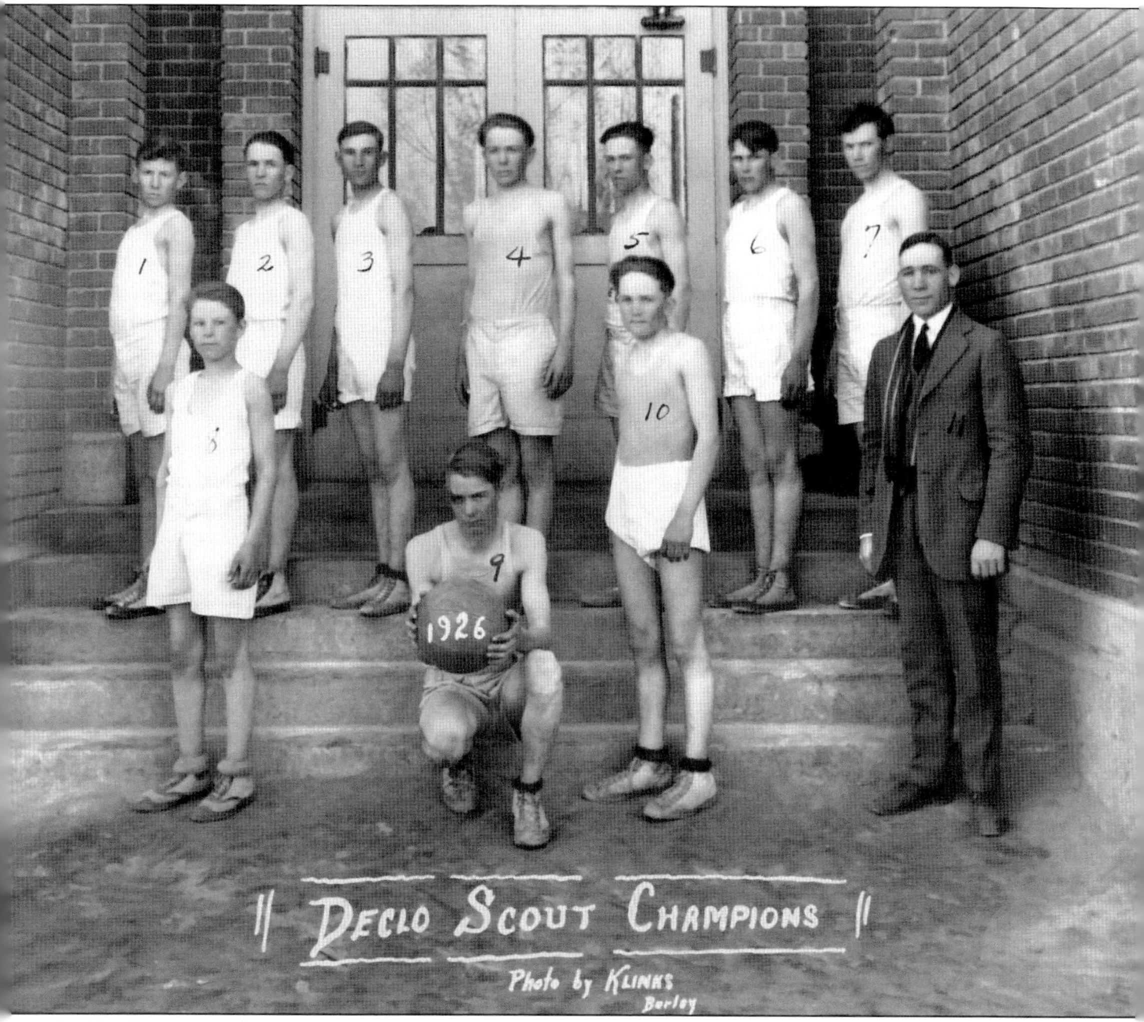

The Declo Scout champions of 1926 are, from left to right, (first row) Jack Anderson, Hyrum Anderson, Ralph Jibson, and coach Vasco Parke; (second row) Devaun Clark, Jasper Richardson, Ned Anderson, Frank Anderson, Lester Jibson, Steven Osterhout, and Eugene Wilcox.

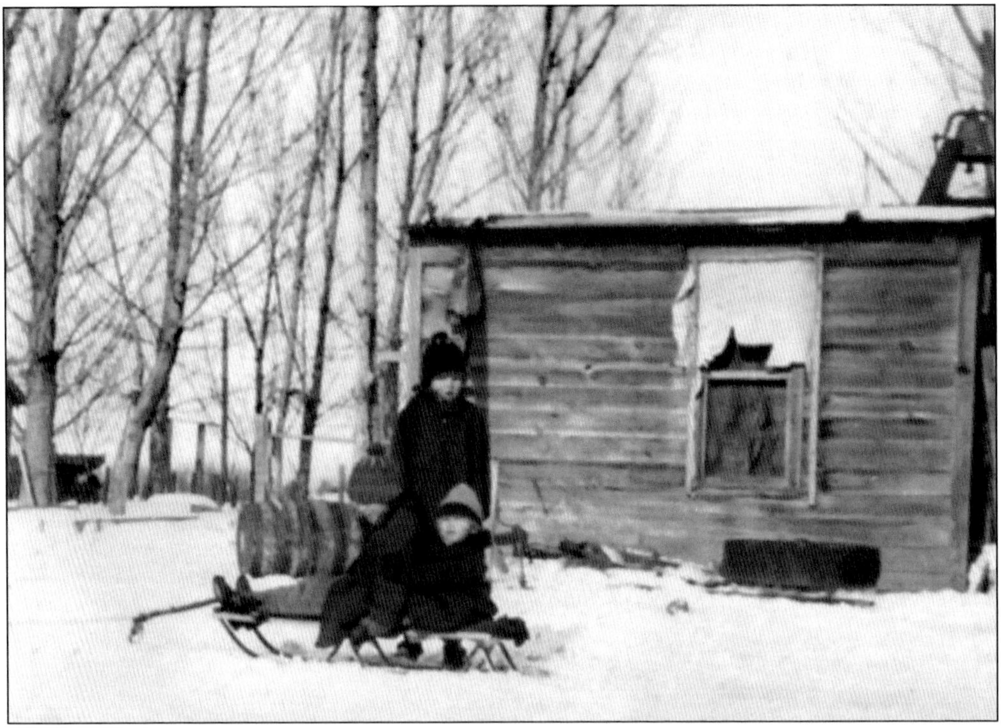

Winter provided a time for fun, as three of the children of Sam and Nettie Richardson played in the snow on their sled. Pictured above are Jasper (left), Bill, and Alta (standing) on Christmas Day 1925. They are in front of the home their parents moved into in 1909 when they moved to Declo. Eighty years later, the wood from this house was used to panel a room in a house in Elba. The picture below shows the children with their pony, Prince. The family won the pony in a raffle and brought him home in their Model A car. (Both courtesy of Nell Richardson Turner.)

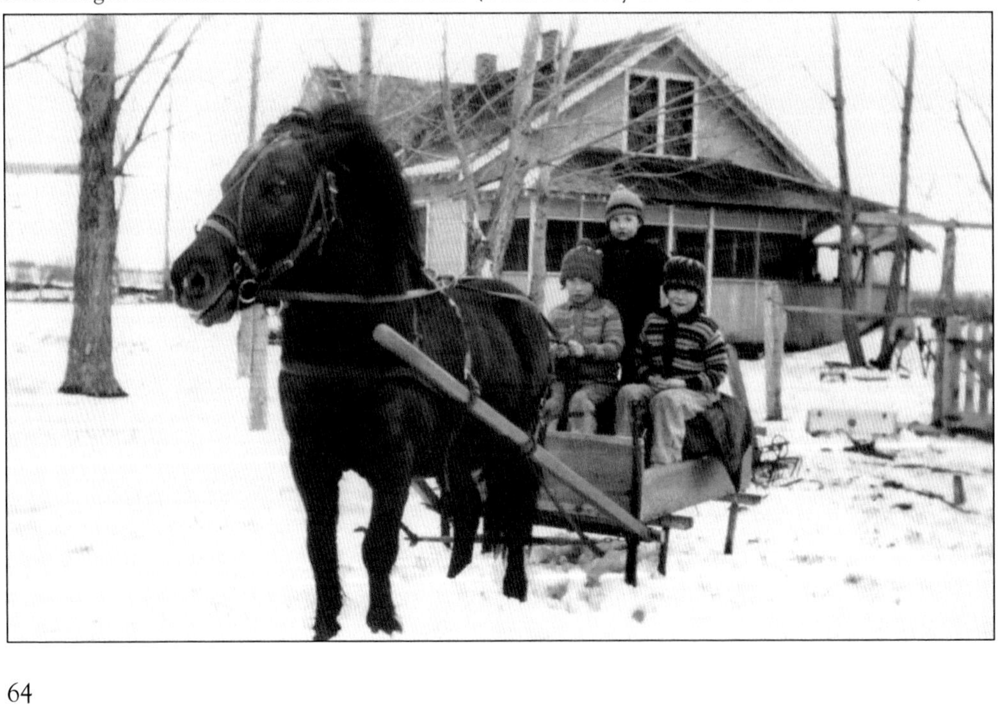

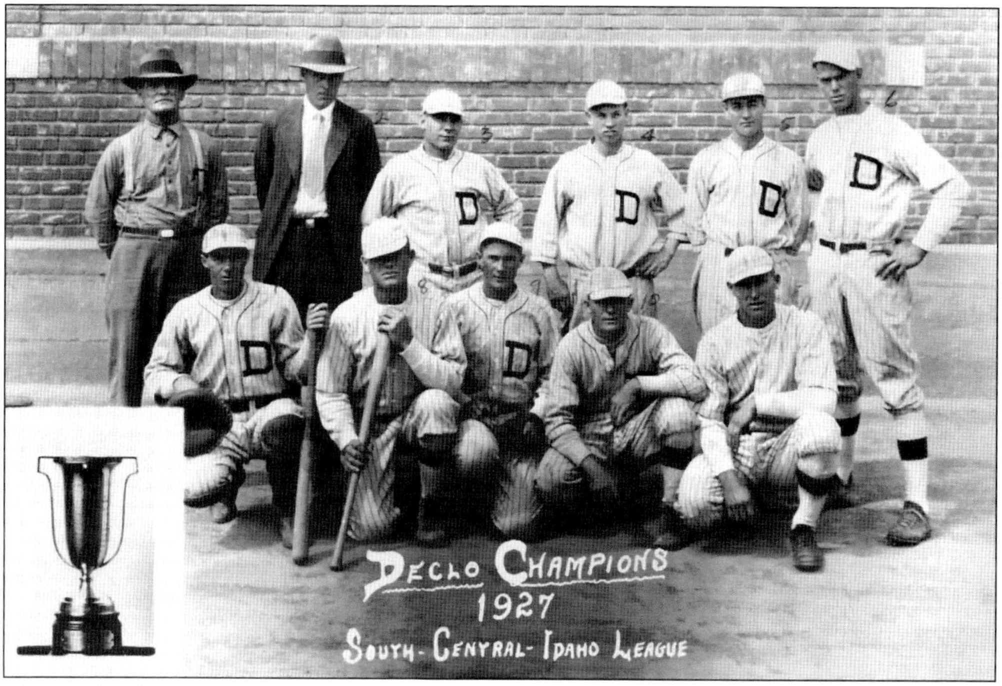

The Declo champions of the South Central League in 1927 are, from left to right, (first row) Doris Anderson, John Braden, Janice Hanson, Earl Osterhout, and John Bortz; (second row) Ben Osterhout, Ray Hasmer, Vasco Parke, Otis Williams, Earl Williams, and Reginald Hamilton. (Courtesy of Cleone Moncur.)

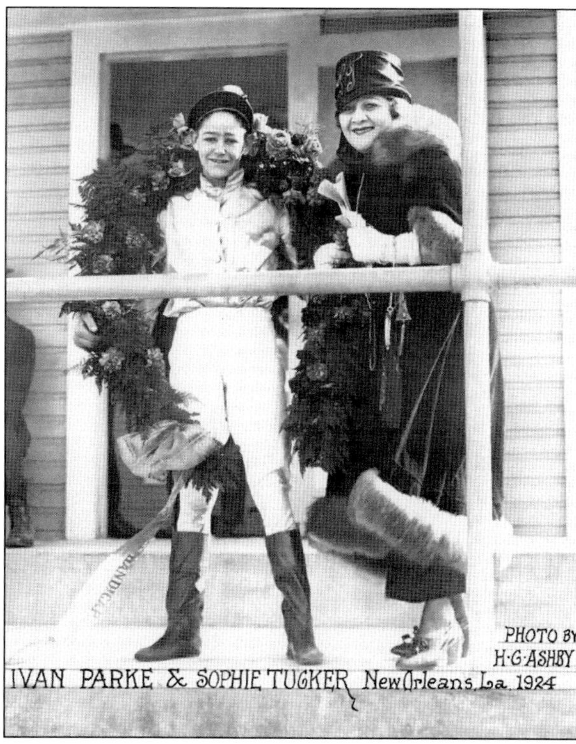

The Anson and Julia Parke family from Declo had eight boys and three girls. Five of the boys were nationally known in the horse racing business as jockeys and trainers. Ivan Parke is pictured here with vaudeville actress Sophie Tucker in 1924.

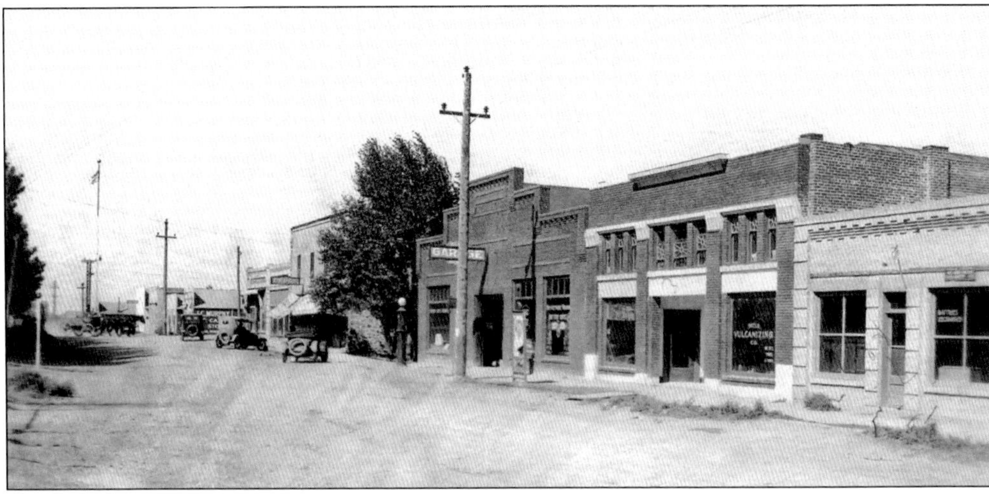

When the town applied for a post office in 1917, the general post office in Washington, D.C., said there were too many towns with the name of Marshfield. No one could decide on a name, so a new group of men visiting in Gillett Mercantile decided to take the initials of the first five men to walk into the store and form a name. The first five men were August Detlef, George Eldredge, James Cooley, Hyram Lewis, and Carl Osterhout. The letters spelled out D-E-C-L-O.

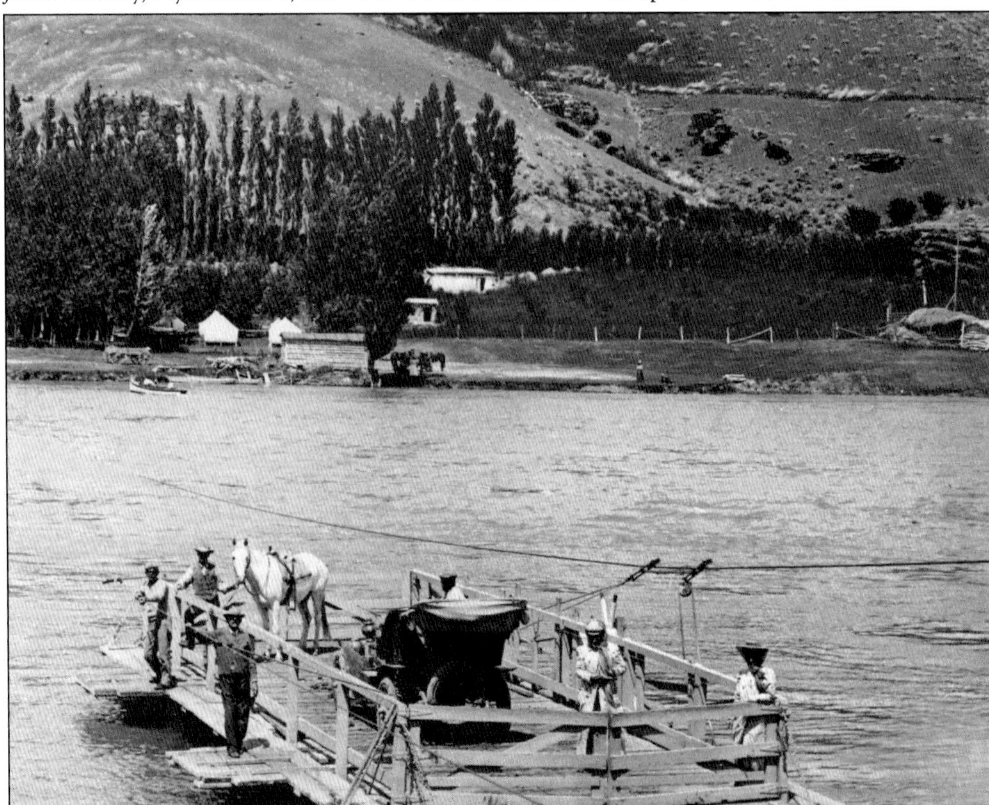

The Marshfield Ferry was near the home of Pete Peterson until bridges were built to cross the Snake River. Ferries were the only way to cross the river. There was another one called the Starrhs Ferry west of Burley.

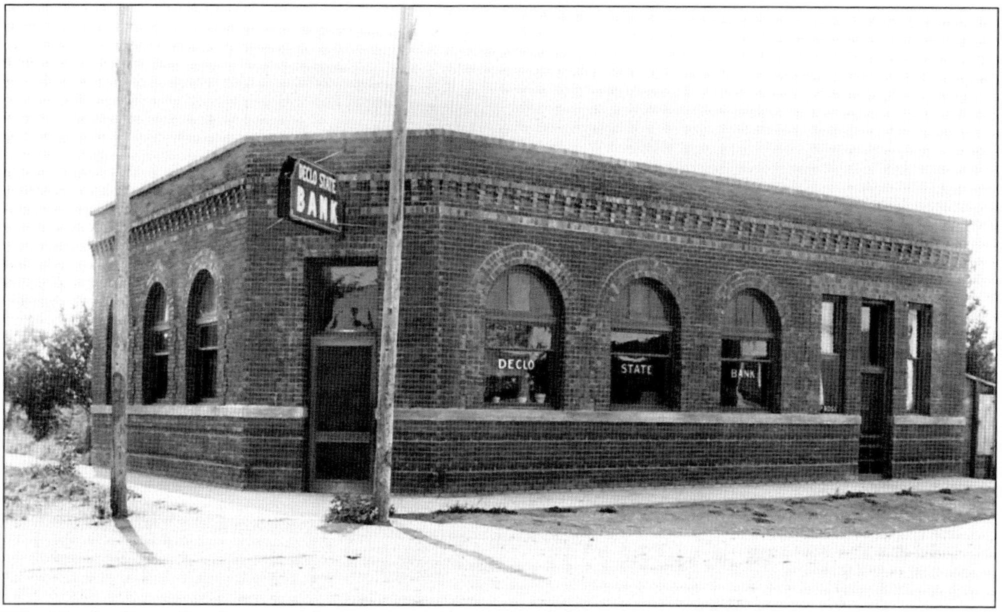

The Declo State Bank opened in 1917 as a branch of the Bank of Commerce of Burley. It had to close in 1920, causing much hardship for the community.

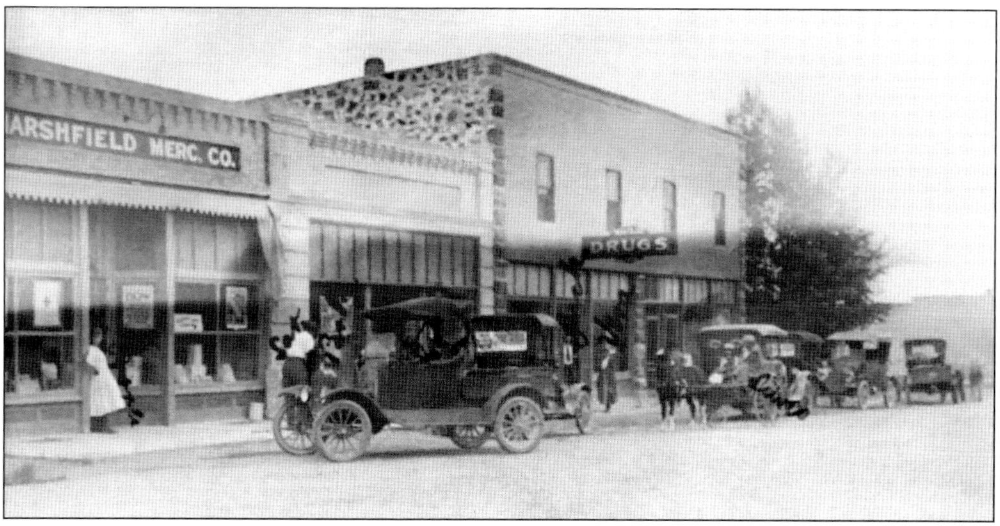

Main Street in Declo in the 1900s had many businesses, such as the Declo State Bank, Gillett Mercantile, hotels, boardinghouses, restaurants, a drugstore, a barbershop, and a bakery. It was a thriving community.

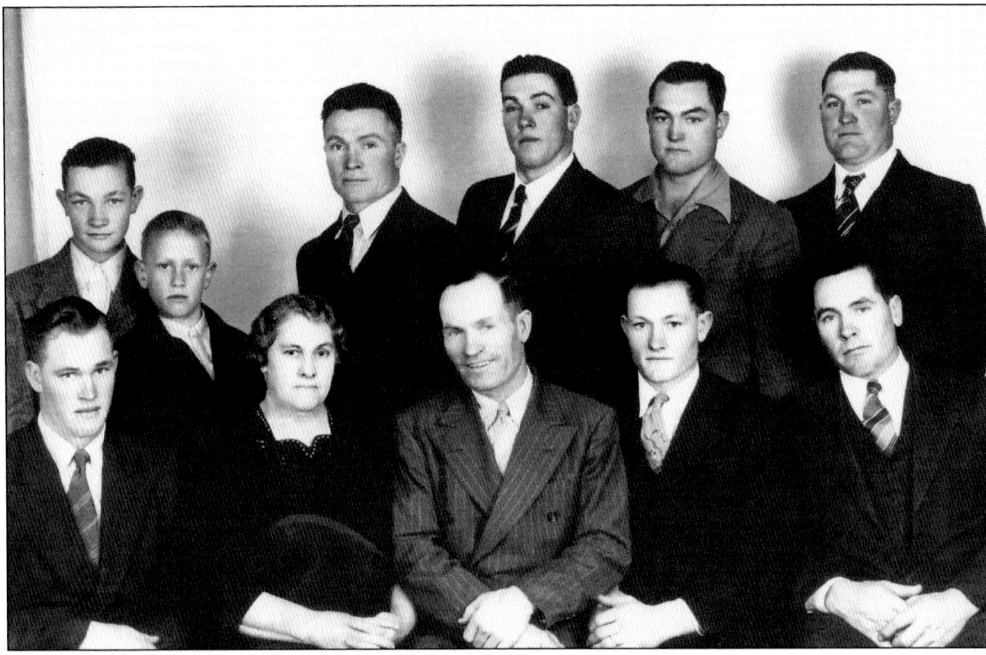

Leon and Katie Osterhout bought a small farm on the Marsh Creek a mile north of the community of Marshfield. Nine sons were born to this family, all at home. All nine sons remained in Declo their entire lives. This was the foundation of more than 30 Osterhout families living in the Cassia County area in 2007. (Courtesy Cleone Moncur.)

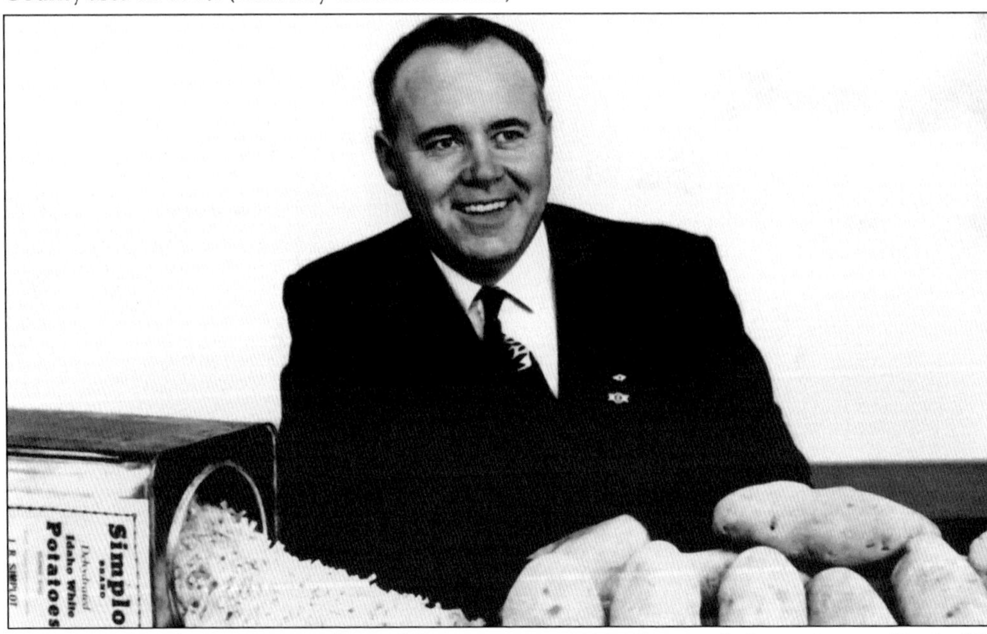

J. R. (Jack) Simplot came to Burley with his parents in 1910. They settled on a farm in Declo. He moved out of his parents' home when he was 14, and he was already learning to recognize good business deals. He became one of the wealthiest men in the country largely through the business side of agriculture. He was a major supplier of dehydrated potatoes during World War II, and he was the first supplier of frozen French fries to the McDonald's restaurant chain.

Five

ELBA

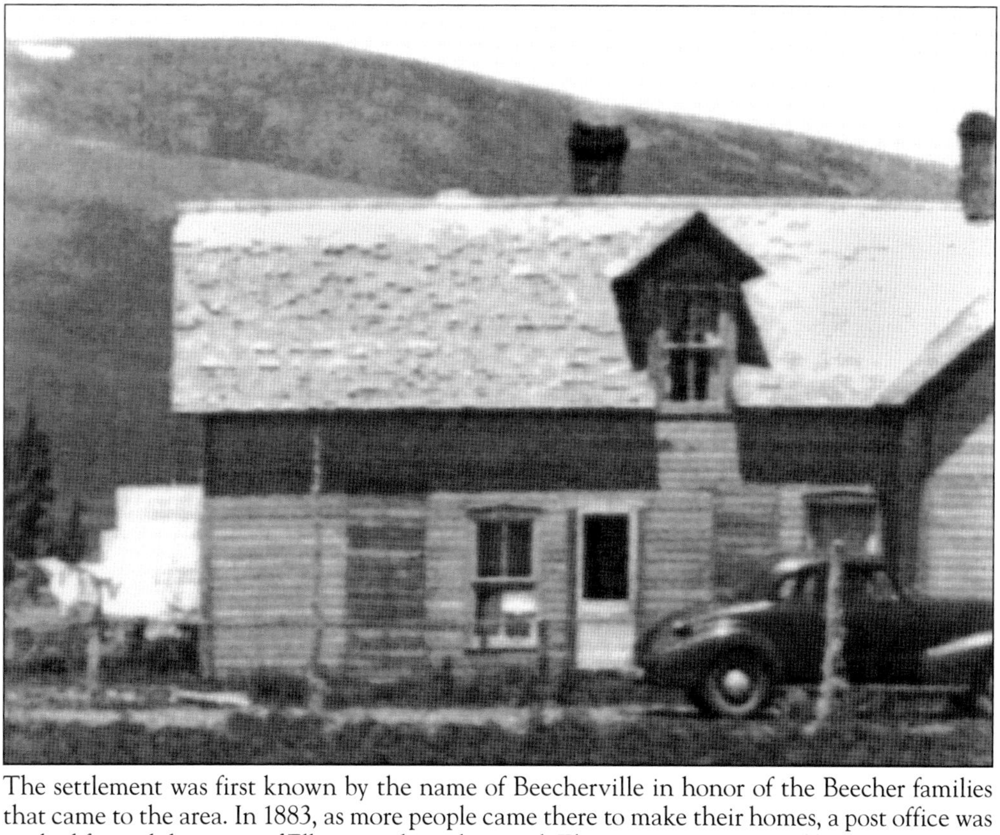

The settlement was first known by the name of Beecherville in honor of the Beecher families that came to the area. In 1883, as more people came there to make their homes, a post office was applied for and the name of Elba was adopted instead. The name was suggested by the postmaster of Albion, Charles Cobb. In the 112 years Elba had a post office, it was always operated in a family home. This is the McFarlane home, the third post office. (Courtesy of Bessie Nye.)

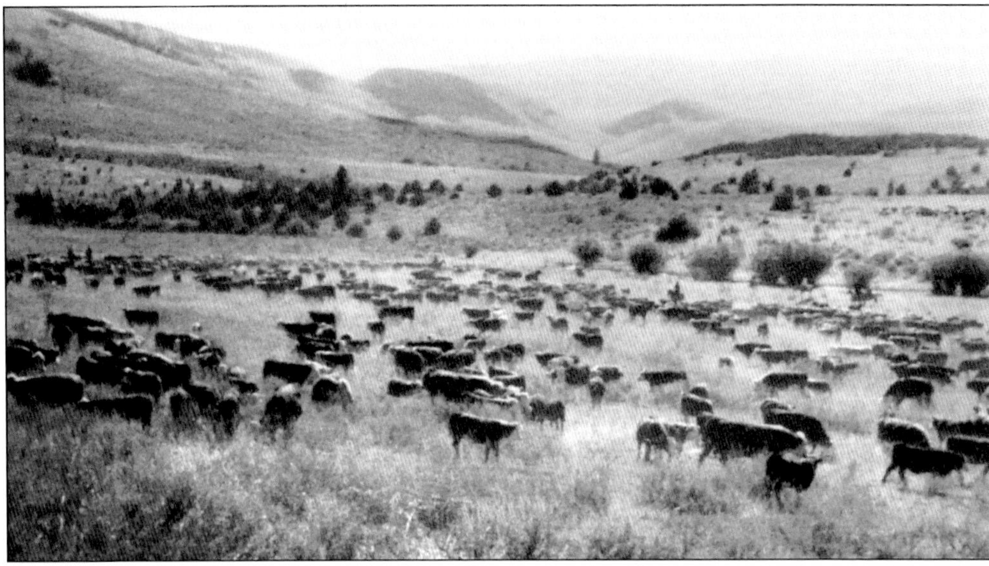

The first white settlers who came to the valley were John Shirley and Andrew Sweetzer from California. They were partners in the cattle business in 1871. This valley was their summer range for 4,000 to 5,000 head of cattle. When Ransom Beecher came from Utah to settle, Shirley said, "You can't live here. The snow will bury you up." However, his partner, Sweetzer, stated, "Since the settlers are coming to homestead, they have the first right. We will move our cattle out of the valley." This they soon did. Before they moved out, however, they killed and dressed a nice, young heifer and divided the meat with the settlers. (Courtesy of Vermoyne Ridenour.)

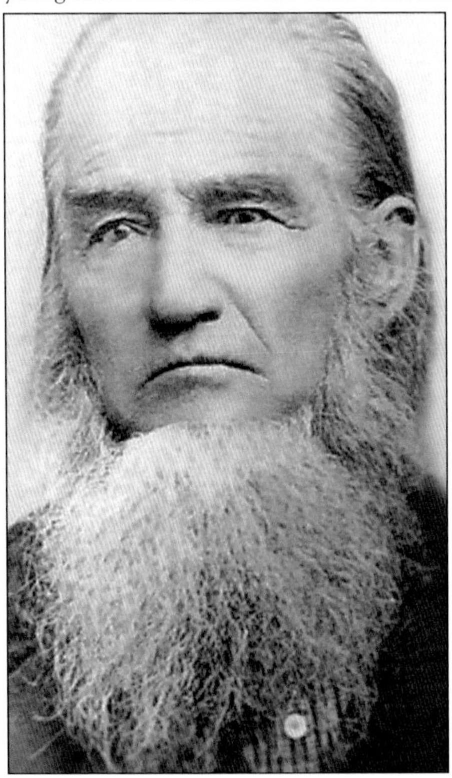

Ransom Asa Beecher came from Willard, Utah, to the valley in 1873 with his family to make their home at Cassia Creek. (Courtesy of Deborah Jones.)

Ransom Beecher and his sister Amelia Searl are sitting on the bank of Cassia Creek with the icehouse, or the smokehouse depending on the season, in the background. (Courtesy of Vermoyne Ridenour.)

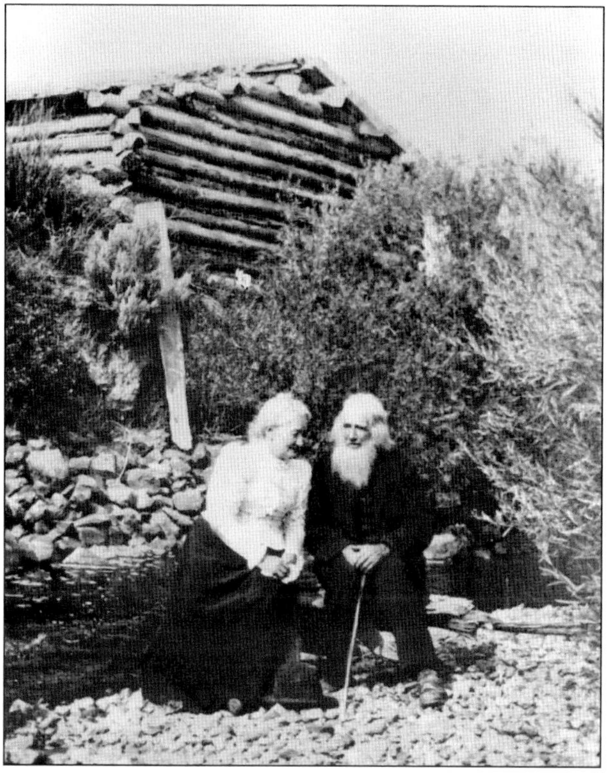

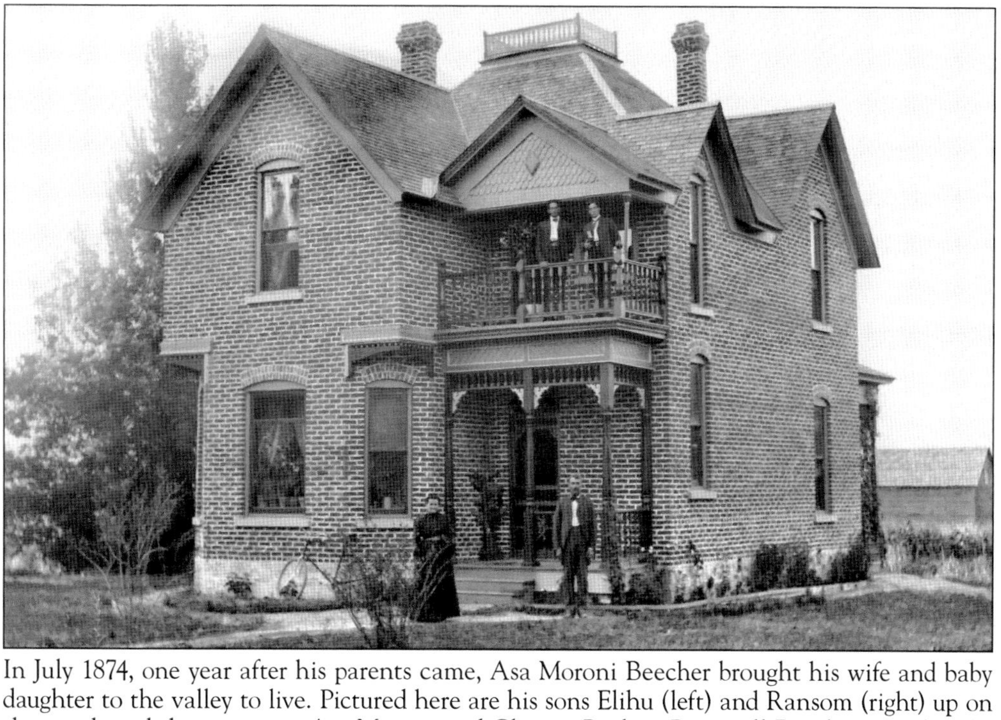

In July 1874, one year after his parents came, Asa Moroni Beecher brought his wife and baby daughter to the valley to live. Pictured here are his sons Elihu (left) and Ransom (right) up on the porch and their parents, Asa Moroni and Clarissa Paulina Pettingill Beecher, standing by the home they built. (Courtesy of Deborah Jones.)

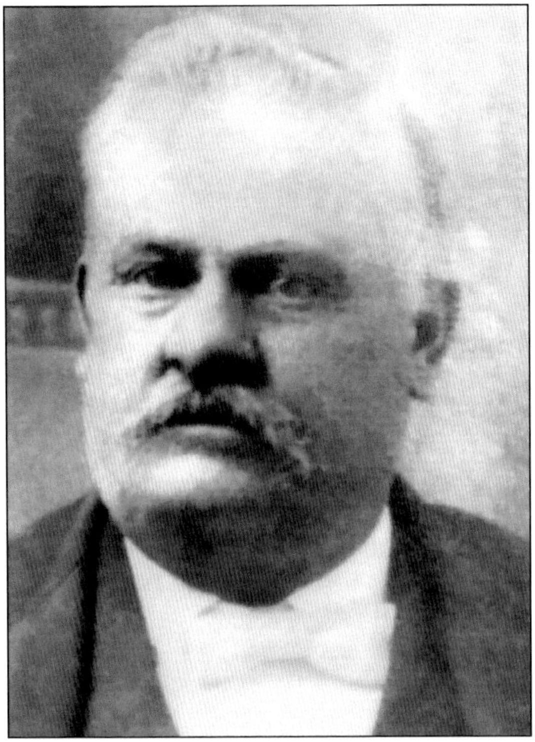

Tom Taylor was a prominent settler in the early days of Elba. He was the first LDS bishop, serving from 1887 to 1910, as well as the first mail carrier. (Courtesy of Deborah Jones.)

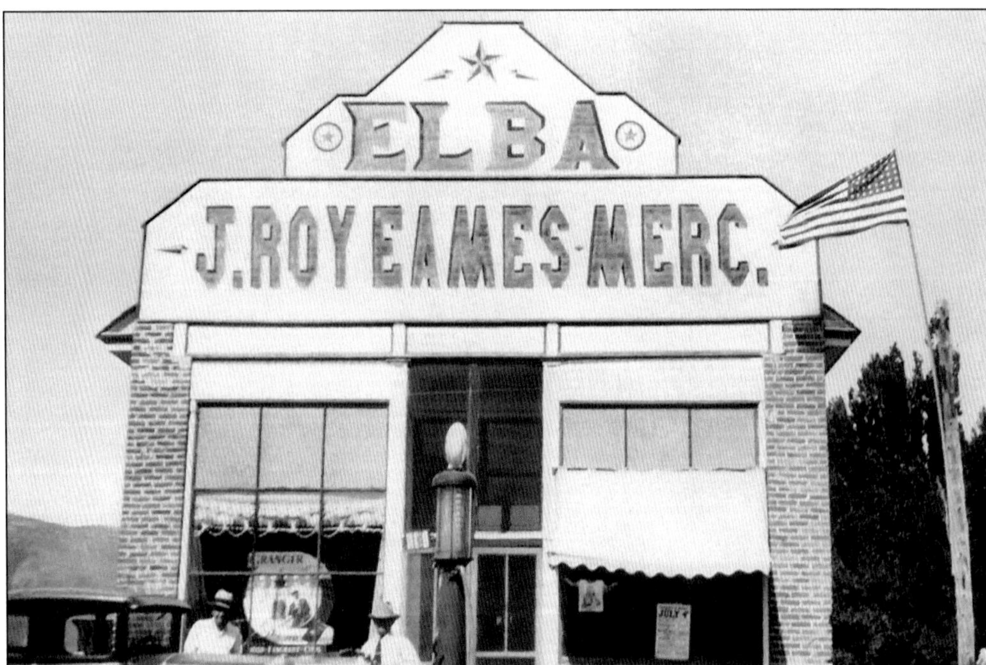

This small store was built and run by Thomas Taylor and George Hadfield. They originally had a frame building built on Taylor's lot. The merchandise for the store was freighted from the railhead in Kelton, Utah. Other merchants who operated this store were Robert Parish, Charlie Bigler, Louis Eames, J. Roy Eames, and Don Musser.

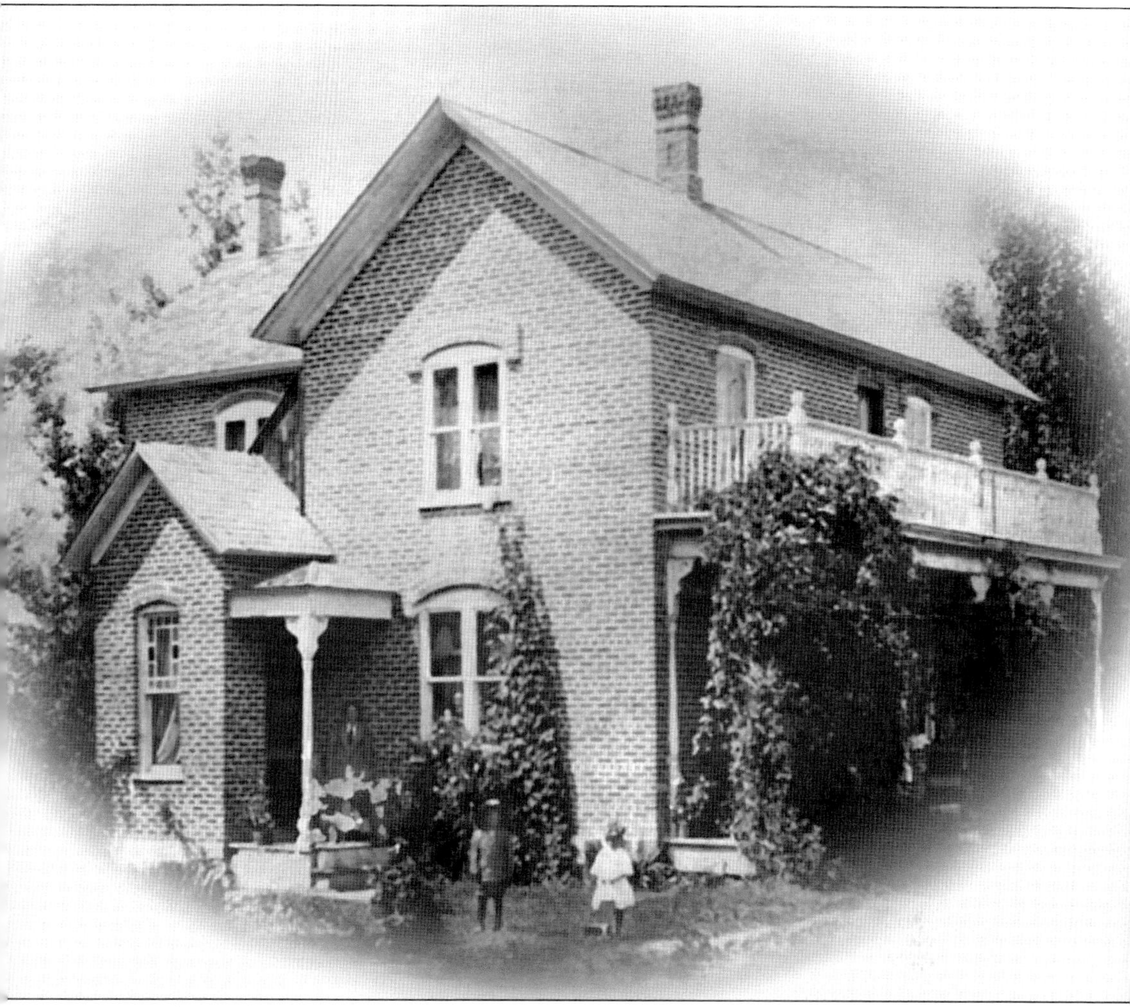

Tom Taylor's beautiful home was large enough for his family as well as renters for two rooms on the second floor. The renters had an outside entrance to their rooms. (Courtesy of Vermoyne Ridenour.)

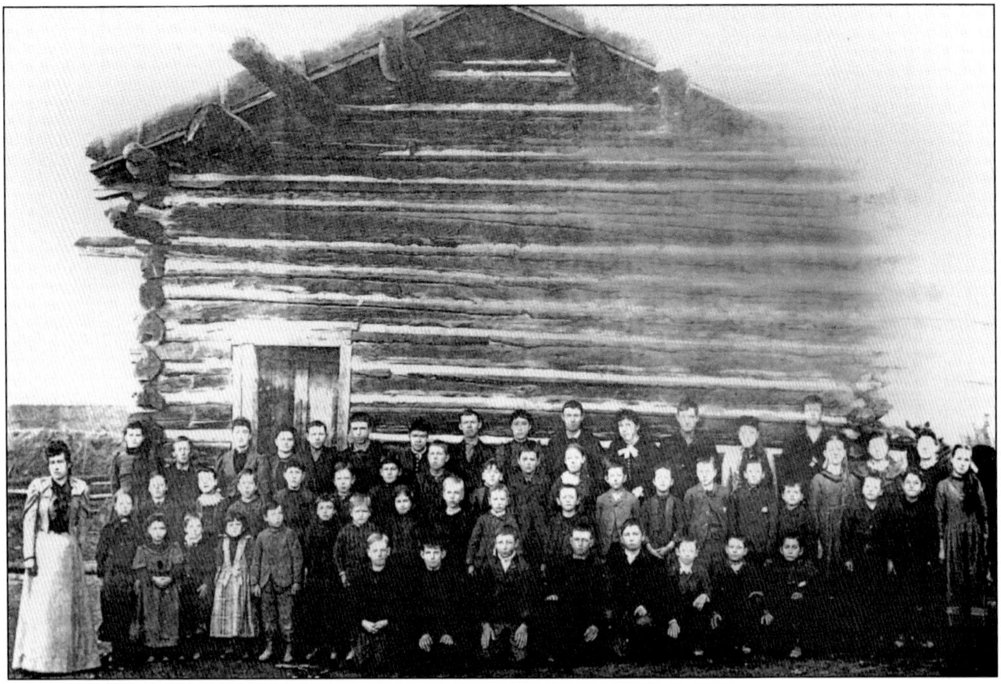

In about 1875, the men hauled logs from the canyon and built a log schoolhouse that was 20 feet by 30 feet. This schoolhouse was the second built in Cassia County. The first was erected a short time before in the neighboring community of Albion. (Courtesy of Mrs. J. R. Hurd.)

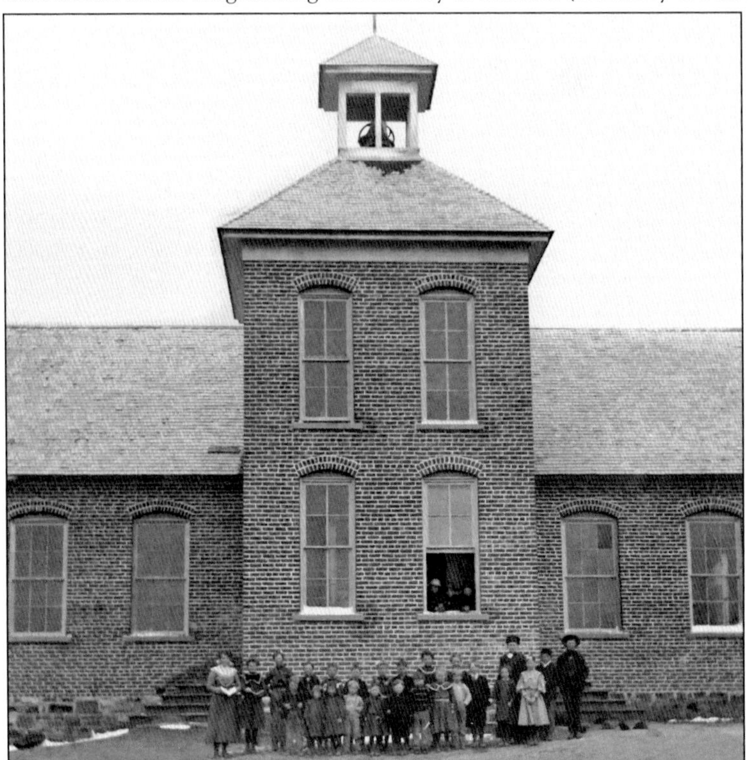

In 1900, a red-brick schoolhouse was built to replace the second log school in the center of the valley, which had only two rooms. This was known as District No. 8. This building has four rooms, two on each side of the hallway that extends the length of the building. In 1926, this building was torn down and rebuilt into the schoolhouse that stands there today.

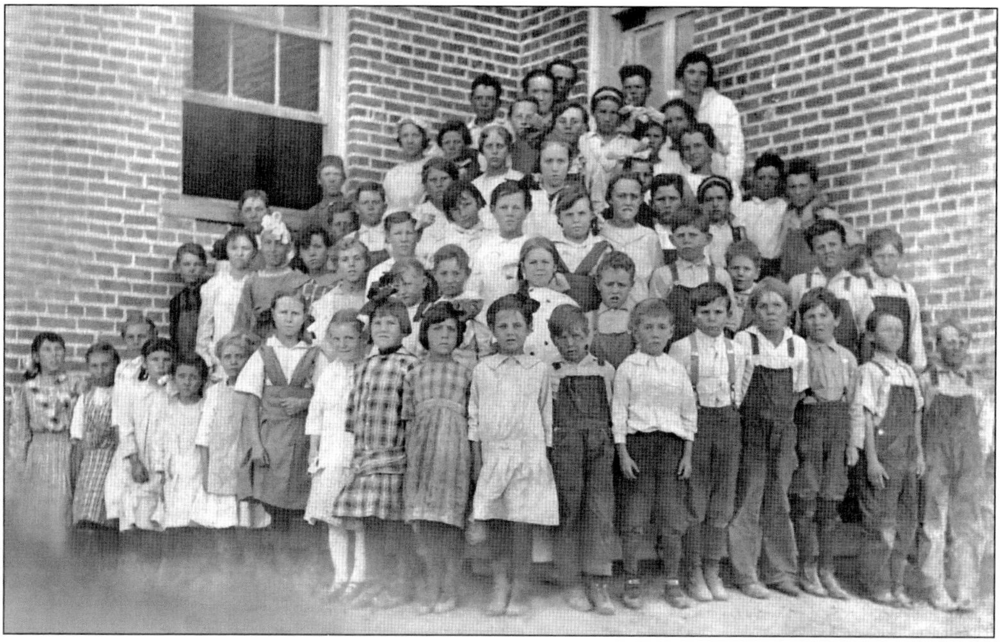

School District No. 8 was how the school in the center of Elba was known. These were the students of 1916–1917. (Courtesy of Bessie Nye.)

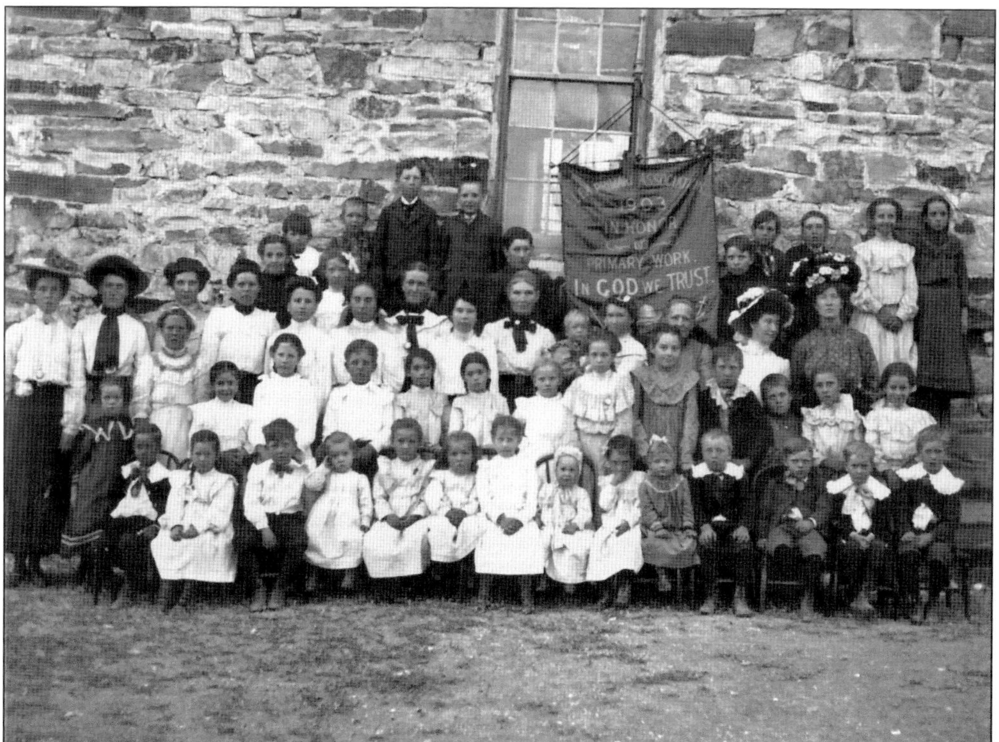

The children of the primary organization of the LDS Church gathered for this picture in front of the church in 1903. (Courtesy of Vermoyne Ridenour.)

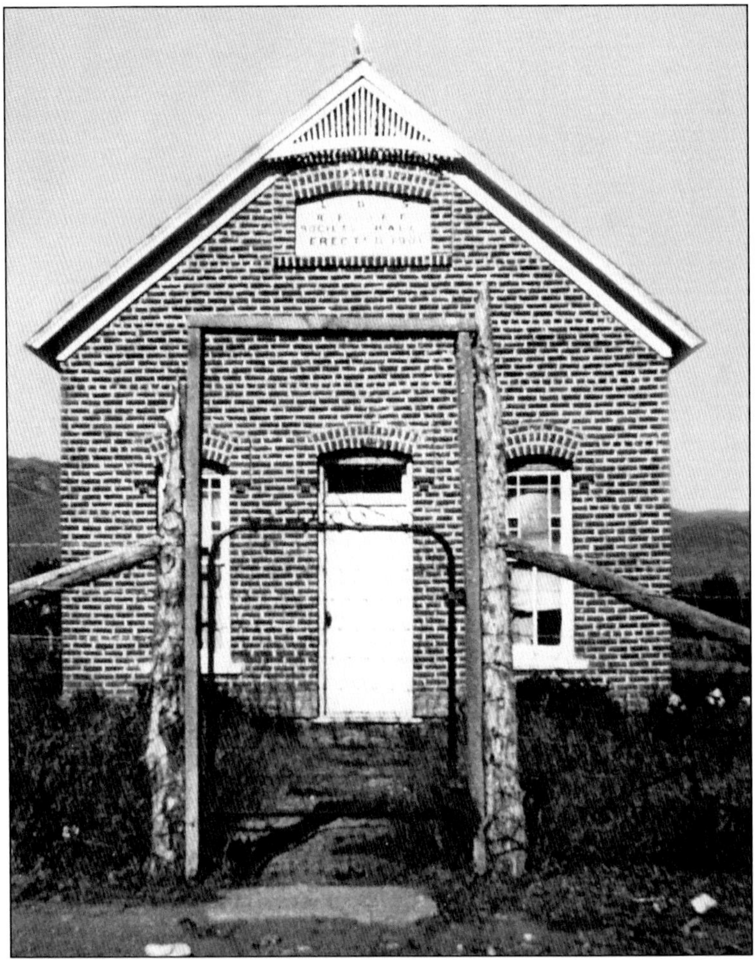

The Relief Society is a women's organization within the LDS Church. This small building was built in 1901 for the women to hold their weekly meetings. (Courtesy of Bessie Nye.)

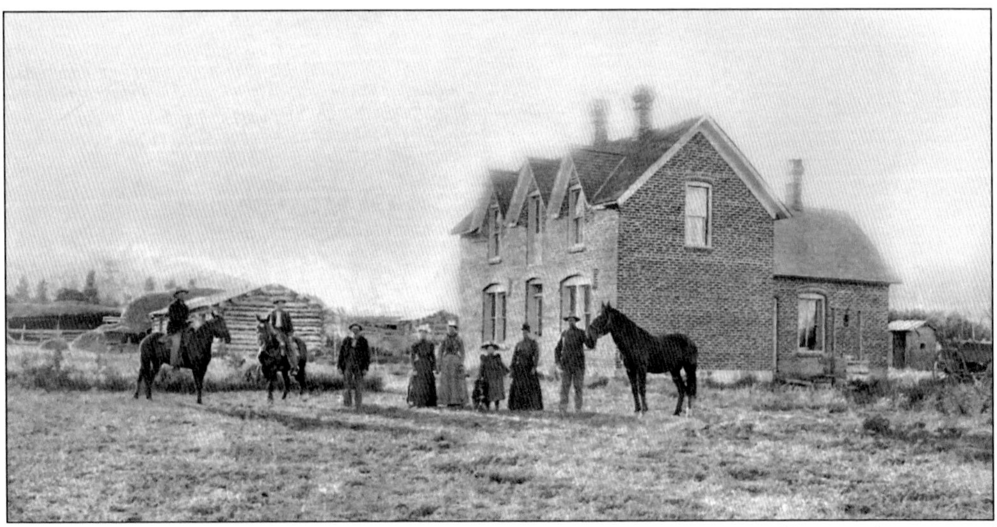

The Dan and Jerusha Savage home is an example of the large and beautiful homes that some of the settlers built. (Courtesy of Janis Carnahan.)

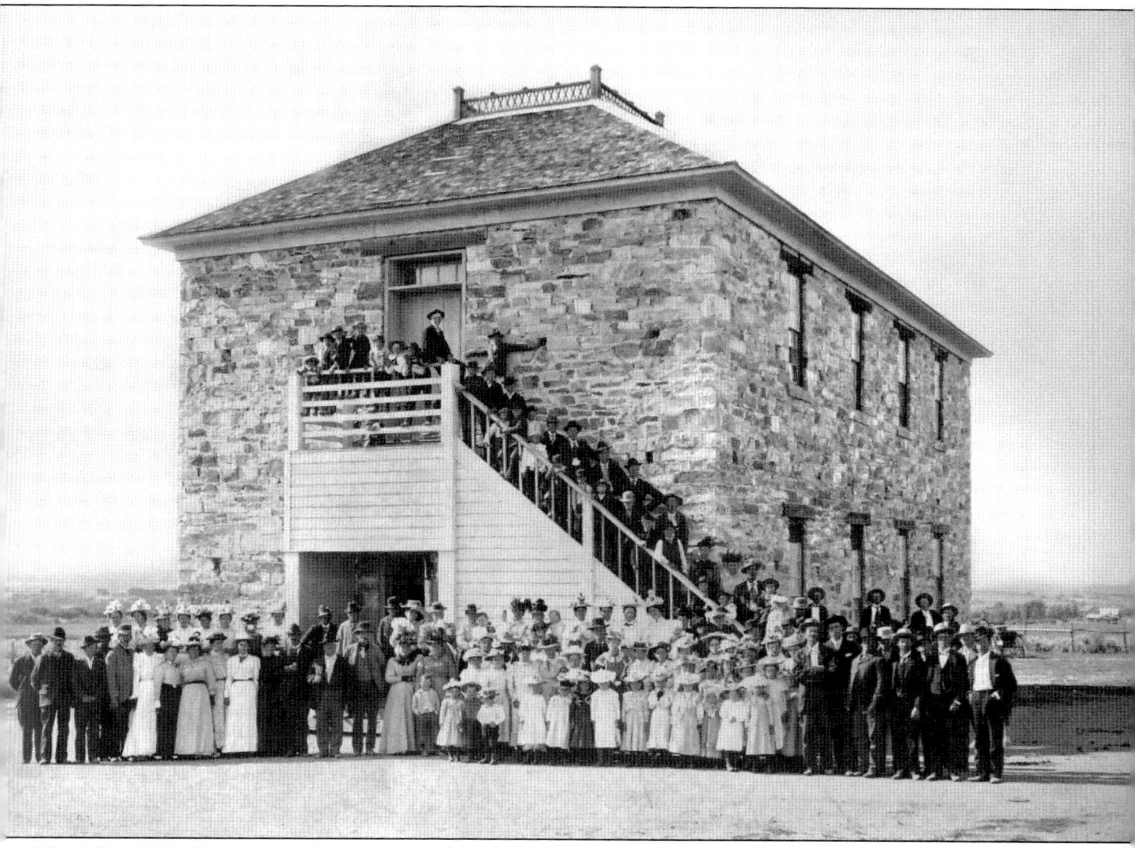

The Elba LDS Church was built about 1890. The rock was white granite hauled from the middle hill west of Joe Savage's home. The men hauled these rocks by team and wagon and laid them up by hand to construct this building. It was two stories tall and 30 by 60 feet in size. In 1950, when the church was being remodeled, Lewis M. Ottley had to use powder to loosen the rocks so the second story could be taken off. The early builders really knew how to mix mortar and lay rock.

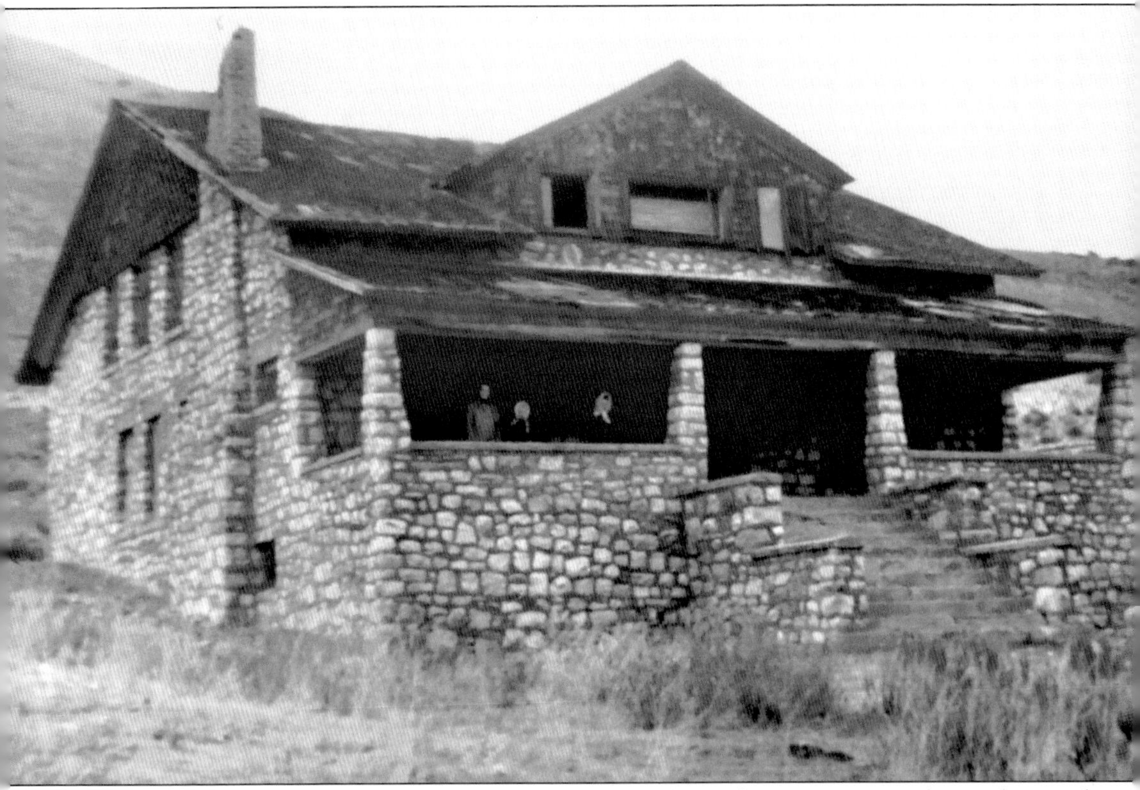

The Melcher Mansion, named after the gold mine, is located in a canyon on the southeast side of Mount Harrison. Built in 1917 by Pier McIntyre, it was an elegant home equipped with all of the decorative and modern conveniences of the day. The McIntyre family lived there for about six months and left when the mine closed, leaving all their furnishings behind. A caretaker lived in it for about seven years, but then it was abandoned until 1996, when Gary Jones bought it and restored it for a summer home. (Courtesy of Deborah Jones.)

Six

MALTA

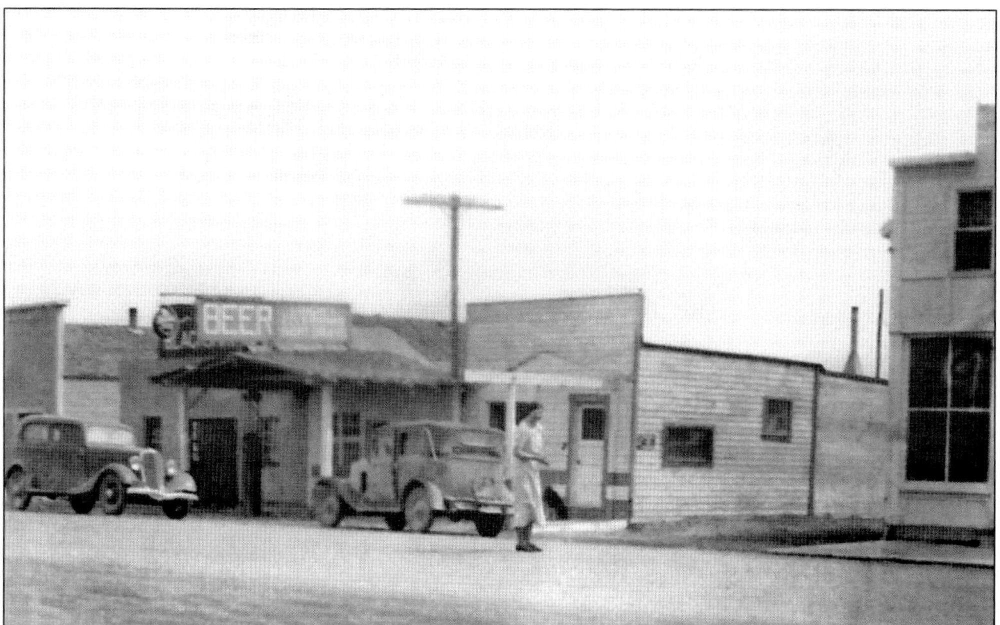

The settlers in the Malta area in the early 1880s had no central location for mail delivery. The mail was delivered in open boxes. The Condit family secured a permit from the U.S. Post Office Department to open a post office and name the community. Apparently it seemed like an island in a wide expanse of sea, so they named it Malta after the island of Malta in the Mediterranean.

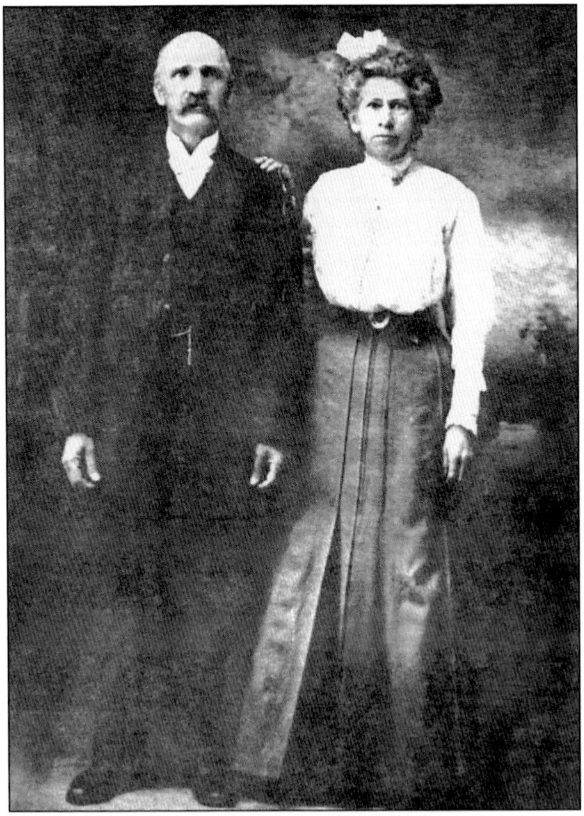

In 1883, the first post office was established in the vicinity of Malta. Addie Condit was appointed postmistress, an office she held for 12 years. She married John Farley on January 29, 1908. (Courtesy of Alvin and Rosella Neddo.)

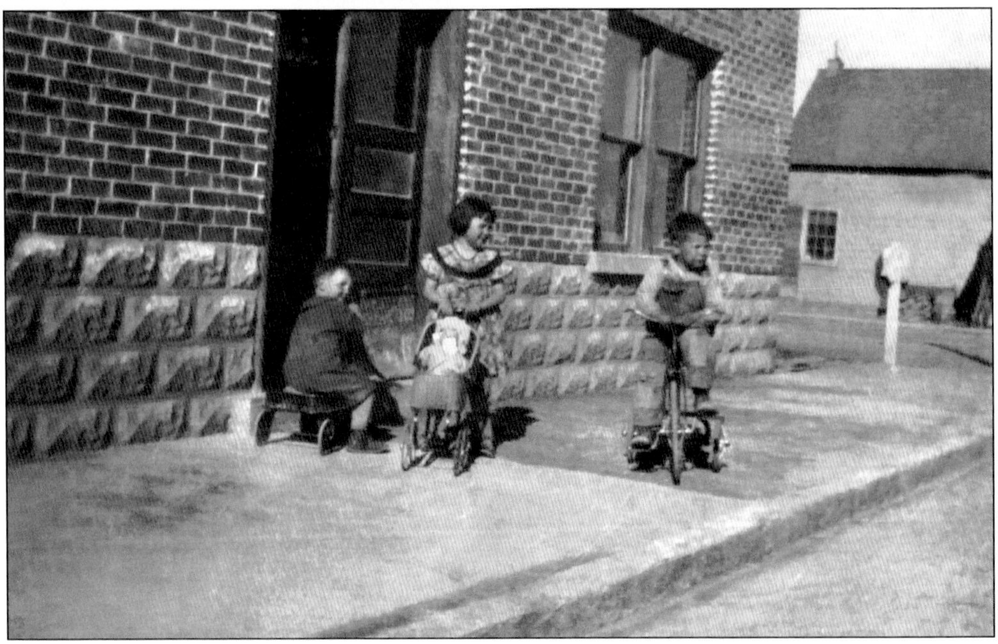

One of the postmistresses of the Malta Post Office was Mrs. J. Henry Thompson (Lora). Her son Robert (left) and daughter Caroline are playing with friend Grant Beyler in front of the post office. (Courtesy of Penny Thompson.)

Pictured from left to right are unidentified, Oscar, Lula, Arthur, Jess, and Eliza Pierce, the mother, holding Nellie. The picture was taken at Pierce Ranch in Malta in 1892. The father, James Pierce, came to Idaho as a young man when he drove cattle up from Texas. He bought into the holdings of brothers Lou and Andrew Sweetzer and later bought them out. Author Edgar Rice Burroughs came to work on the ranch in his youth. (Courtesy of Ann Wight.)

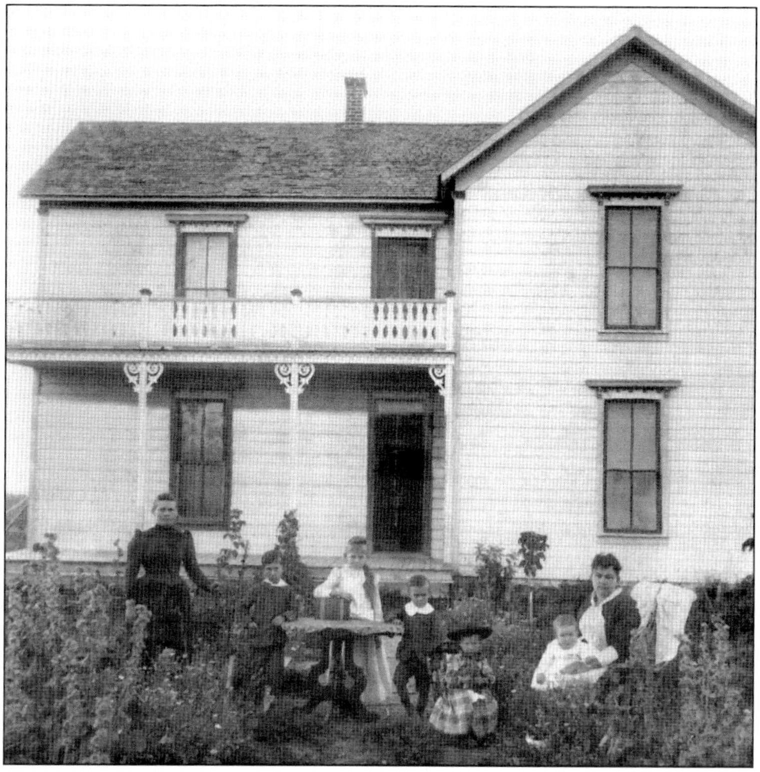

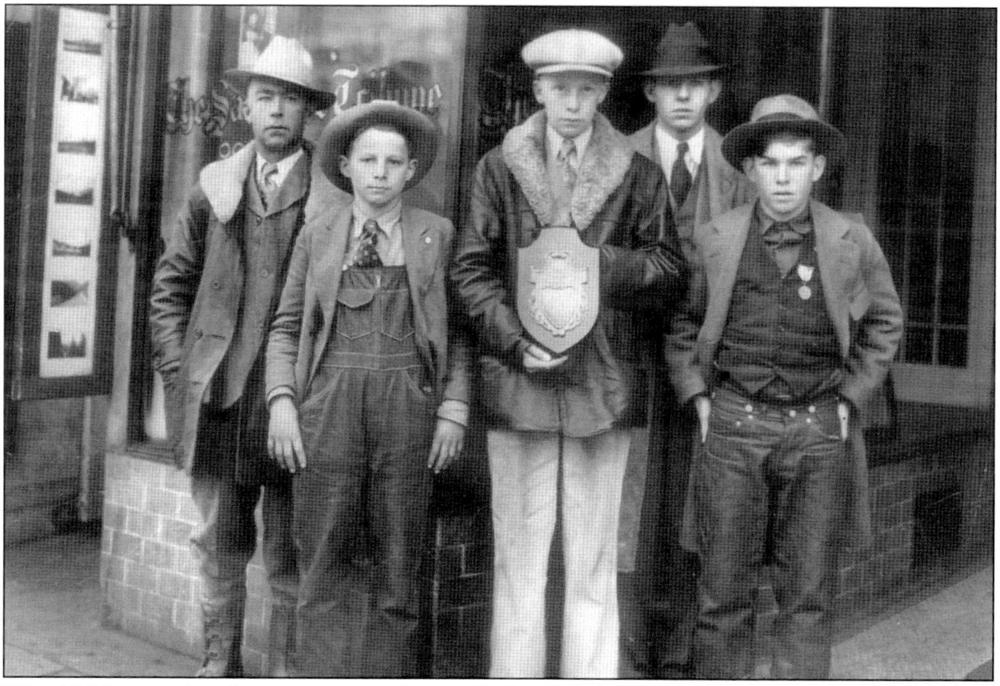

The 4-H livestock judging team traveled to Ogden, Utah, in 1931. They won the top judging award. From left to right are Art Pierce, Jack Hitt, Jack Pierce, Mr. Warren (the county agent), and Glen Parke. (Courtesy of Ann Wight.)

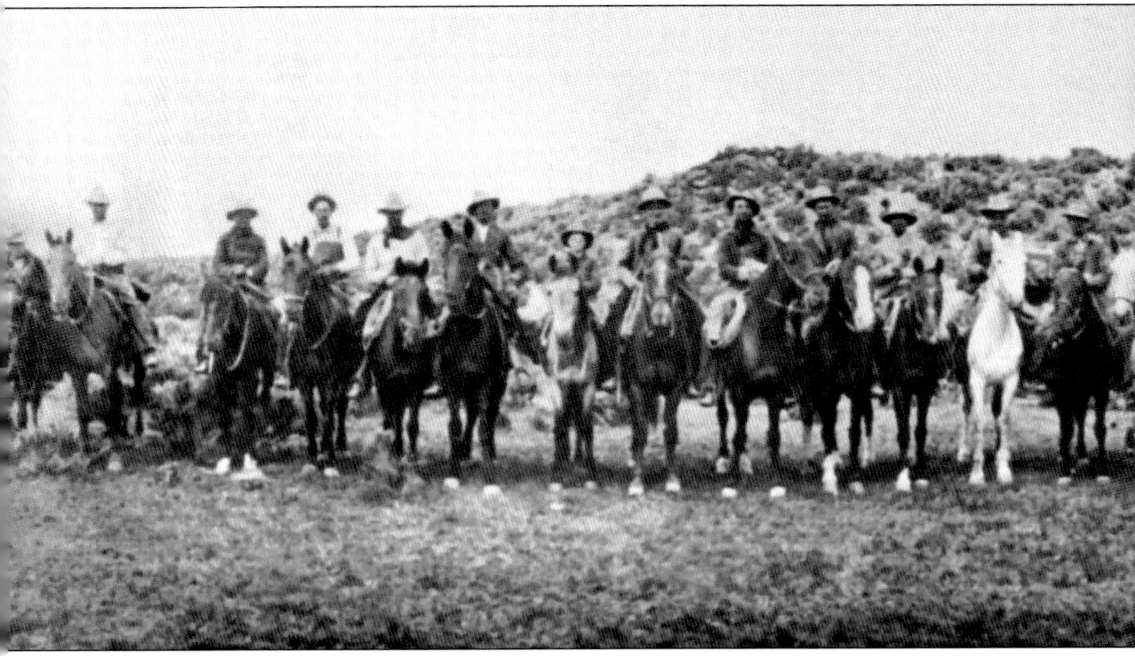

The cattle ranchers of Malta ran out of hay during the winter of 1917 and drove their cattle down to Raft River at Heglar Lane to feed. The men in the picture are, from left to right, Ollie Anderson, Frank Johns, George Chatburn, Harrison Powers, Ralph Lounsbury, Jim Hitt, Floyd Taylor, Joe

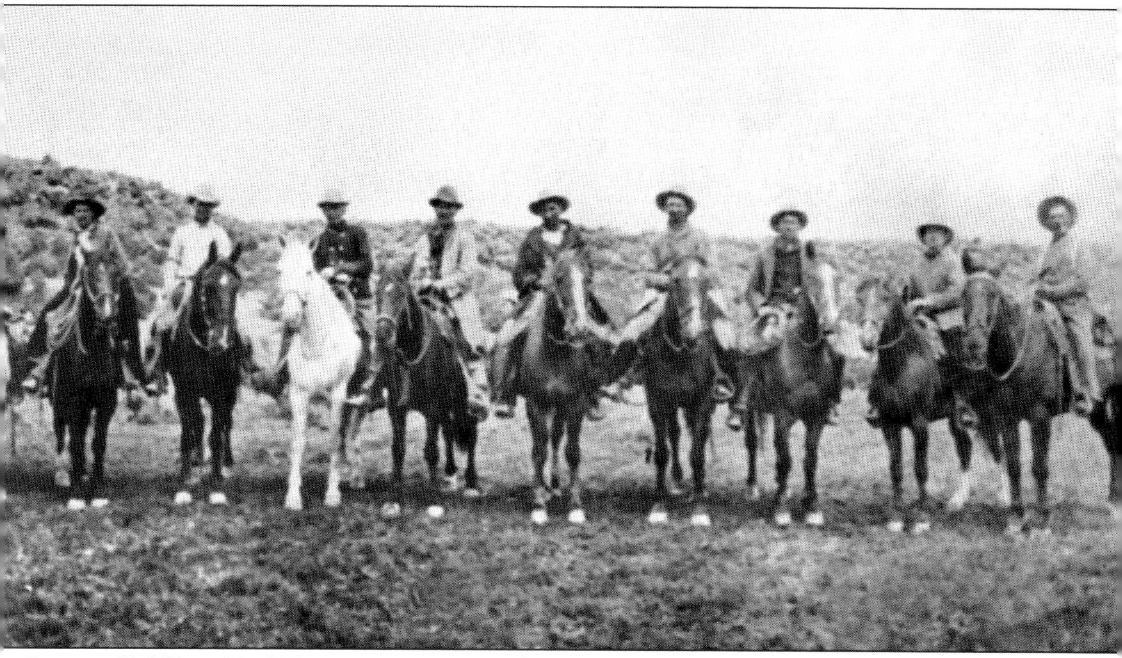

Stewart, Ted King, Fred Kossman, Tommie Taylor, Sam Cottrel, Ed Kossman, Bill Pierce, Buck Peterson and his brother ? Peterson on one horse, Allen Batch, Frank Shodde, Dick Anderson, Bert Cottle, John Hitt, Ether Parke, and three unidentified. (Courtesy of Ada Parke.)

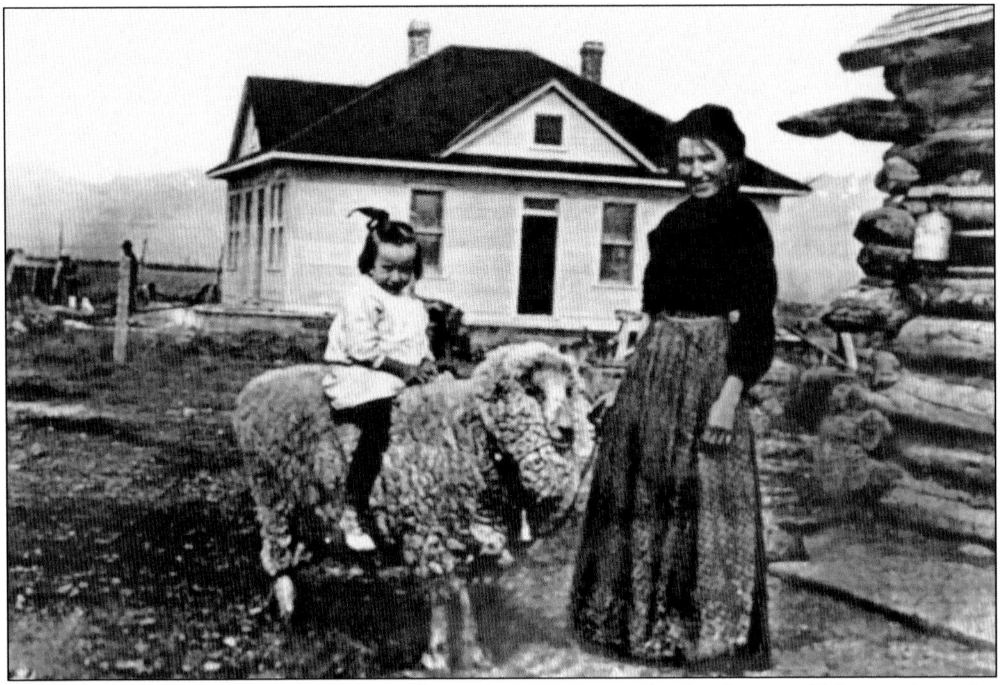

This log home could be the first one in the Malta area. It was the first home of Ether and Cecilia Hutchison Parke. Daughter Eunice is sitting on the sheep. They built the frame house, which is the home of Ada Parke in 2009, to replace the log home. (Courtesy of Ada Parke.)

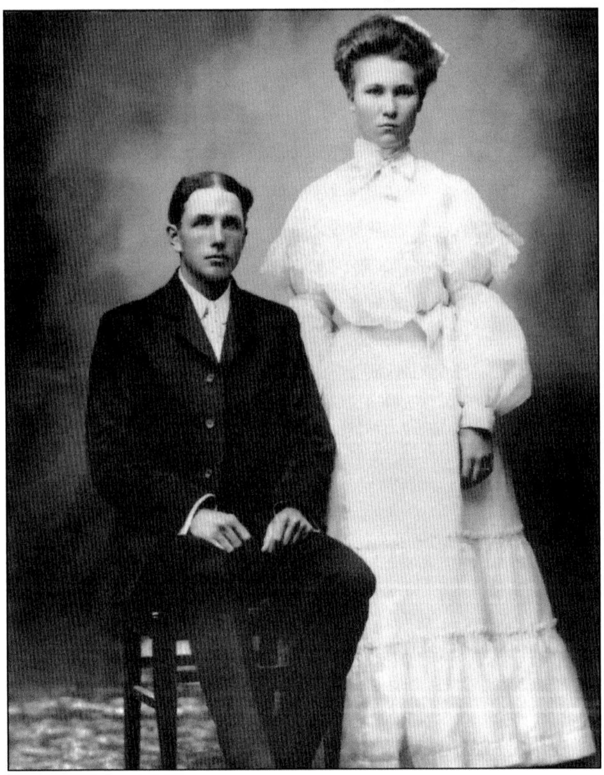

Isaac James Neddo Jr. came to Malta in 1902 and purchased a ranch with his father. He married Alice Osterhout on June 2, 1905, in Logan, Utah. Alice Osterhout was raised in Conner Creek, Idaho. The ranch is still in the family. It is owned by their granddaughter and her husband, Trudy and Kevin Tracy. (Courtesy of Alvin and Rosella Neddo.)

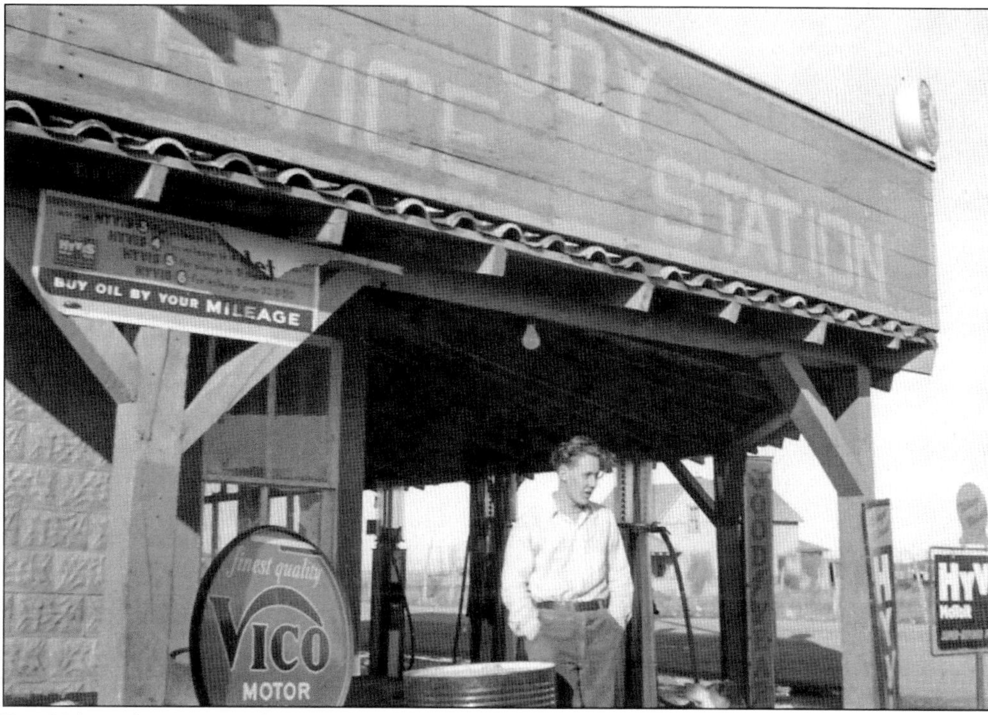

Rex Udy is shown at Dad's Service Station.

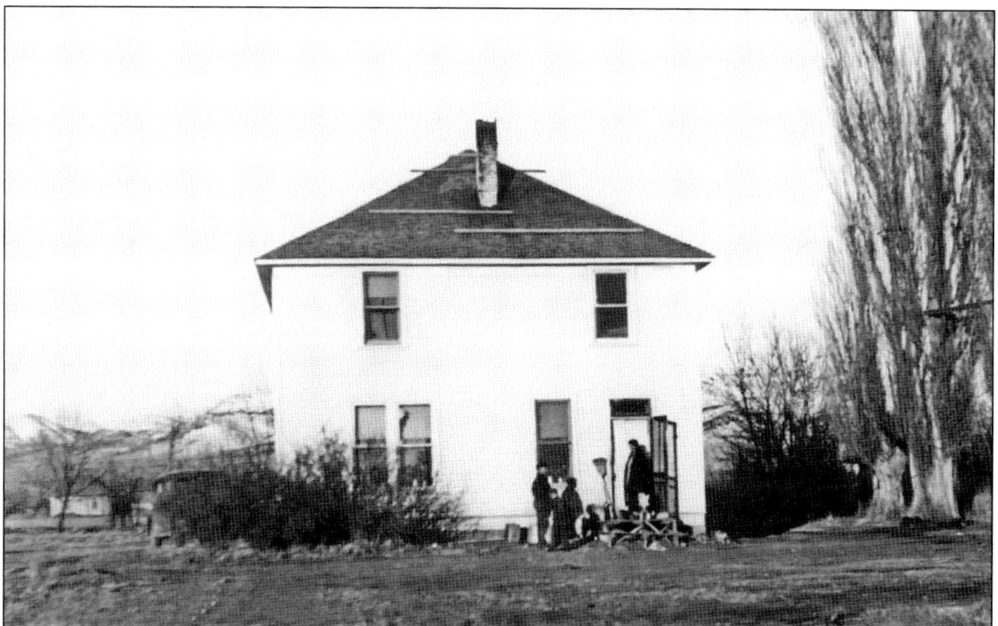
The Ivan J. Neddo home was built in 1906. (Courtesy of Alvin and Rosella Neddo.)

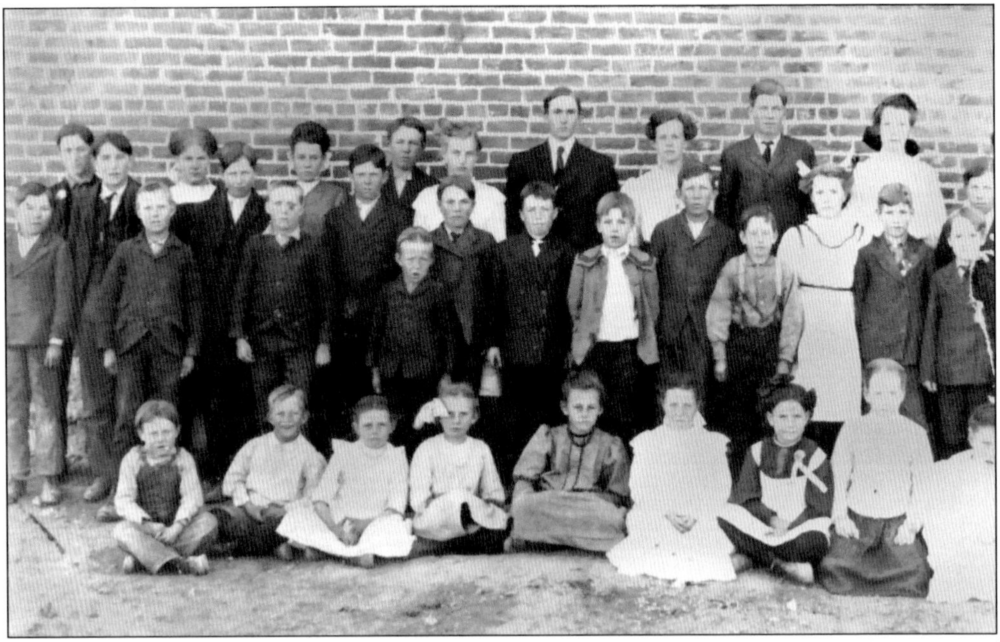

The Malta School class in the early 1900s appears to be all the grades together. (Courtesy of Kaye Carson.)

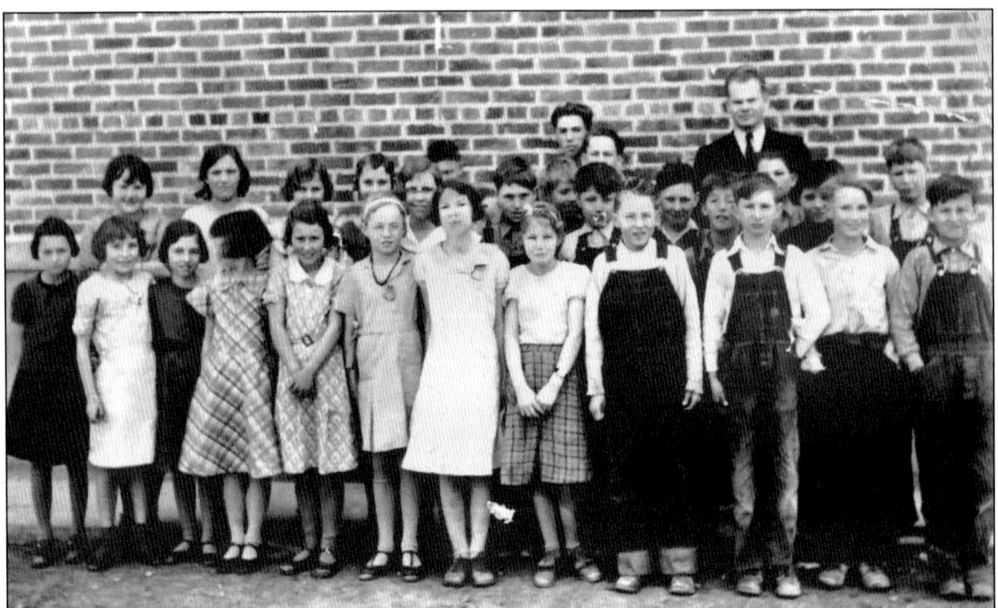

Pictured here is the Malta fifth- and sixth-grade class of 1934, taught by Fred Anderson. (Courtesy of Kaye Carson.)

Seven

OAKLEY

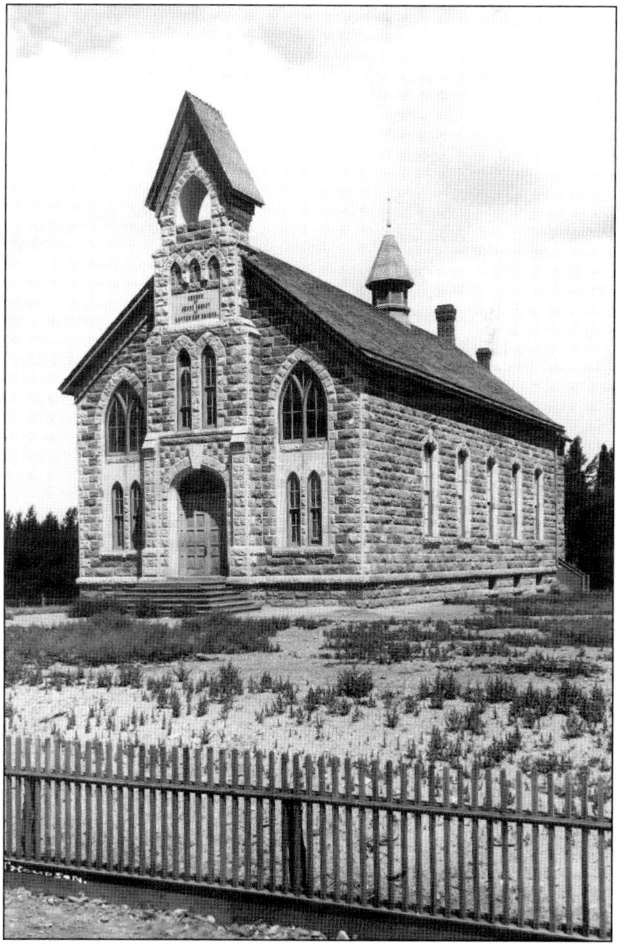

The Cassia LDS Stake Tabernacle was started in 1895. This beautiful building was constructed of basalt from a quarry 2 miles east of Oakley. The walls were 18 inches thick. It was completed in 1902 at a cost of $12,000. The church had a seating capacity of 700 people and was used for a variety of meetings, such as graduations, patriotic gatherings, and musical programs. Funds were raised to purchase a beautiful pipe organ. The building was abandoned in 1956 and burned down in 1966.

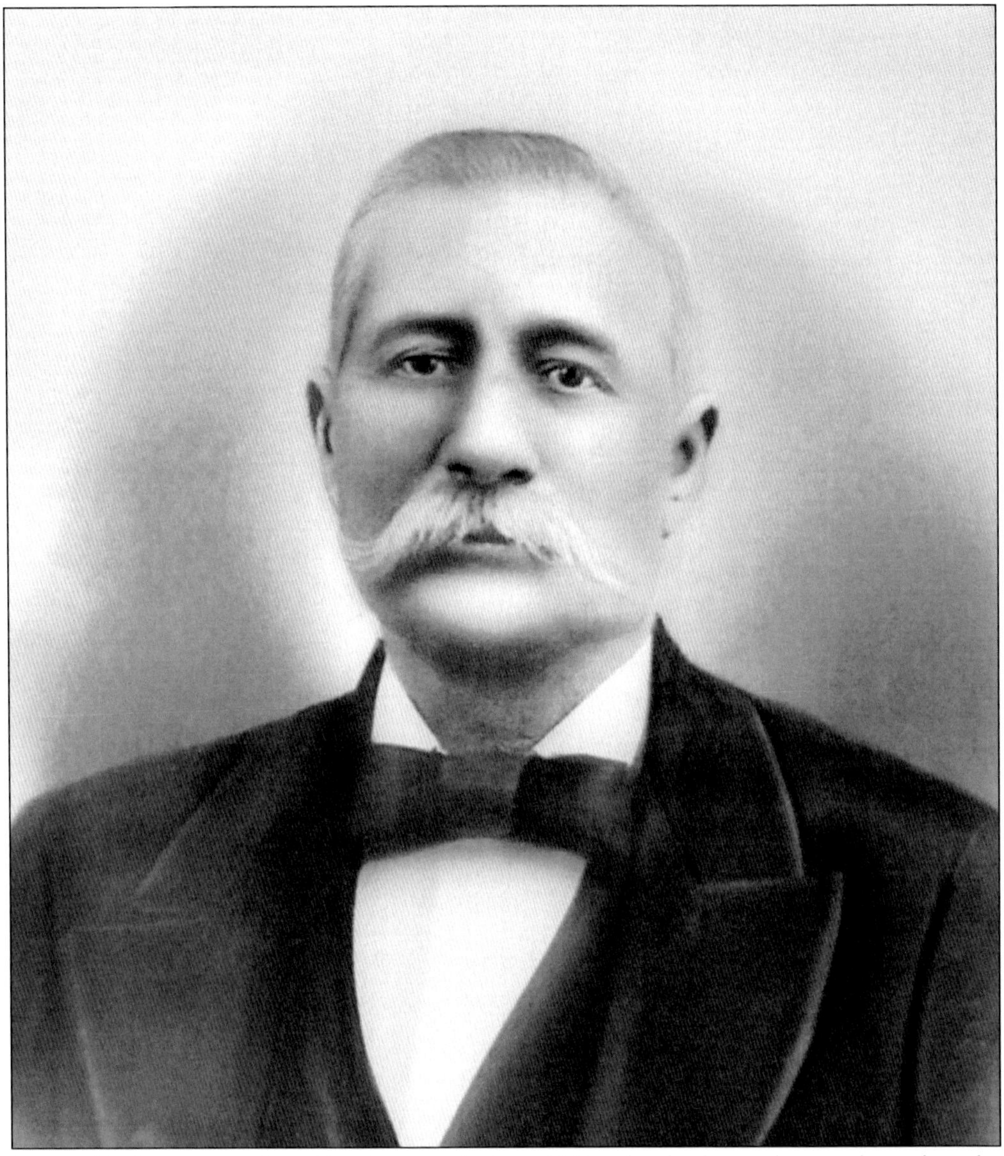

Horton D. Haight came from Farmington, Utah, in 1882 to be the first stake president when the Cassia Stake of the LDS Church was organized. It included all the towns of Cassia County. Each community had its own congregation. He brought with him nine children, including his married children and their spouses. He and his family became prominent leaders of the community. David B. Haight, a grandson, grew up in Oakley and became an apostle for the worldwide church in 1976. (Courtesy of the Oakley Valley Museum.)

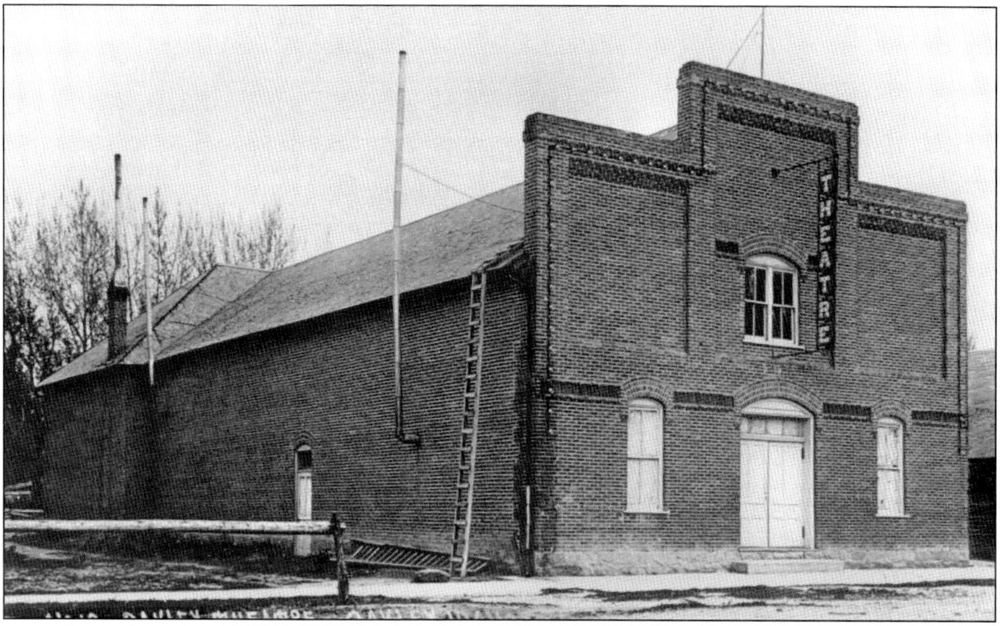

An editorial in the *Oakley Eagle* in 1906 may have prompted B. P. Howells to build an opera house. This well-constructed building served the community for many years. Although most of the productions were from local groups, during the 1910s, traveling troupes would stop in Oakley for a week on their way to and from Salt Lake City and Boise. It is still used for live performances of the Oakley Valley Arts Council. (Courtesy of Jamie Larsen.)

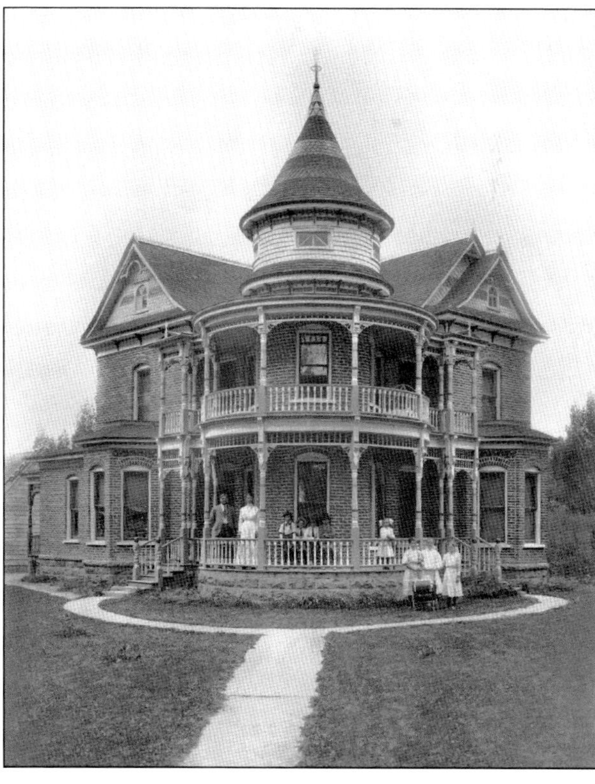

Benjamin P. Howells was just 12 years old when he came to the Oakley Valley in 1875. He had helped a man, P. M. Niles, drive a herd of cattle from Tooele, Utah, to the Goose Creek Valley. Niles, an educator, tutored him, and Howells went on to become a teacher and an attorney at an early age. By 1900, he was a judge and a prominent member of the community. His home, called "the Castle," is a beautiful example of the Victorian architecture that many of Oakley's affluent citizens used from the 1890s through 1910. (Courtesy of Jamie Larsen.)

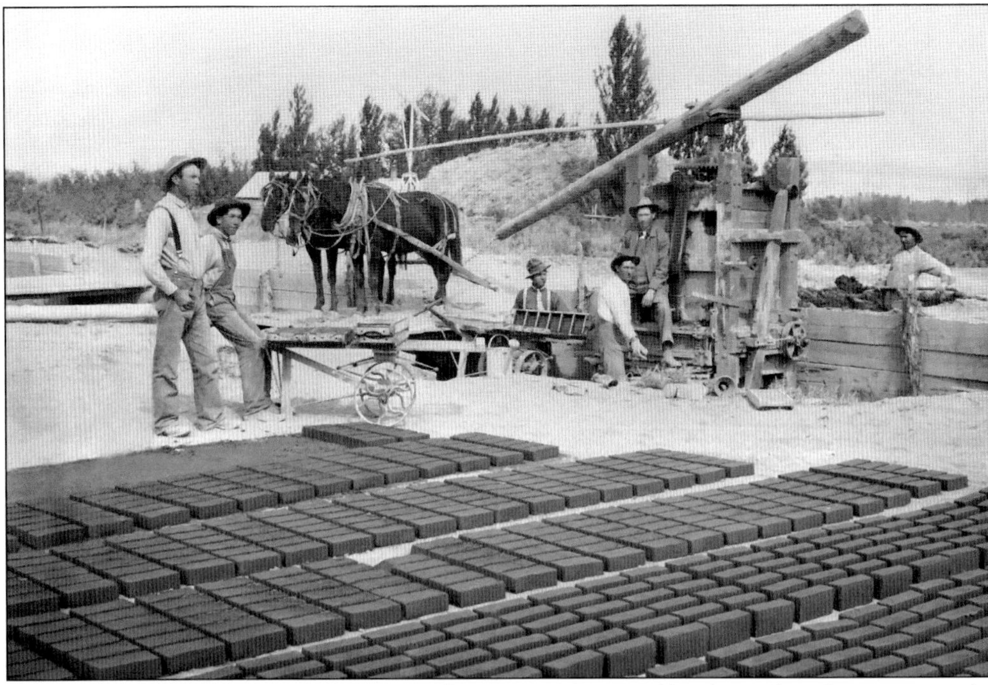

Many of the buildings, including the Howells Opera House, used bricks made right in town at the Oakley brickyard. George Bunn, a mason, was also talented at making the brick. His chimney work was unique and easy to identify. He celebrated a finished house by standing on his head on top of the chimney once at the age of 60. (Courtesy of the Oakley Valley Museum.)

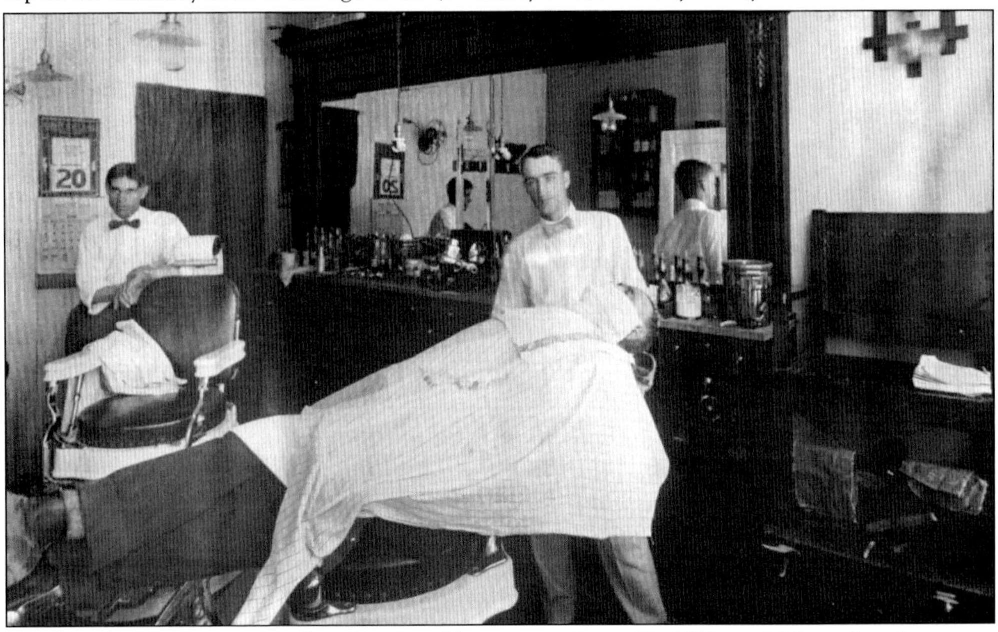

This gentleman was getting his shave and haircut on June 20, 1913, at 2:30 in the afternoon. Calendars and clocks posted prominently help to identify the date so precisely. Like most small towns, this was the spot to catch up on the local news and gossip. (Courtesy of the Oakley Valley Museum.)

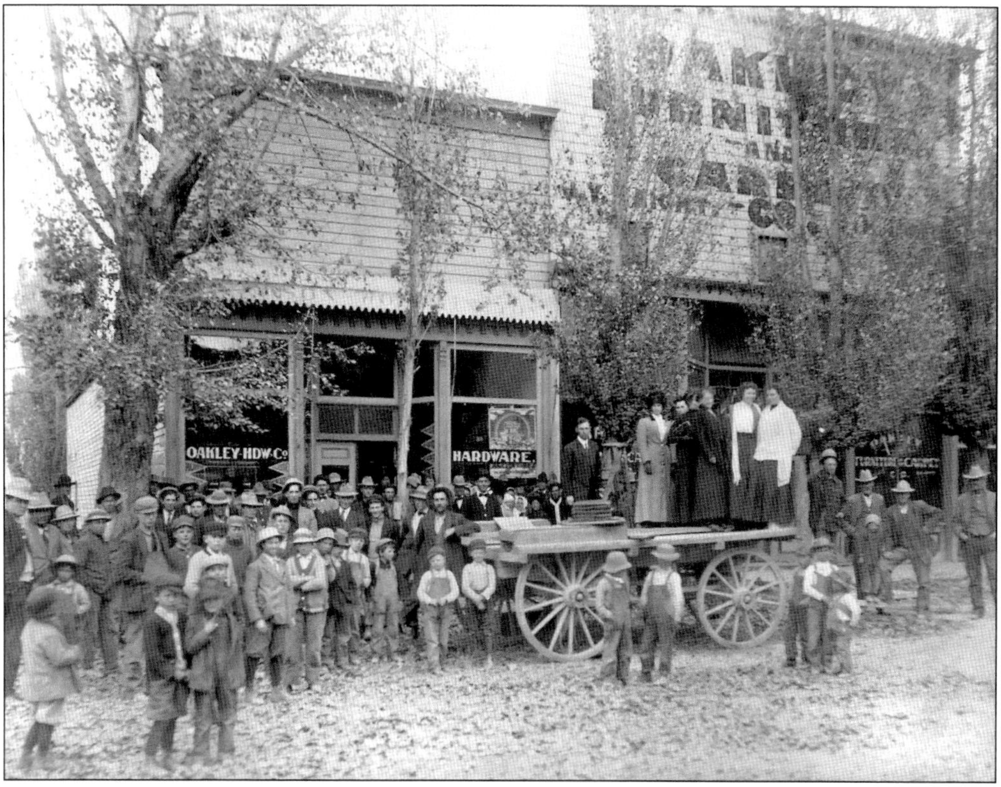

This is a downtown scene on Main Street taken in front of Oakley Hardware and the Oakley Furniture and Carpet Company in 1914. (Courtesy of the Oakley Valley Museum.)

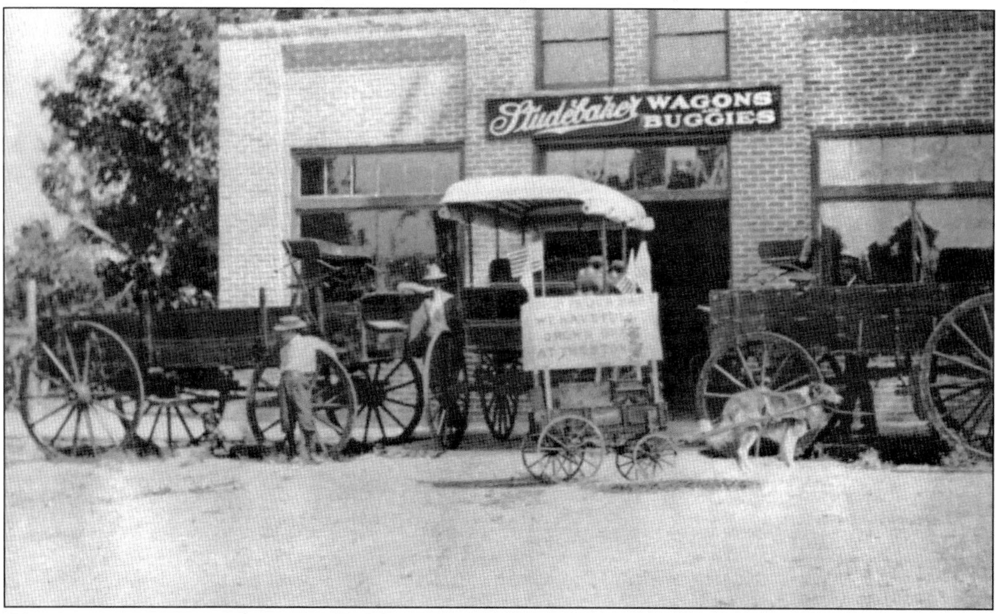

The miniature wagon being pulled by a dog was apparently ready for a parade. The sign says, "This is our baby. We have grown ones at the store." Studebaker Wagon Company was located on Main Street east of the co-op. (Courtesy of the Oakley Valley Museum.)

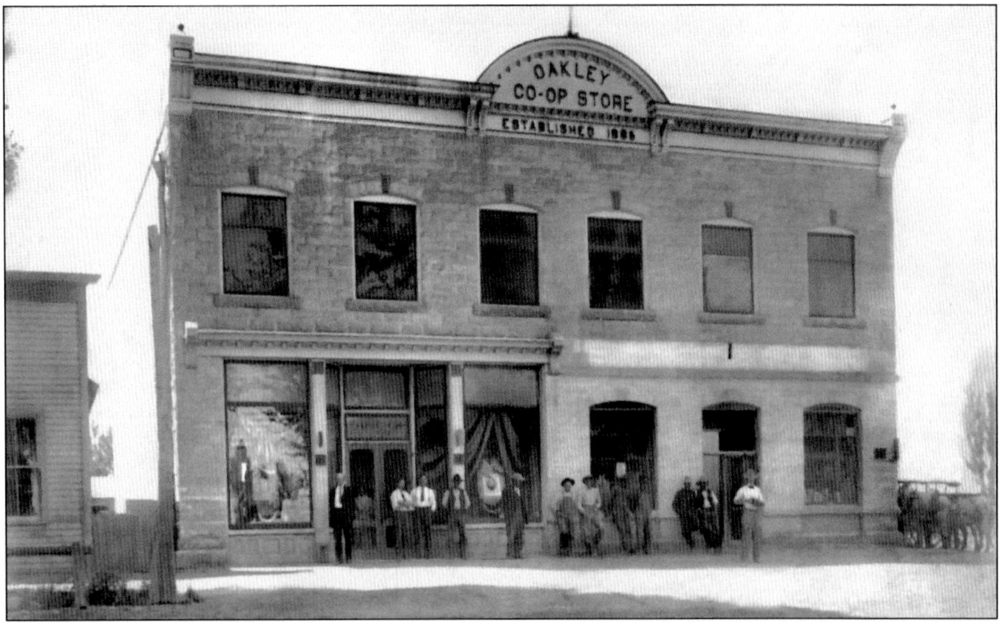

The Oakley Co-op grew from a small log store started by George Grant. In 1883, a group of people led by Horton Haight bought an interest in it and formed the Oakley Cooperative Mercantile Institution. The stone building in the center of town was built in 1889. It is one of a few businesses in the county that has been in continuous operation for so long. (Courtesy of the Oakley Valley Museum.)

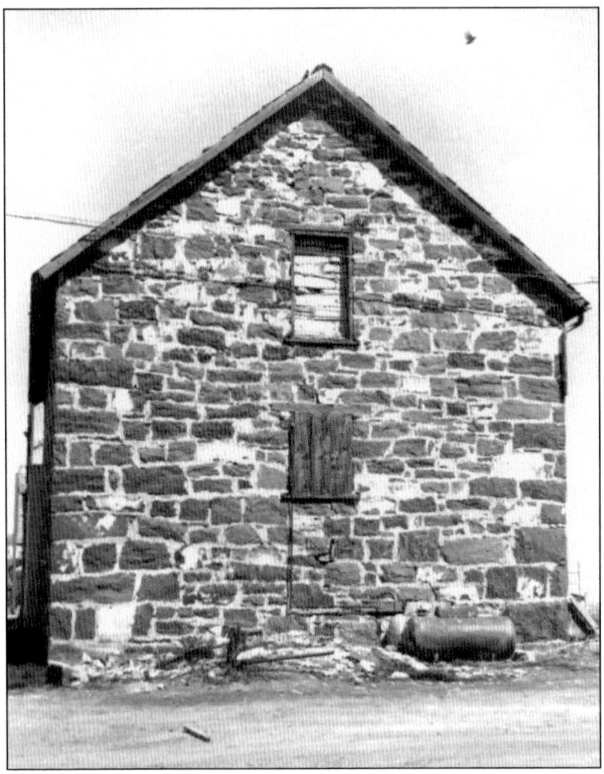

This well-insulated building behind the Oakley Co-op is made of lava rock and is still used for cool storage.

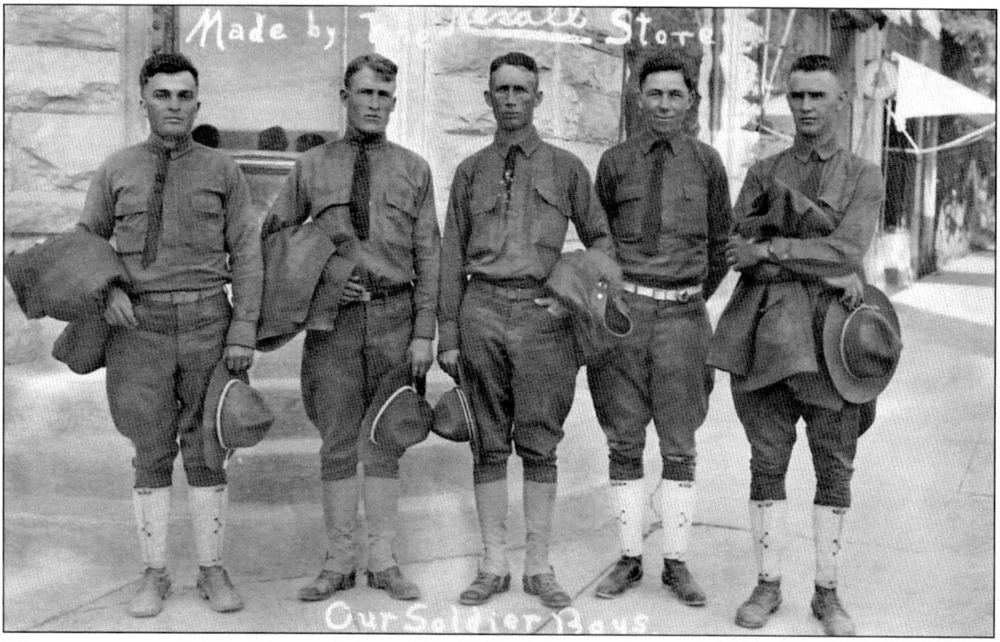

Many young men left Oakley to fight in World War I. Pictured from left to right are Edgar Puckett, Bill Ambler, Frank Hunter, Elis Dahlquist, and James Dayley.

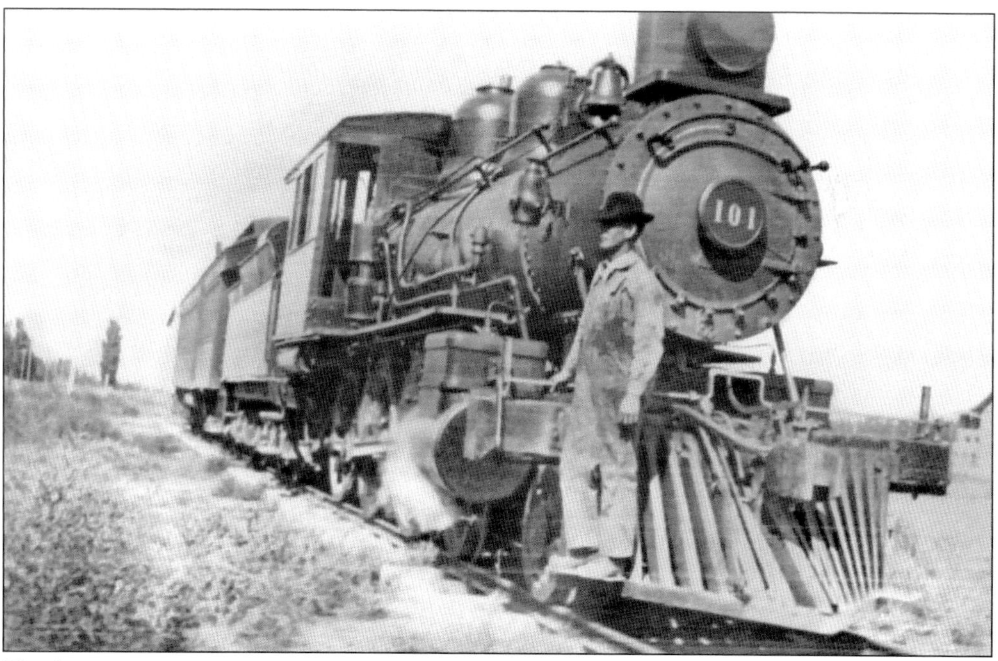

The first train to come into Oakley was the short-lived Idaho Southern Railroad, which traveled from Milner to Oakley. It first entered the town in 1910. People would come from Milner to shop because Oakley had a better variety of stores. When the Oregon Short Line Railroad built its line from Burley in 1911, the Idaho Southern couldn't compete, and it closed a few years later. (Courtesy of the Oakley Valley Museum.)

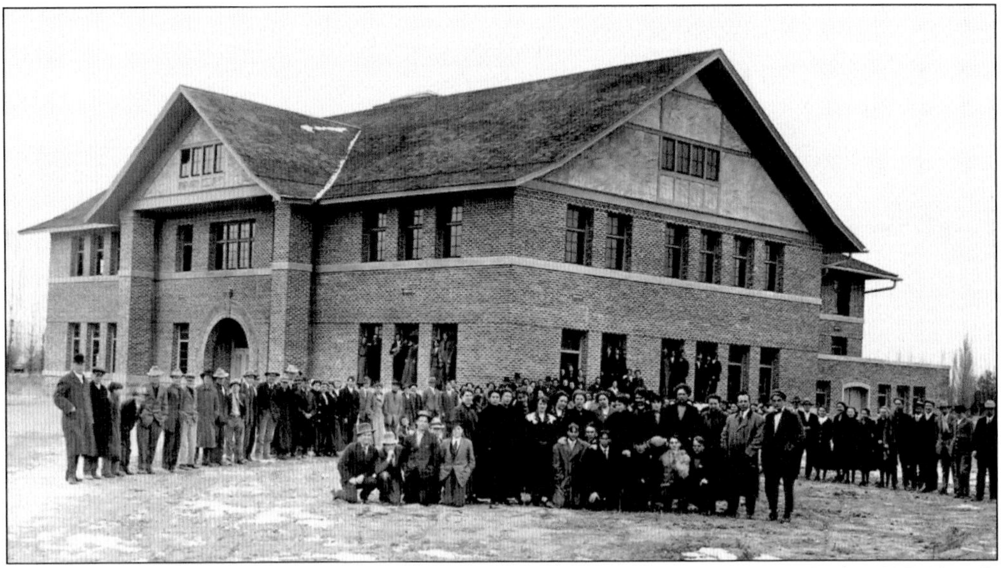

High school education was not available in the early years of Cassia County. In 1887, the LDS Church opened the Cassia Stake Academy for high school courses. Pictured here is the Cassia Stake Academy in 1910. In 1920, the state bought this building and carried on the high school experience.

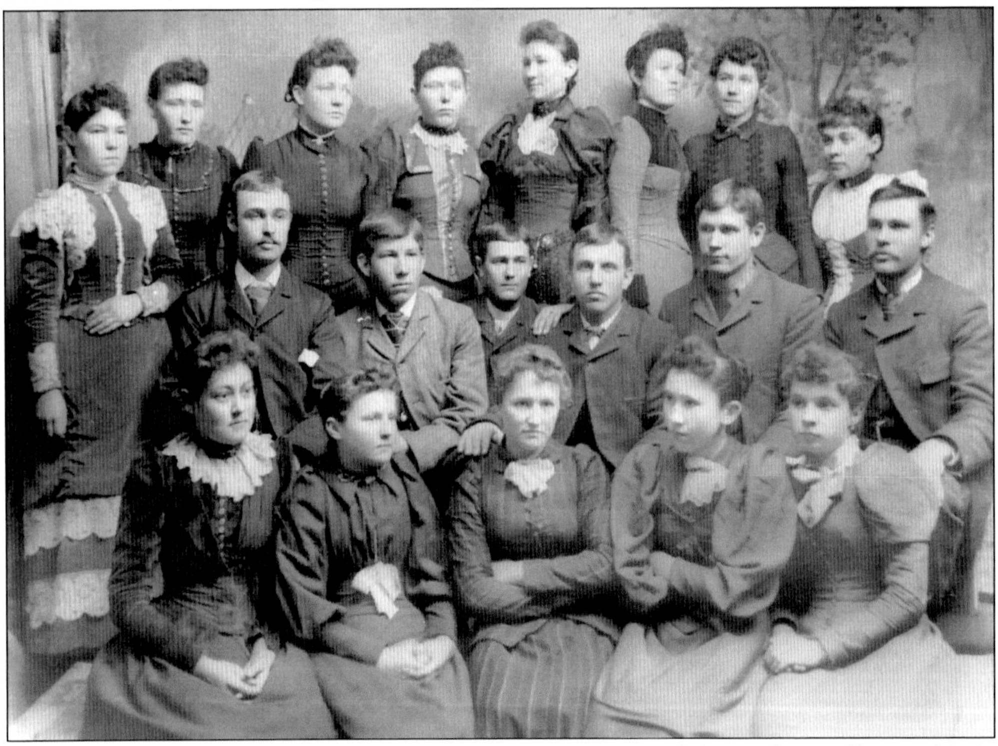

This was a group of students of the Cassia Stake Academy. From left to right are (first row) Lola Haight, Stella Eliason, Clara Mechem, Edith Worthington, and Agnes McBride; (second row) Lewis King, Fred Critchfield, Orson Bates, Oliver Picket, Frank Wilson, and Arthur Dummer; (third row) Matilda Dayley, Lizza McMurray, Etta McMurray, Levana Samuelson, Geneva Worthington, Lottie Curtis, Ammas Marcus, and Eva Dunn.

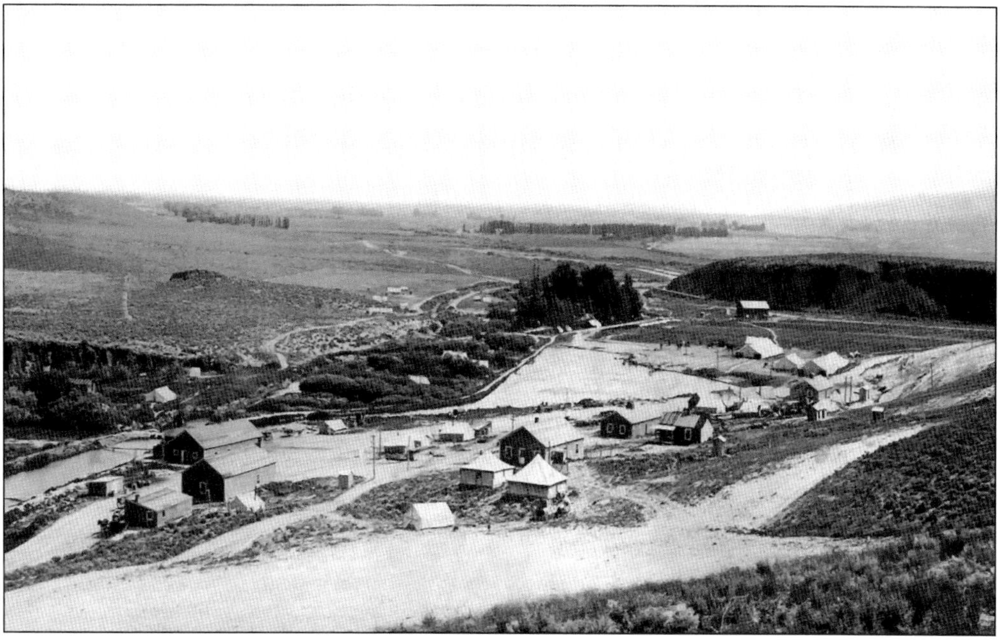

The Oakley Dam was under construction from 1909 until 1913. At the time, it was one of the highest earth-filled dams of its kind in the world. A small temporary town was built just below the dam during the construction. Two steam engines carried about 700 cars of dirt a distance of a quarter of a mile to get it close enough to the site to transfer to wagons that brought it closer to the dam.

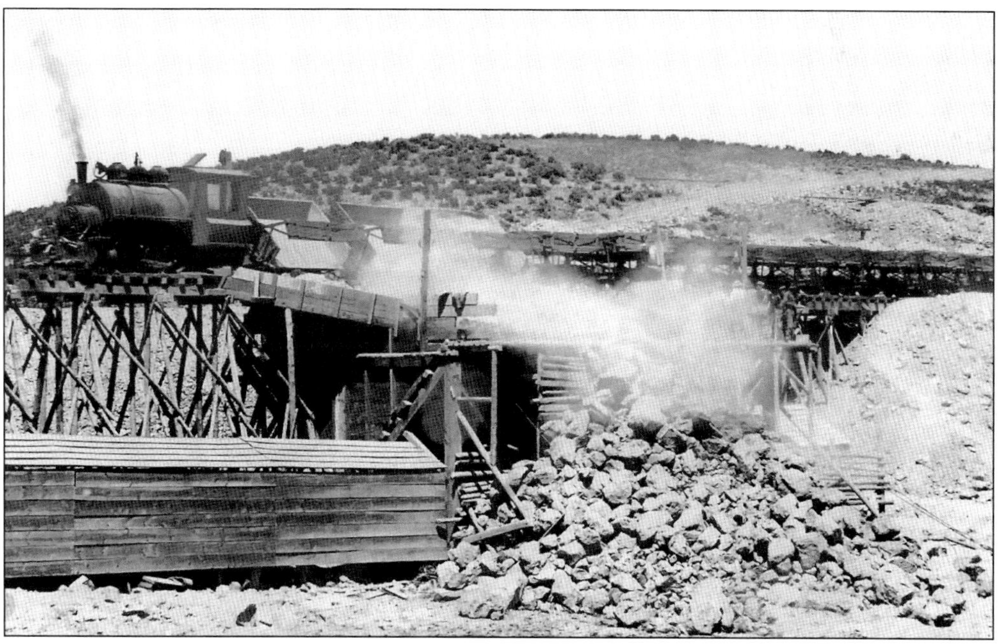

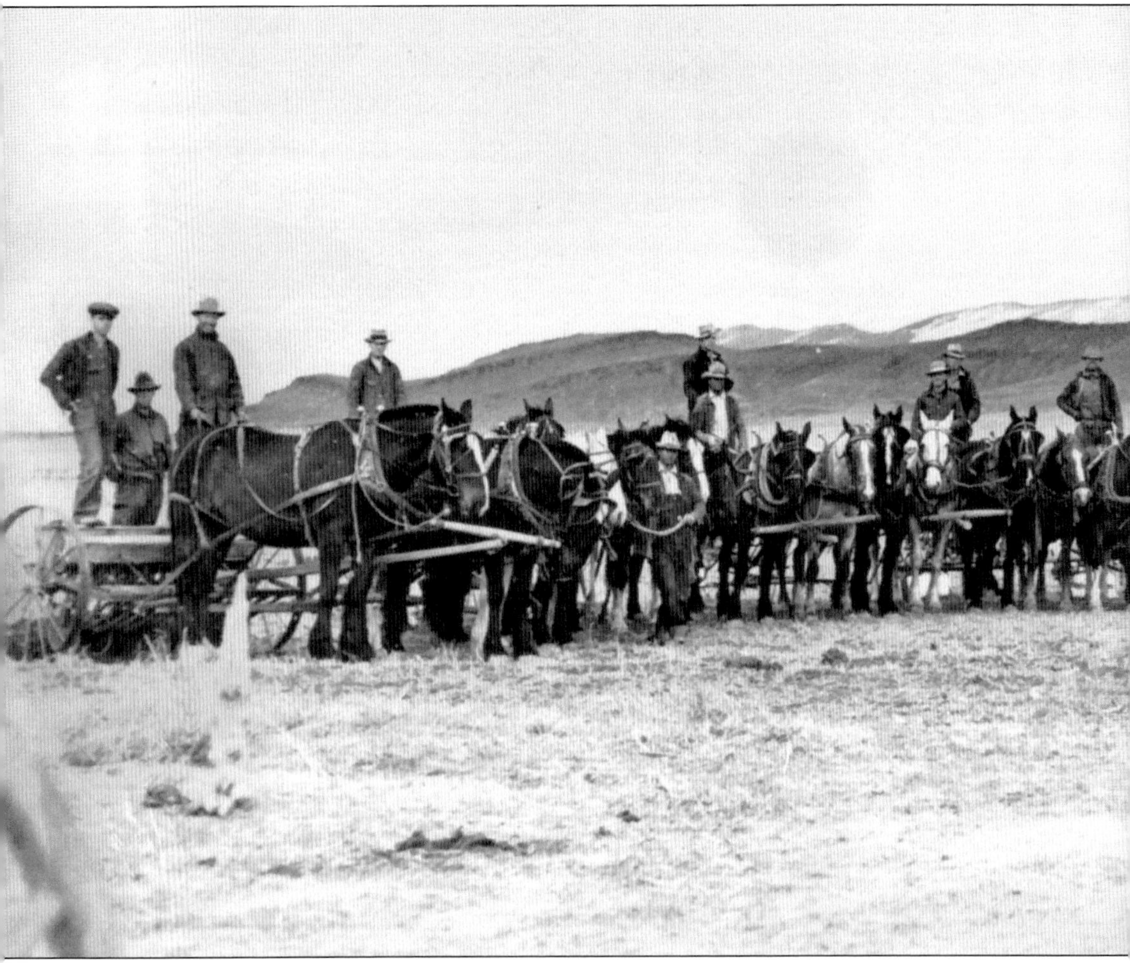

The LDS Church had welfare farms in 1937 just as they do today. Here are the Basin Ward members getting ready to work on the farm. Pictured from left to right are Omro McIntosh, Stanley McIntosh, Vern Heiner, Ashel Fairchild, Theodore Taylor, Thurman Martin, Rex Martin,

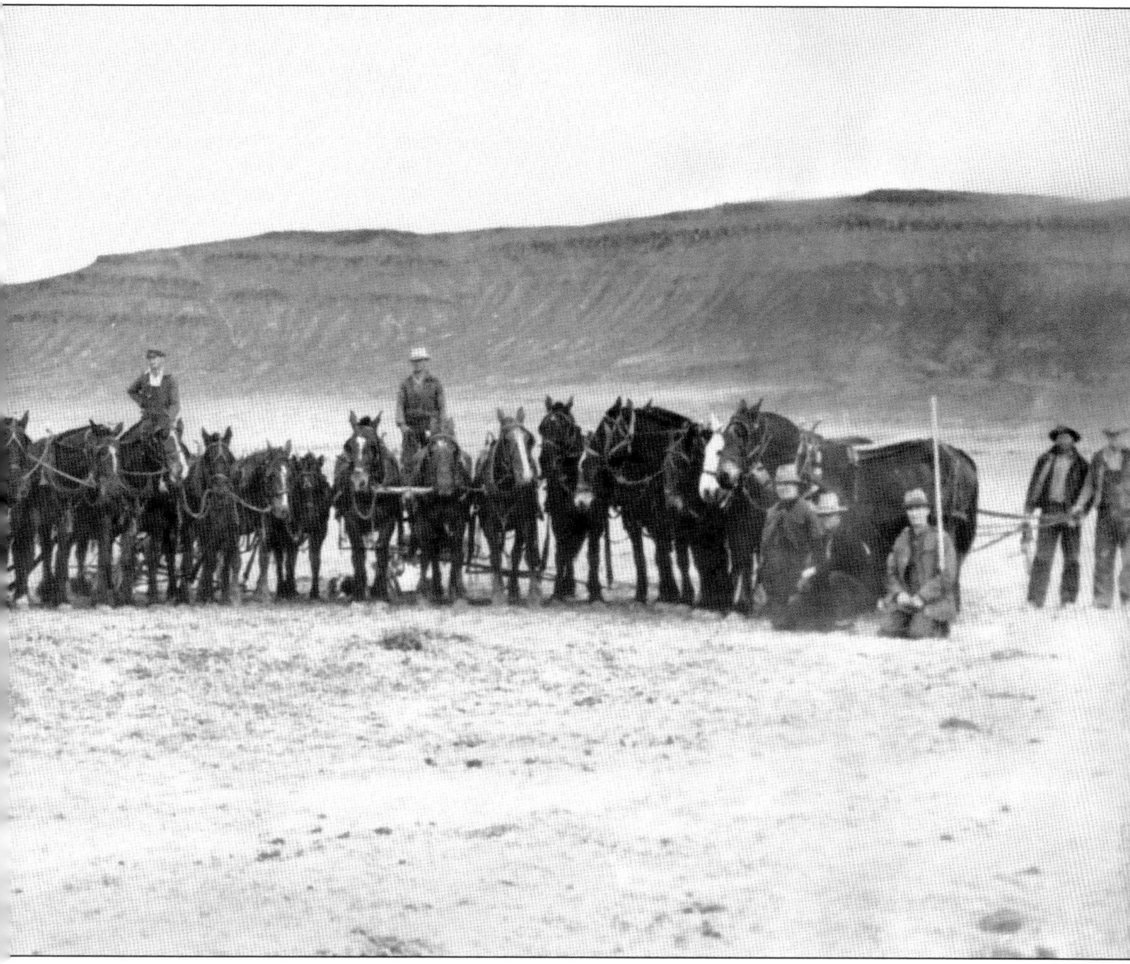

Albert McIntosh, Ray Bates, Mose Martin, Vern Steel, Ray McIntosh, James S. McIntosh, John Martin, Sam McIntosh, Lloyd Martin, and Bartoe McIntosh.

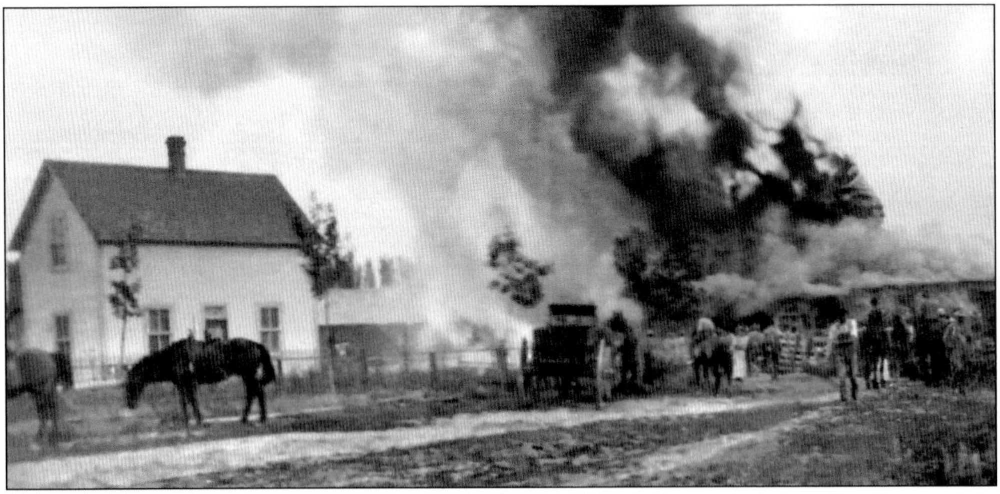

The Light Air Park was a recreation complex built around 1901 that included a roller skating rink, horse race track, swimming pool, ball diamond, and dance hall. The skating rink burned down in 1912 when it was hit by lightning. The Light Air Park was plowed and planted with wheat in 1918 to help the war effort.

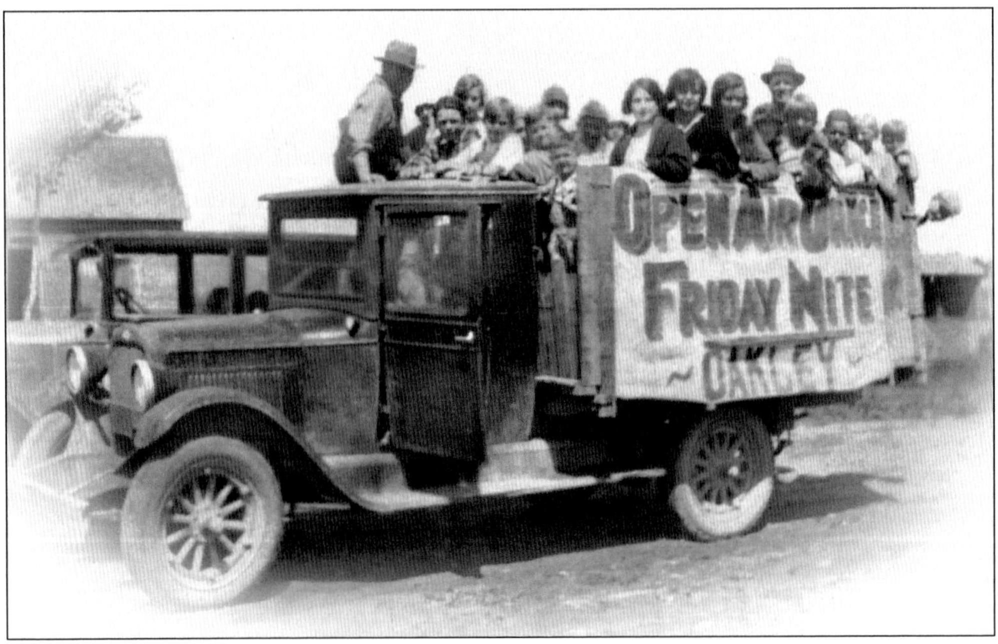

Dances were a popular attraction in Oakley. Before 1900, there were at least two dance halls in operation. Around 1910, three more dance halls were constructed. At first, the dances were known to last all night. (Courtesy of the Oakley Valley Museum.)

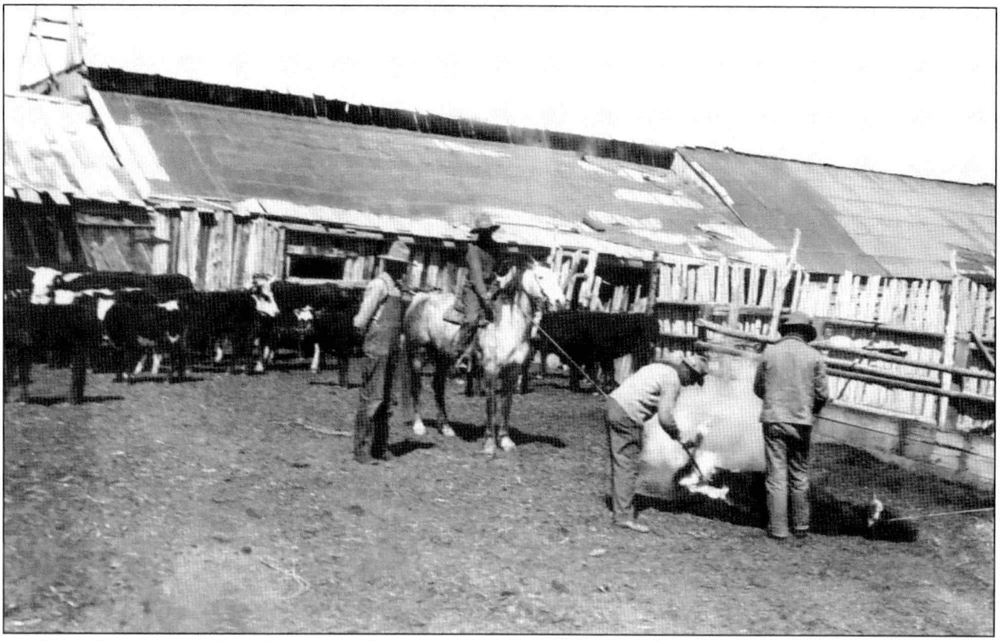

It is branding time at the Warm Creek Ranch about 1917. Pictured are, from left to right, Will Rivers Jr., Lafe Poulton, William Poulton, and George Poulton. (Courtesy of Maxine P. Adams.)

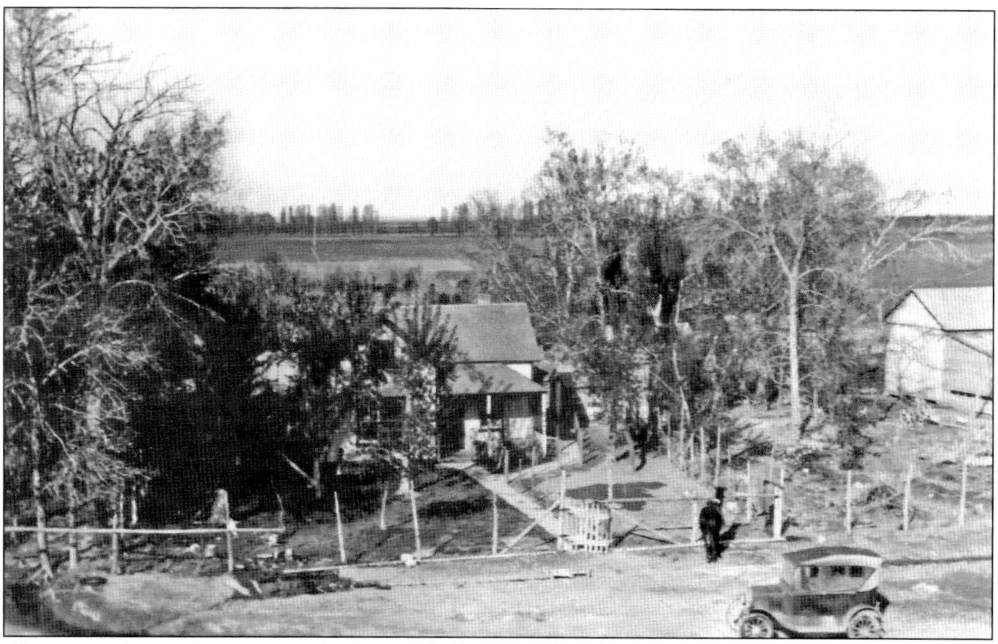

This was taken in 1923 at the Warm Creek Ranch. The photographer got on the top of the barn to take this picture. Lilburn Foster came in 1864 and was the first man known to stay longer than the summer season in what is now Cassia County. (Courtesy of Maxine P. Adams.)

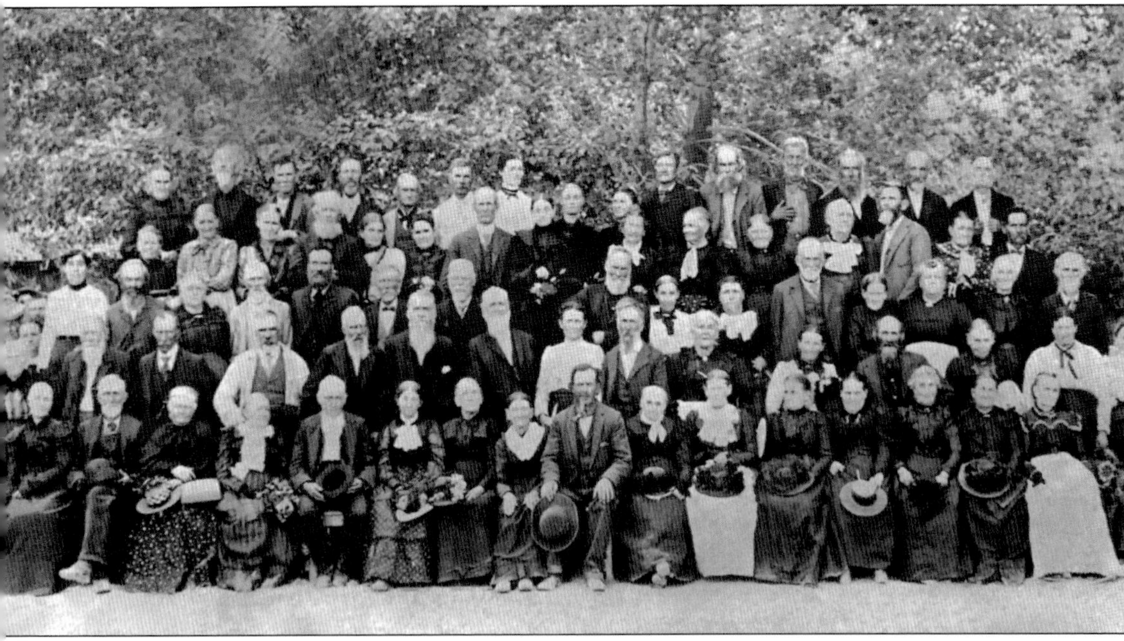

In 1901, many of the original settlers gathered for an old folks' reunion in Oakley. They came from all over the county to renew acquaintances.

Eight

Irrigation, Farming, and Ranching

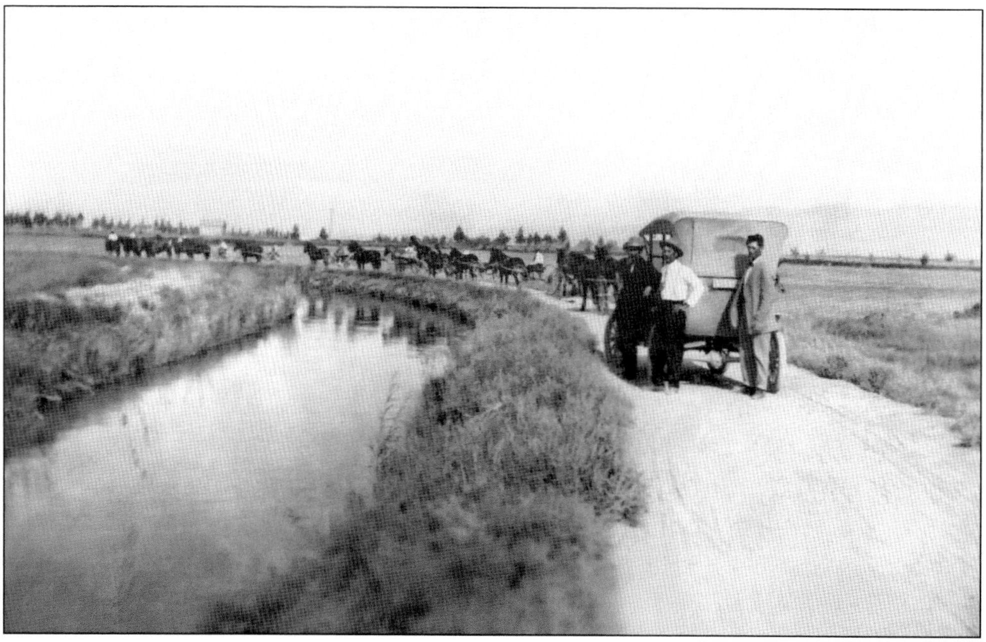

The building of the Minidoka Dam in 1906 and the southside canal system in 1908 changed the face of the land south of the Snake River. This scene is of county and water district officials inspecting the canal system and surrounding farms just a few years later.

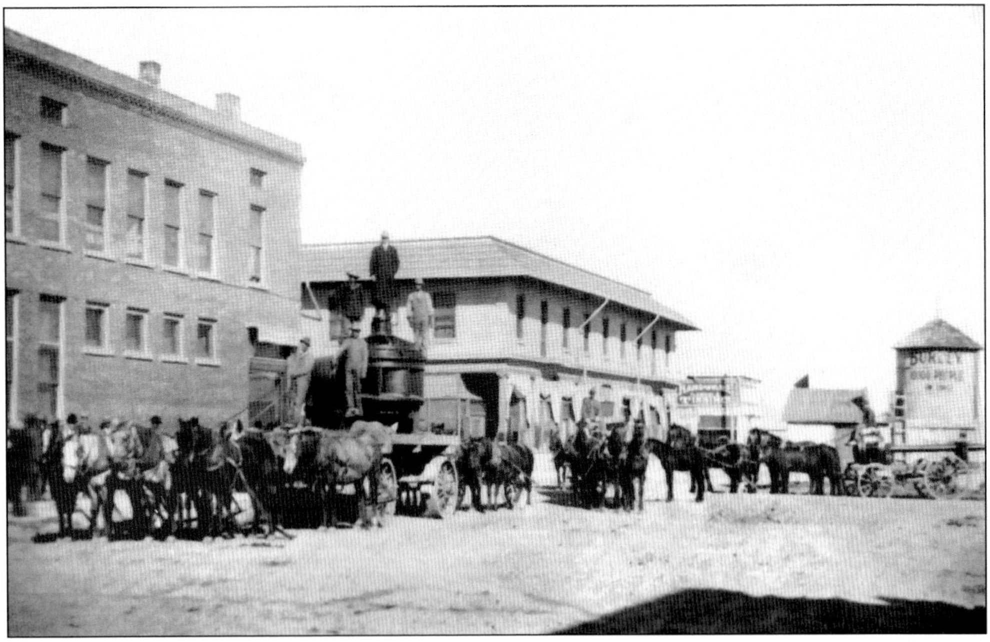

When the canals and lift stations were being built in the Declo area, the closest railroad was in Burley. The big equipment came in on the railroad and was loaded onto wagons to haul out to the pump station sites.

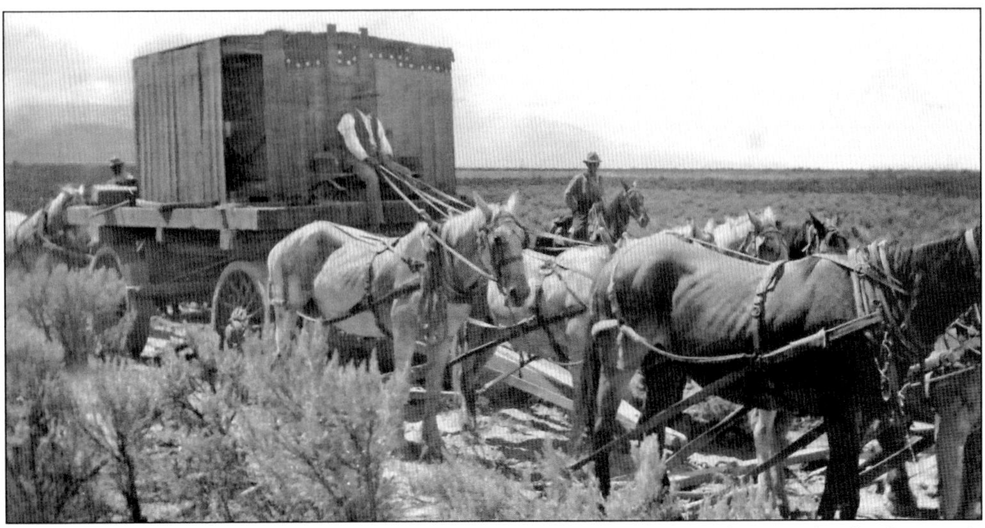

The loads of equipment were so heavy that it took teams of horses in front and in back to push and pull the wagons.

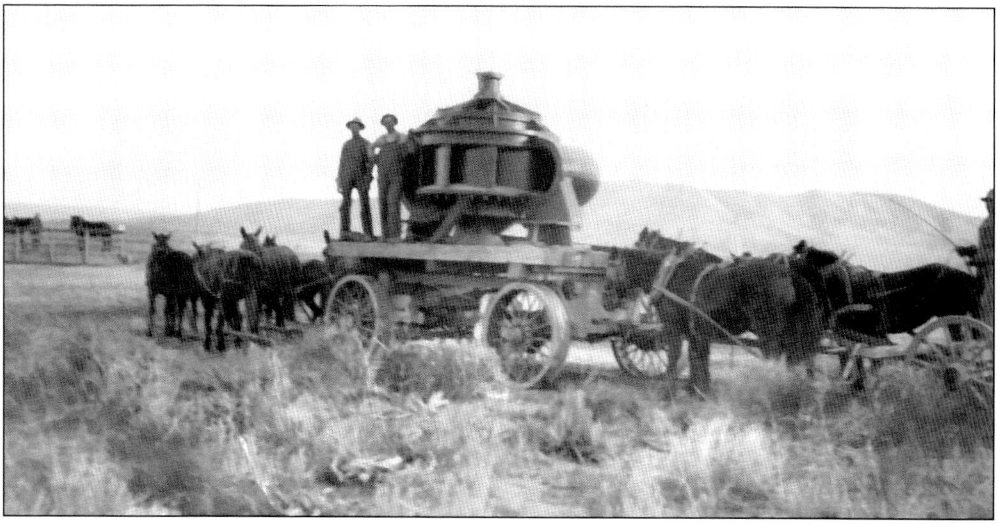

The wagons used to haul the heavy equipment were specially made with wide steel wheels and extra-sturdy construction to carry the loads across the flat but rough terrain.

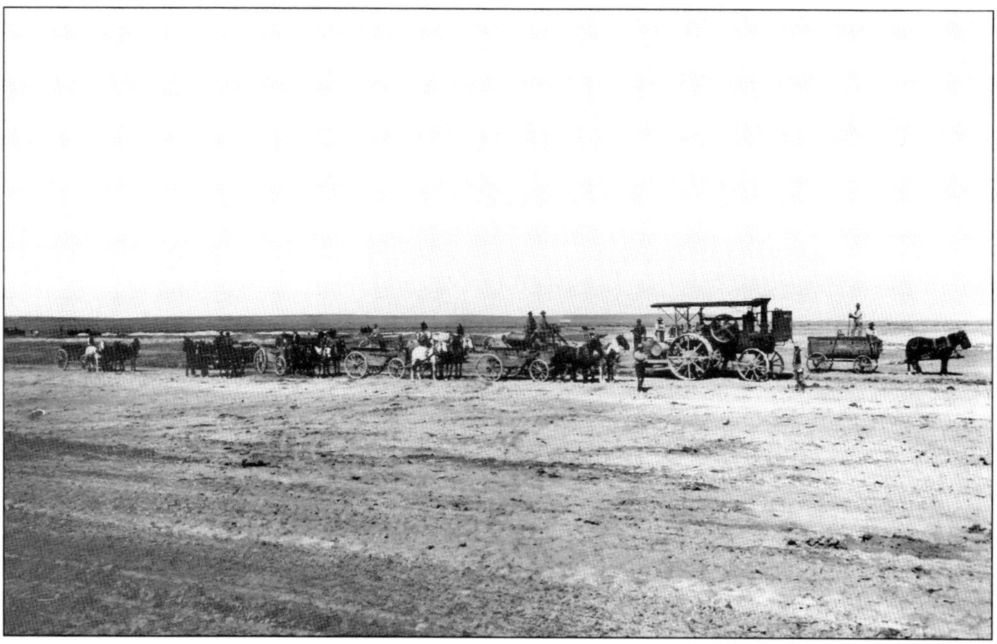

Ninety miles of canals were built in Cassia County in 90 days. The homesteaders worked with their horse-drawn equipment around the clock and finished on June 22, 1908. An inspection the next day by James Garfield, the secretary of the interior, preserved their water rights.

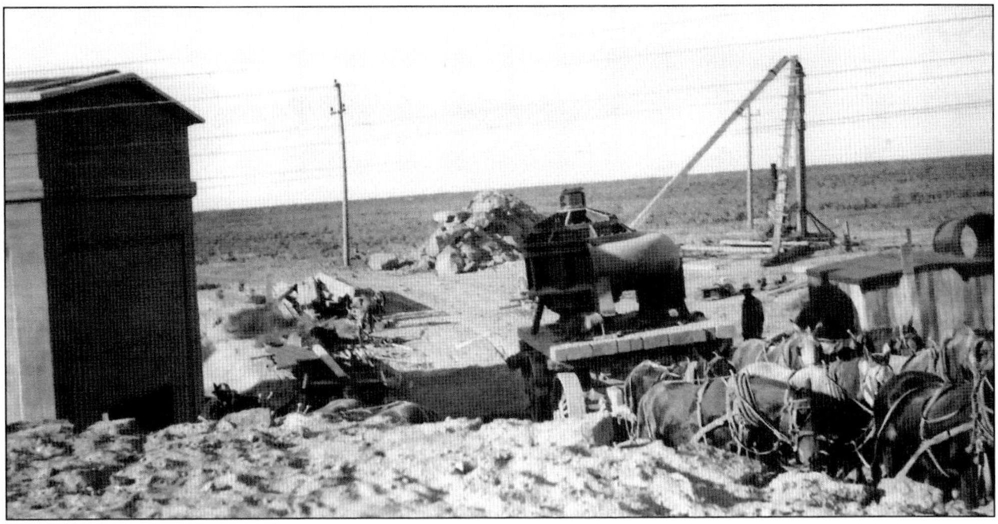

In this photograph at a lift station, the horse-drawn wagon is being driven into the area to unload the power turbine.

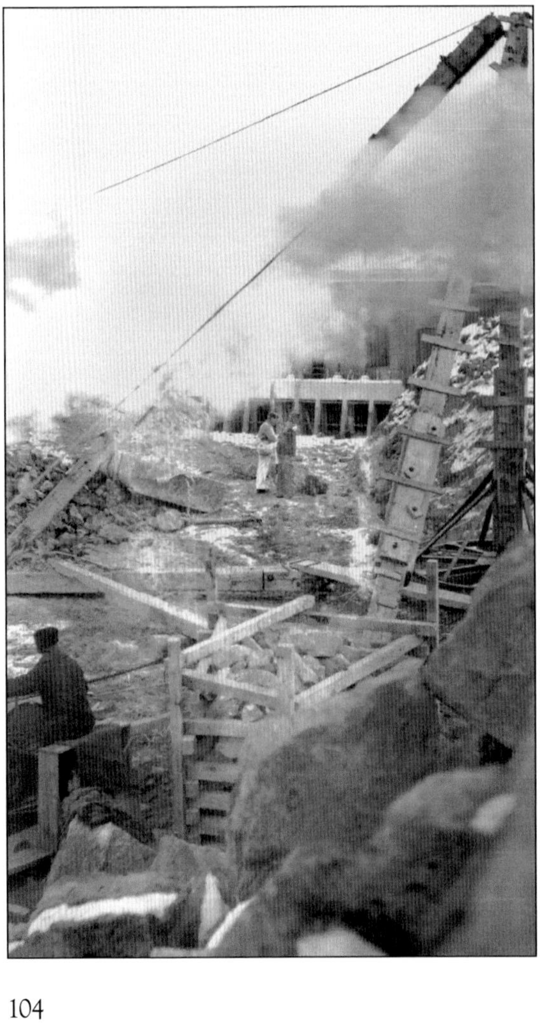

This is at the Minidoka Dam site. Work on the dam started in January 1905. In November 1906, the diversion gates were closed and the reservoir began to fill. It was built with the purpose of providing a way to irrigate the south side of the river.

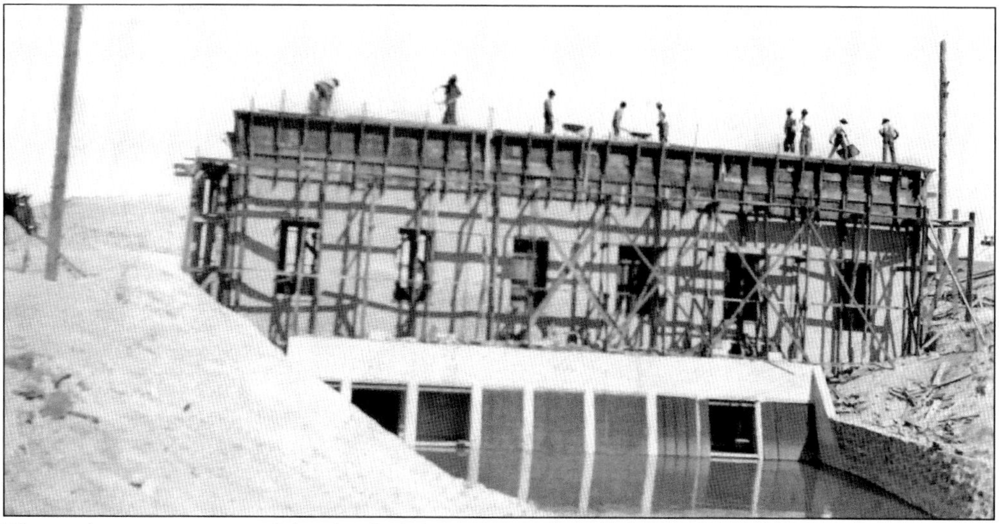

This is the construction of the third of three lift canals built in 1908. By 1910, over 50,000 acres were irrigable with this system.

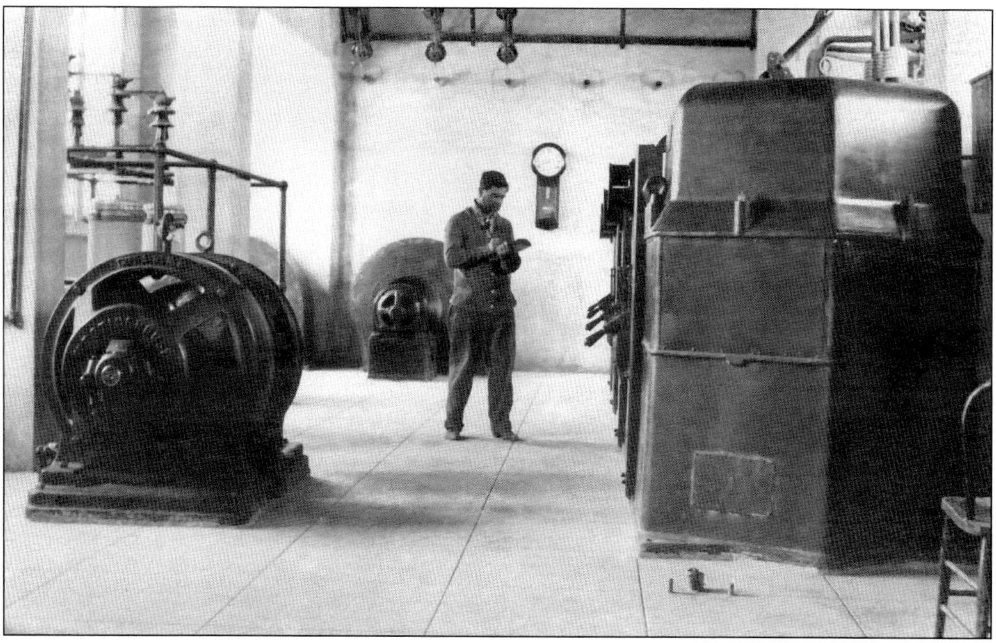

Ferd Fuqua is looking at a bank of air-cooled transformers that were original to the lift station. These were replaced in the early 1930s.

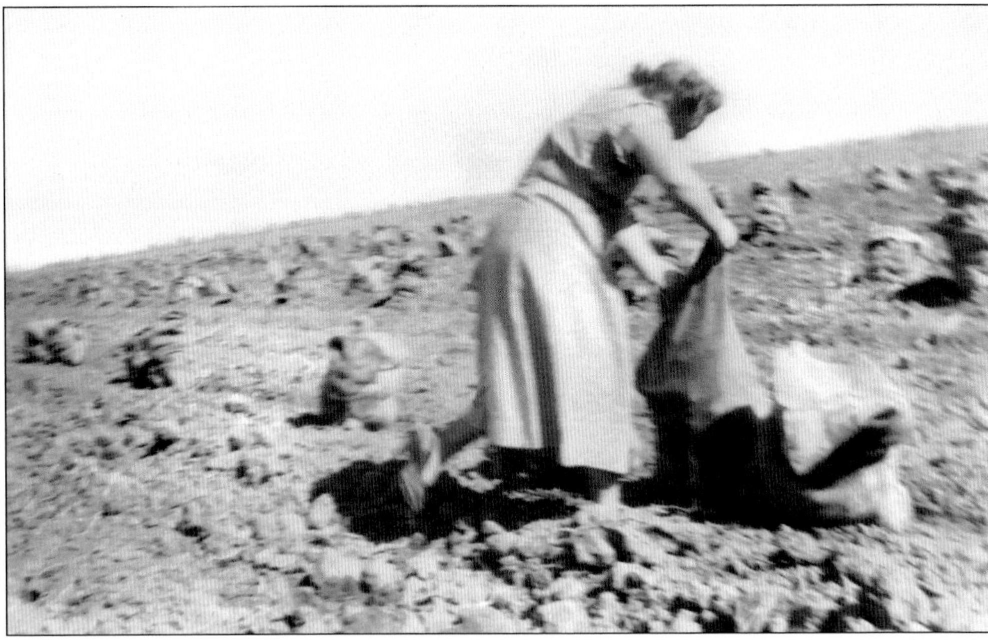

Afton Garner Baker helped her husband, Wade, with the potato harvest. Here she is sacking the potatoes by hand. Notice her choice of shoes. Next the workers would come in a truck or wagon and pick up the sacks to take to the cellar.

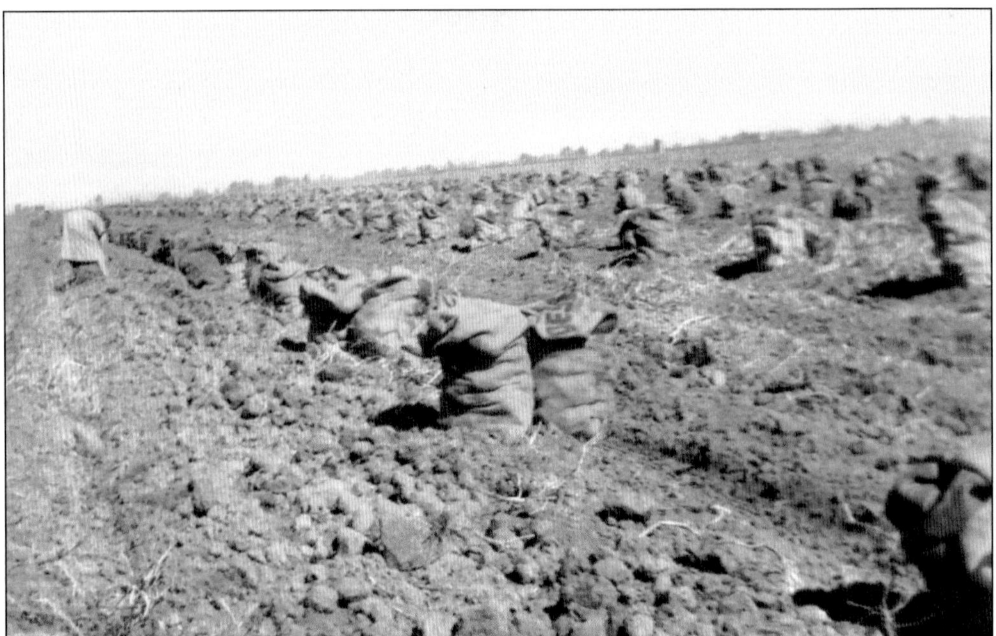

On February 18, 1910, well-known potato expert Eugene H. Grubb predicted, "Irrigated Idaho can and will become the greatest potato-growing section on the American continent." During the last 50 years of the past century, Burley was known as the "Potato Processing Capital of the World," making Grubb's prediction a reality.

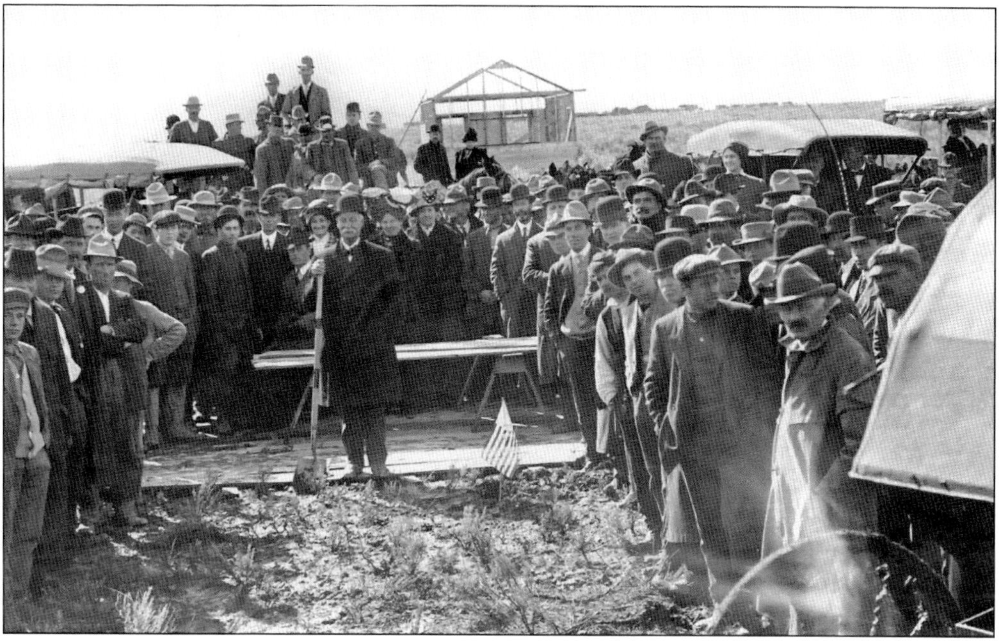

The Amalgamated Sugar Company broke ground in Burley on March 7, 1912. Mayor Josiah E. Miller is in the center. The company moved its factory from La Grande, Oregon, and was ready for beets on October 12, 1912. Five thousand acres were planted that first year. The opening of the Amalgamated Sugar Company gave the settlers another cash crop to market and was the beginning of the agricultural era of Cassia County.

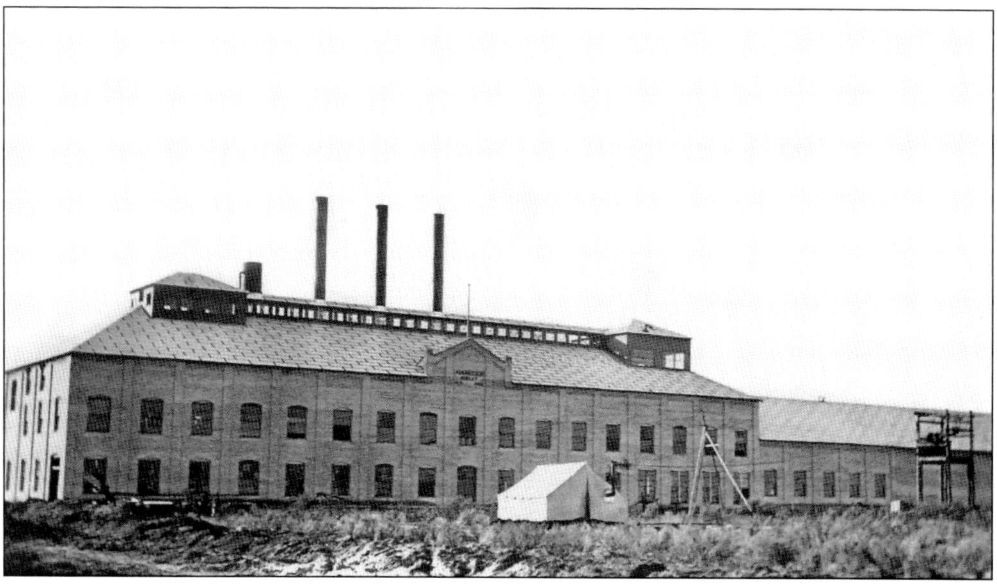

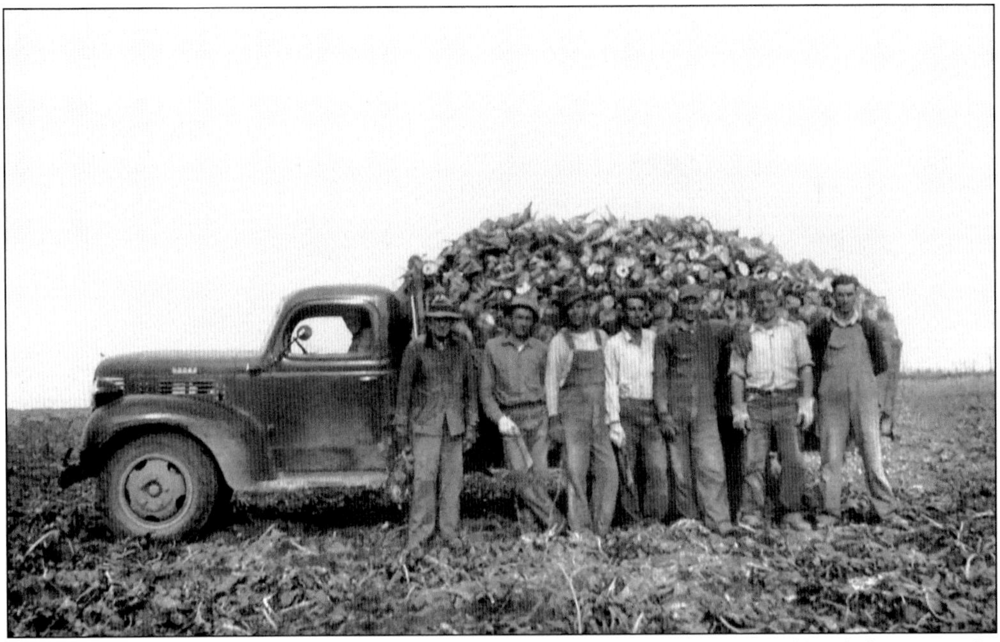

At harvest time, the beets were topped by hand with special beet knifes and loaded onto trucks or wagons for the trip to the sugar factory. This backbreaking work is shown at the Wade Baker farm in the Unity area south of Burley. (Courtesy of Shirlene B. Anderson.)

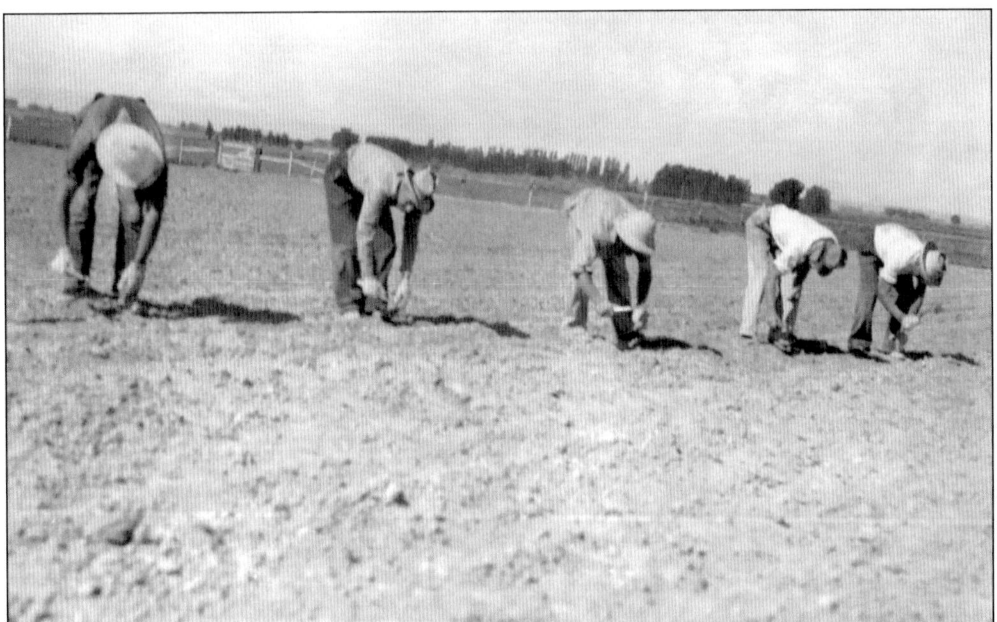

Sugar beet seed was closely planted in the rows. Then the workers came along and thinned them out with short-handled hoes. This was very labor-intensive work.

Clayton Beck came to Burley from Spanish Fork, Utah, in 1919. He farmed south of Burley in the Starrhs Ferry area. He and his sons grew sugar beets. One son, William Beck, later became the president of the National Sugar Beet Growers Association.

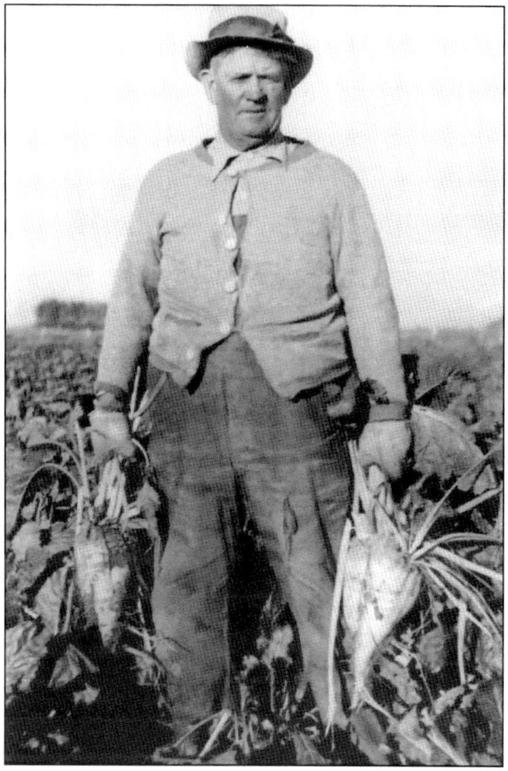

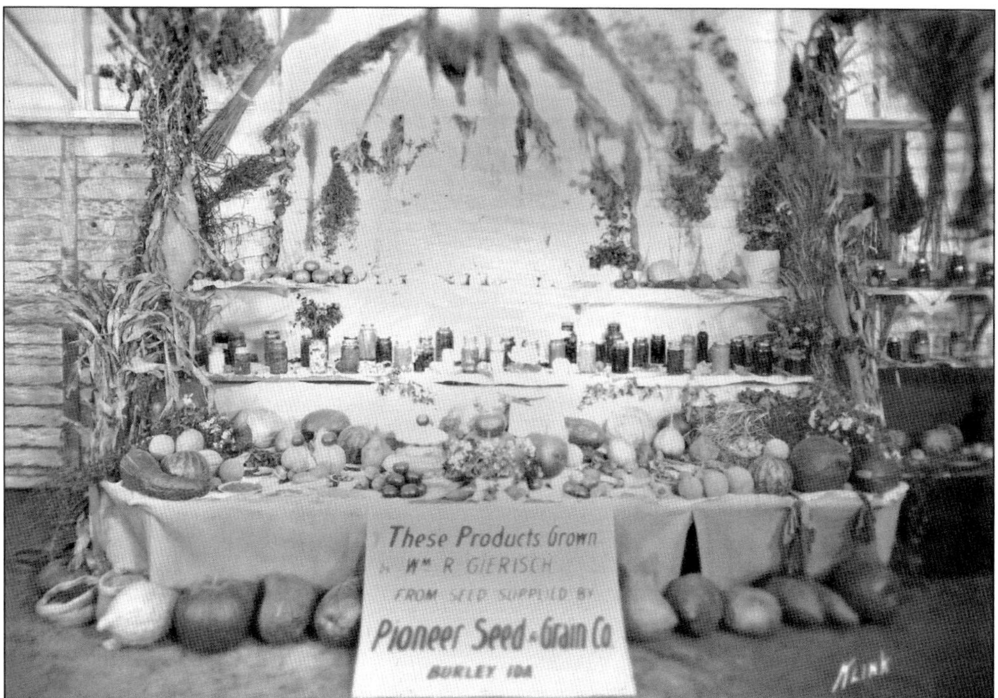

The county fair, first started in 1910, was an opportunity for the farmers to display their crops and produce. William Gierisch came from Utah in 1918.

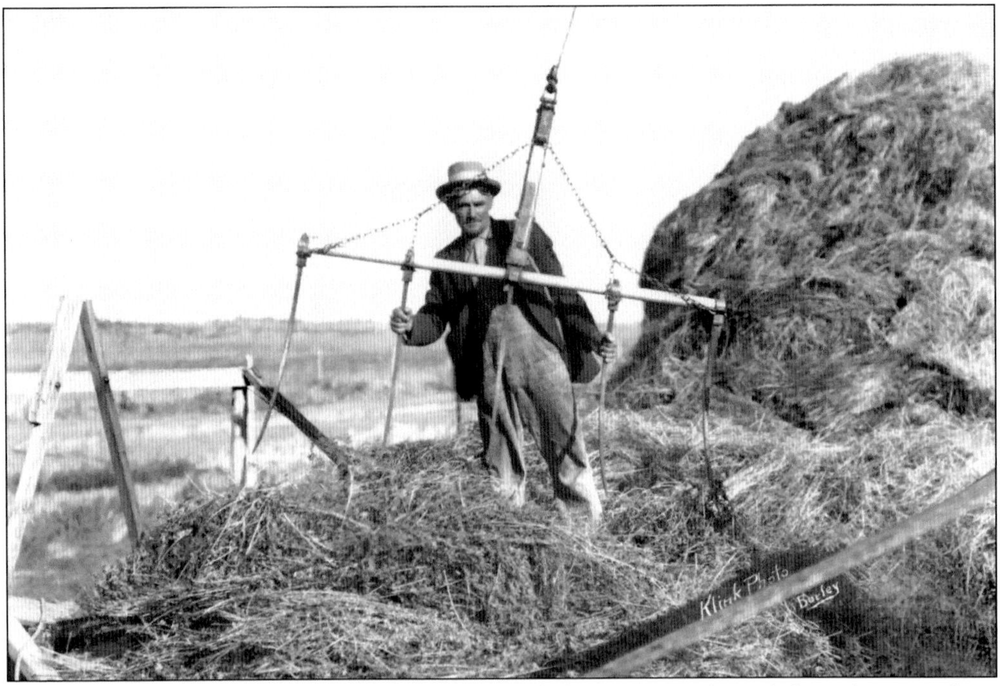

Robert McBride developed a special type of Jackson fork in 1918. He farmed along the river where the Burley golf course is now. He began the first ice company in Burley in 1912. He operated it for five years.

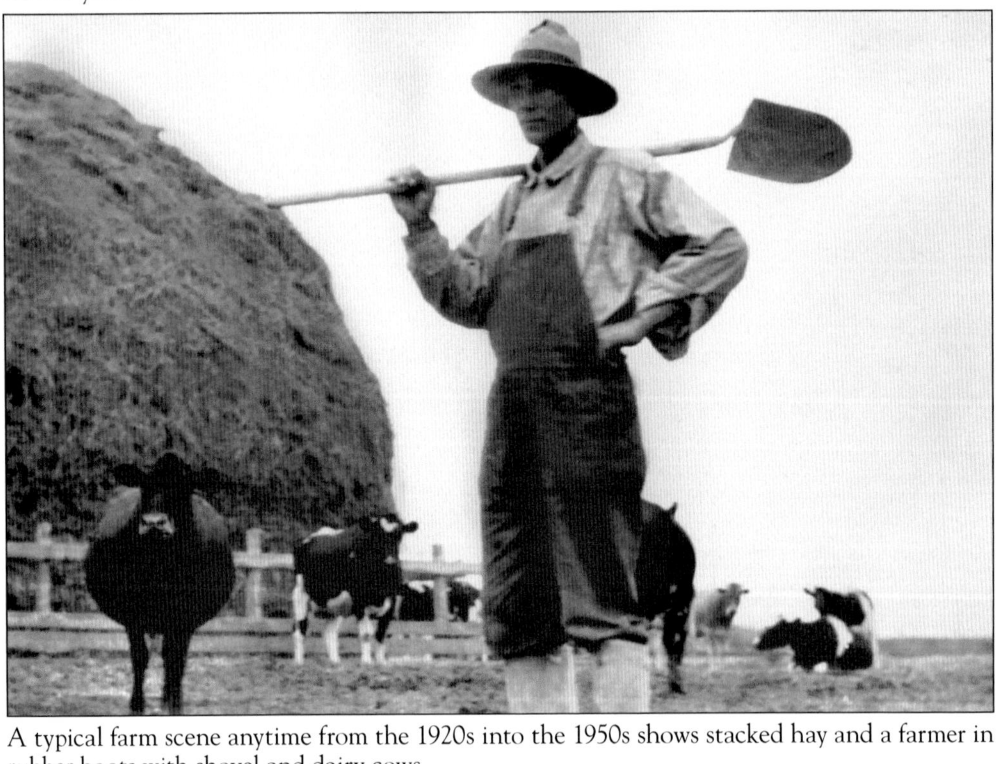

A typical farm scene anytime from the 1920s into the 1950s shows stacked hay and a farmer in rubber boots with shovel and dairy cows.

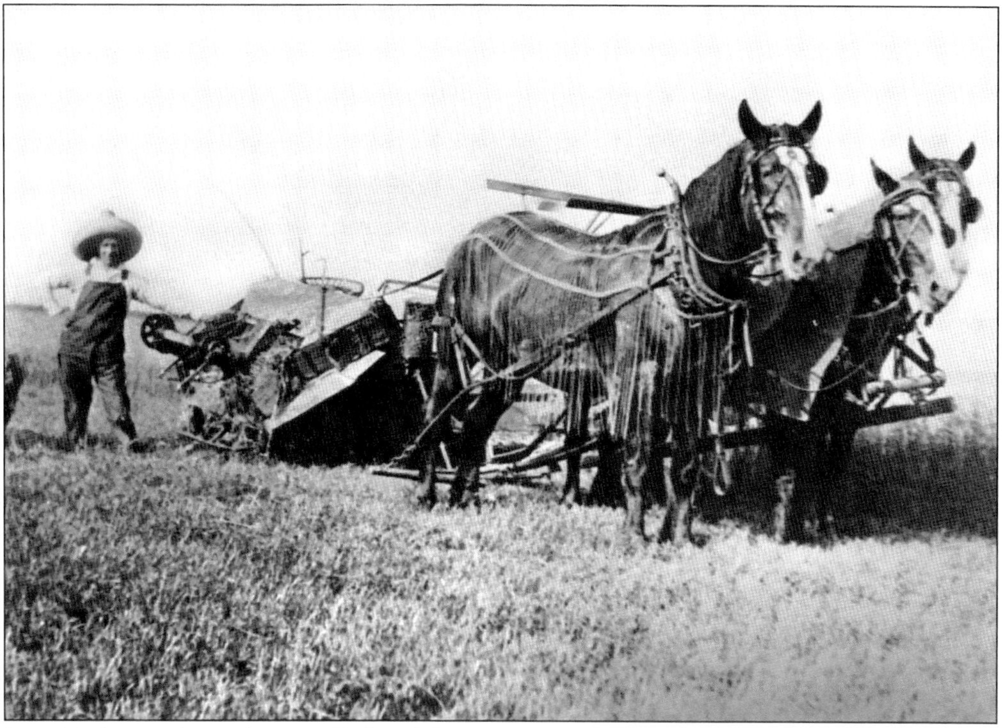

Otto Paulson is shown here in 1910 with his team at grain harvest time.

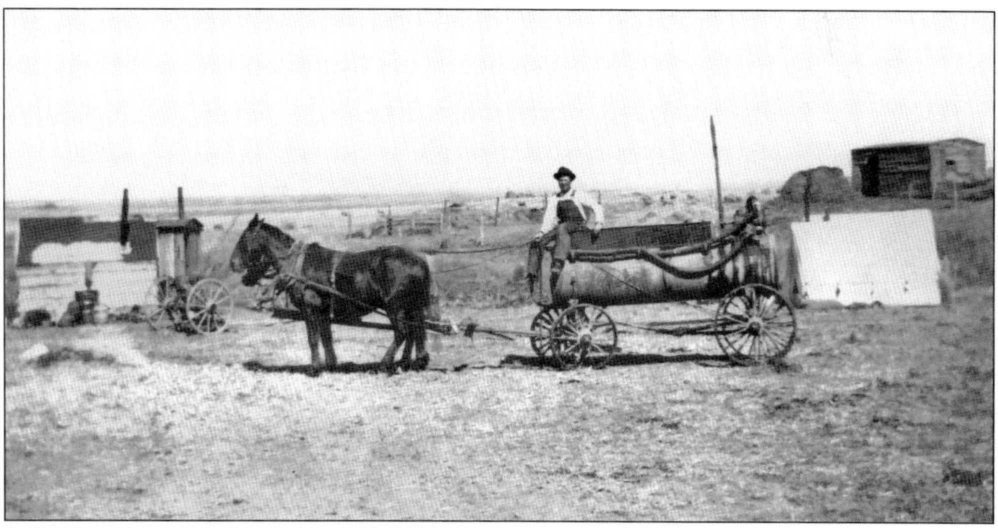

Before the canal system was finished, the farmers and ranchers had to get water for their livestock and crops. Lowell Cummins, seen in this picture, is on the water wagon they used to get water from Goose, Trapper, and Birch Creeks. He was the son of Francis Marion and Sarah Deseret Severe Cummins and grew up on a farm southwest of Oakley.

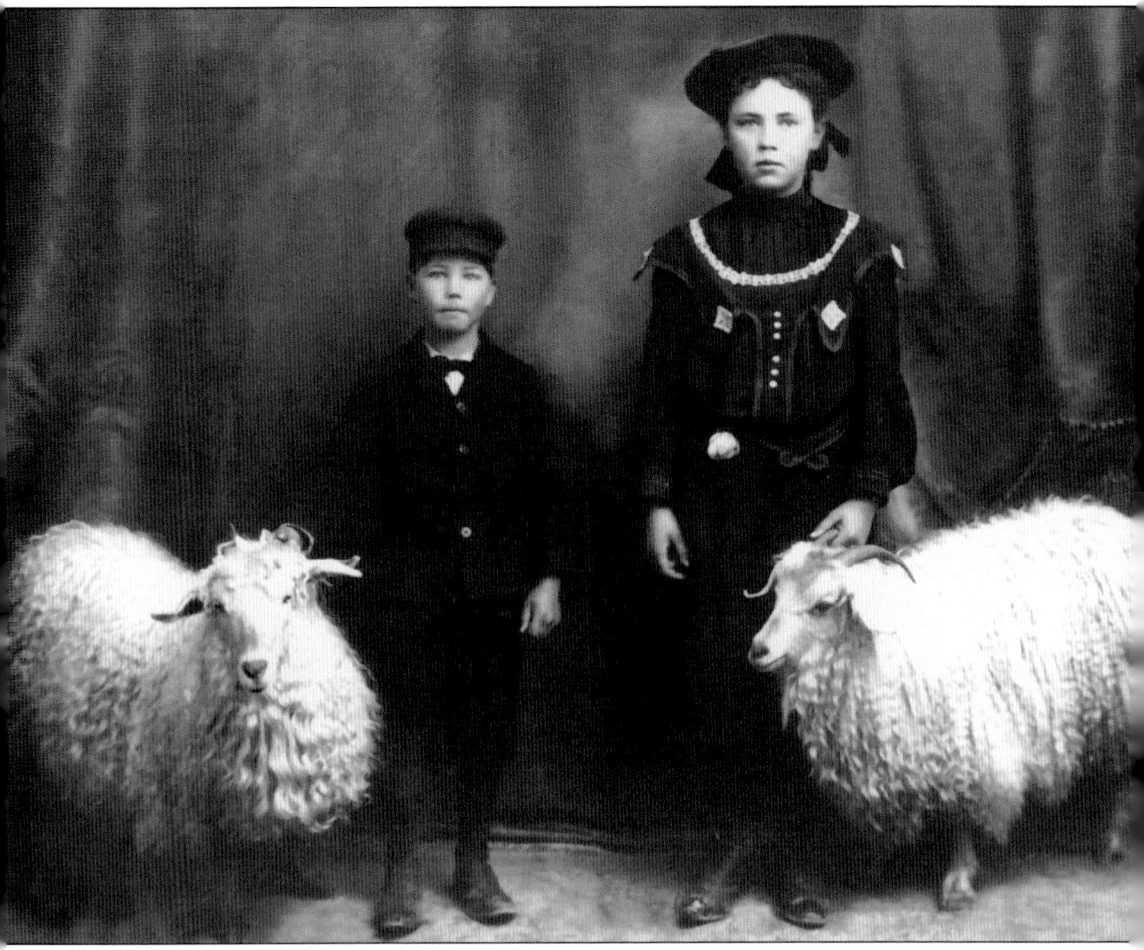

Phillip and Irene Cummins, children of Francis and Sarah Cummins, are pictured here about 1902 with two Angora goats from their father's herd. The family had a large herd of Angora, which were often herded on horseback in the foothills west of Oakley. The Angora breed is an excellent producer of fine-quality fleece. (Courtesy of Jamie Larson.)

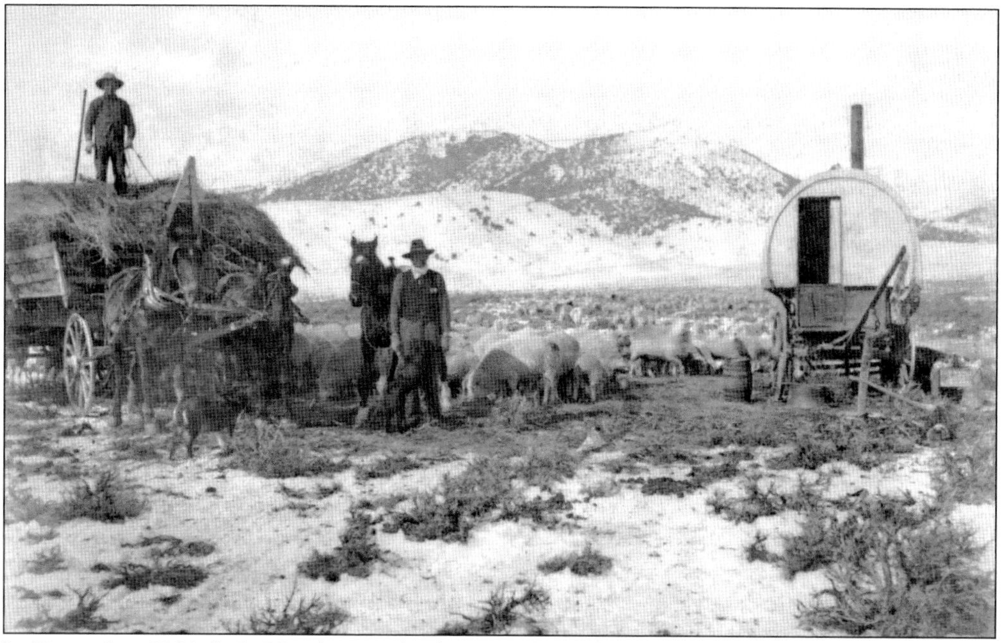

In December 1901, J. A. Handy was the foreman for the A. J. Hack Sheep Company of Boise. Raft River was their winter quarters. He is standing by the horse (note the meat hanging from the wagon tongue). Handy married Pear Condit on December 16, 1903. She was tending the post office at Malta, and J. A. met her while picking up his mail. They had two sons, Leo and Ernest.

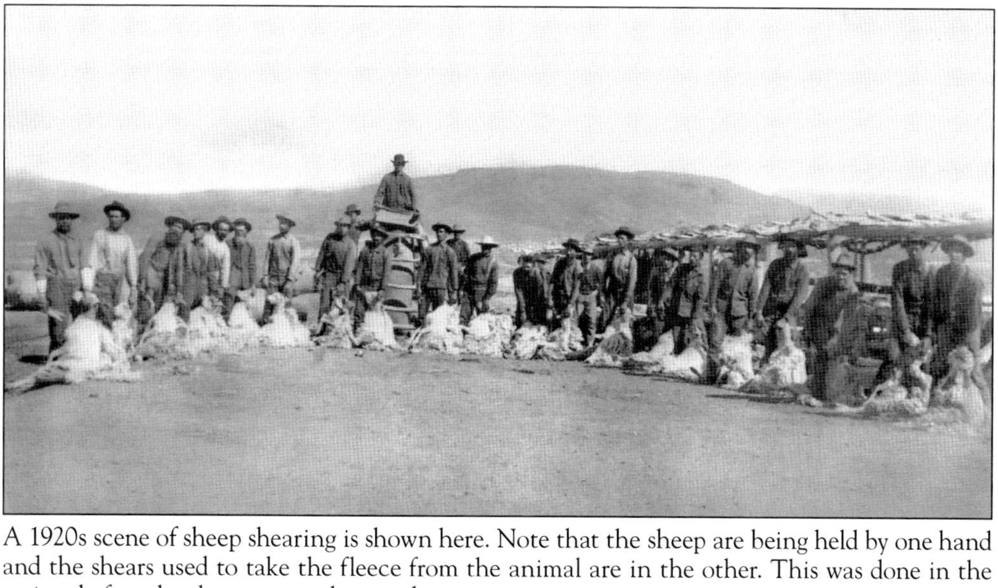

A 1920s scene of sheep shearing is shown here. Note that the sheep are being held by one hand and the shears used to take the fleece from the animal are in the other. This was done in the spring, before the sheep were taken to the summer range.

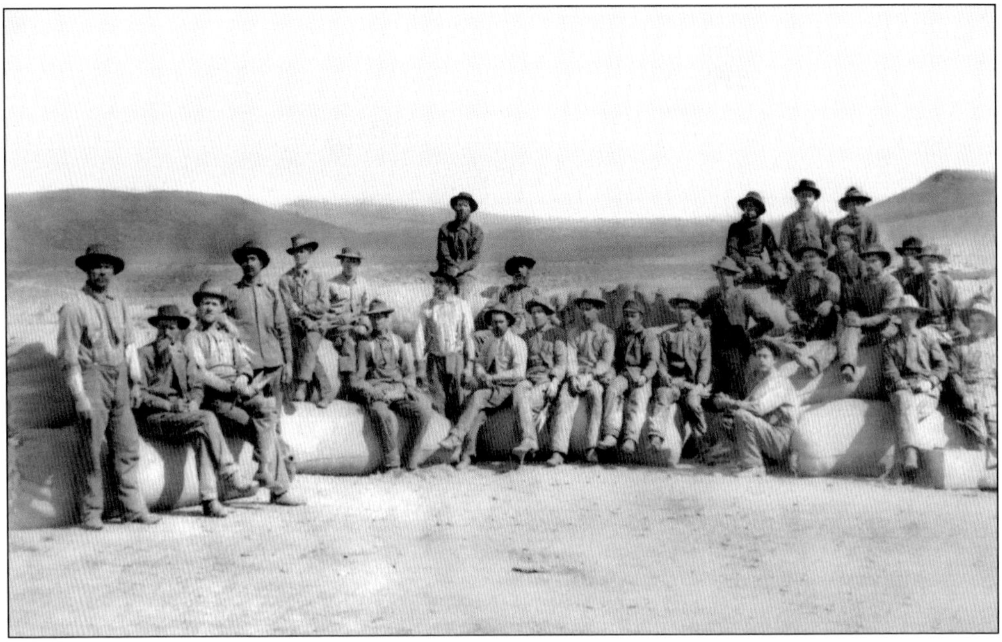

These huge sacks of wool weighed between 500 and 1,000 pounds. After the shearing, the sacks of wool were loaded onto wagons and taken to market.

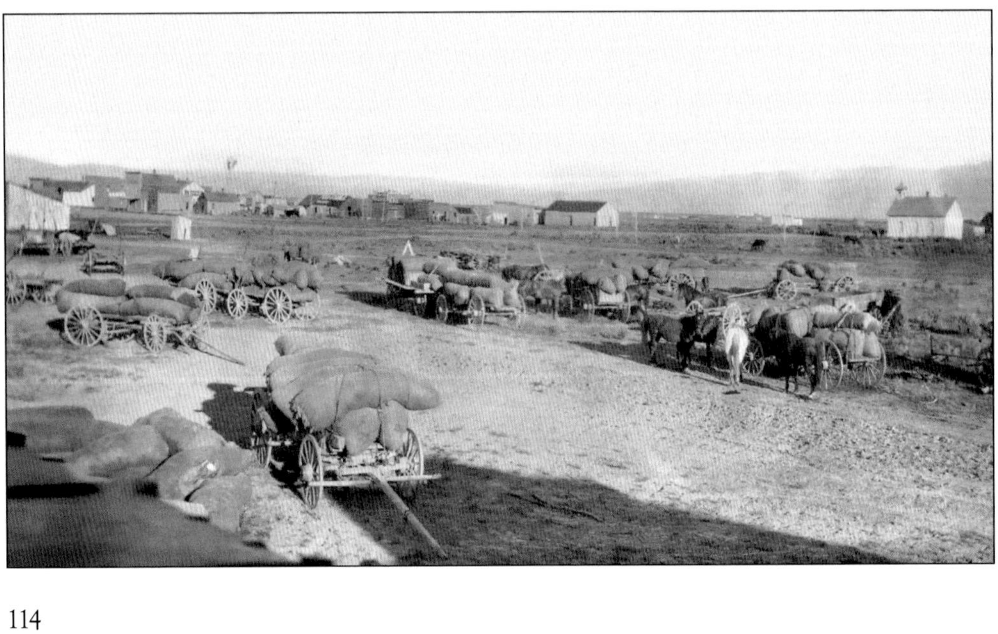

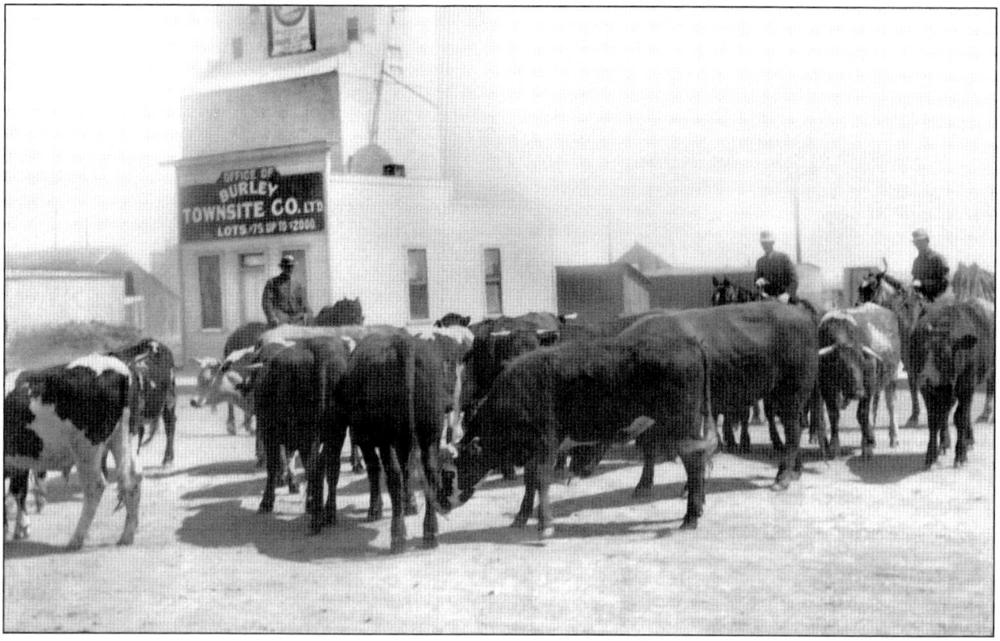

The first carload of cattle to be fattened on the Minidoka Project is shown here. The herd was purchased by Art Rosencrans in 1910 from Mr. Gillette at the price of 5¢ per pound.

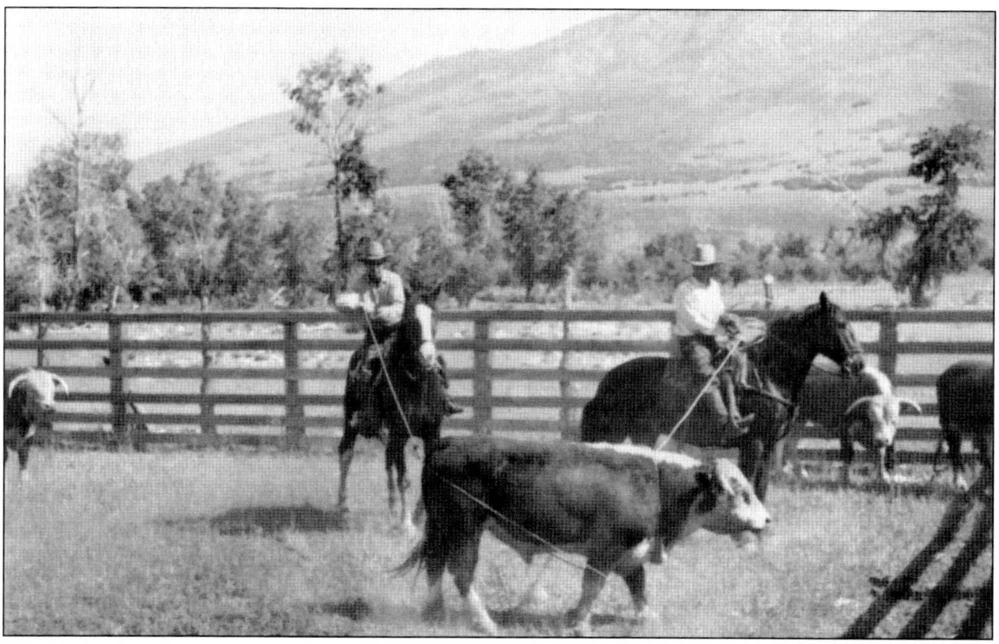

The Parke families were ranchers drawn to the Malta area because of the wide expanse of grass and the wide flowing Raft River. Pictured here are Glenn (left) and Ether Parke. (Courtesy of Ada Parke.)

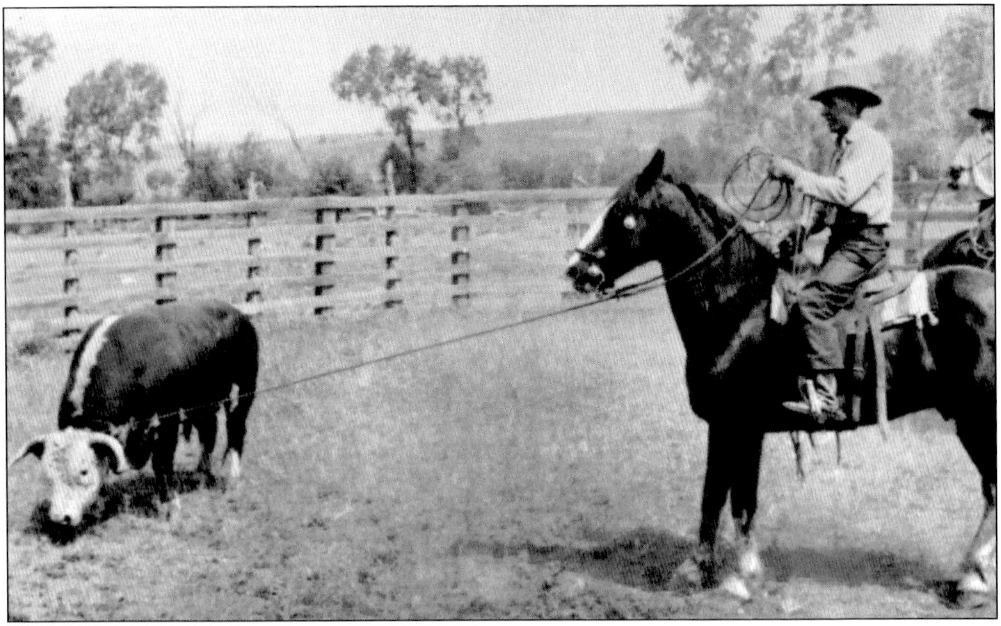

These pictures of brothers Glenn (on the horse in both) and Ether Parke were taken at a branding at the Browning Ranch. (Both courtesy of Ada Parke.)

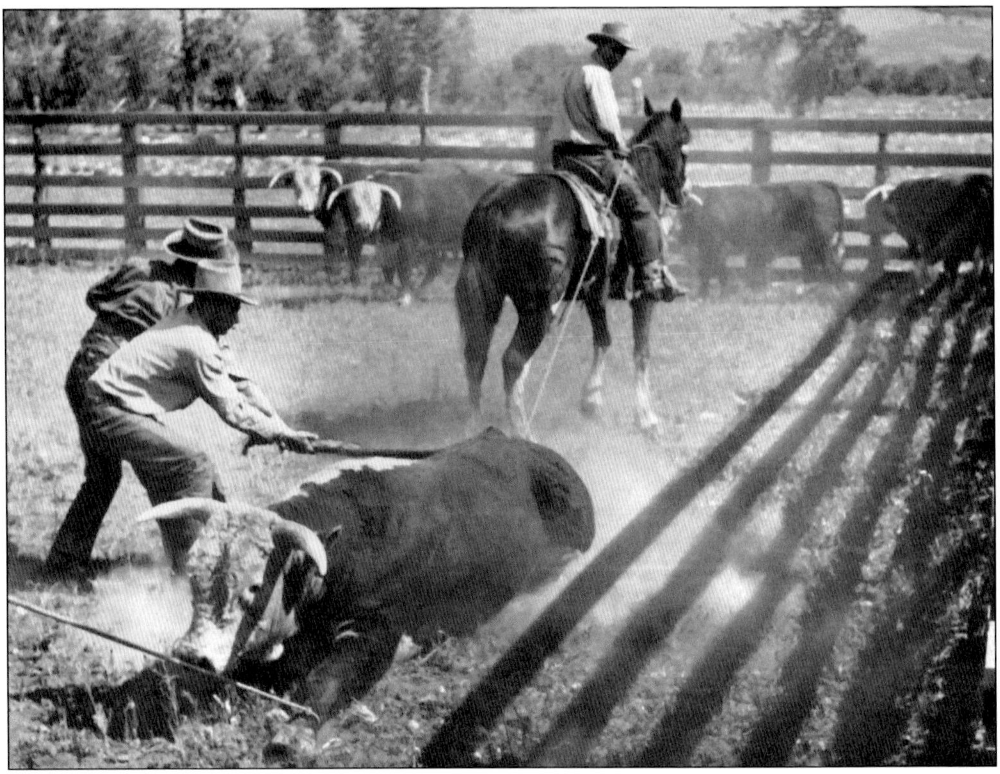

Nine

TRANSPORTATION

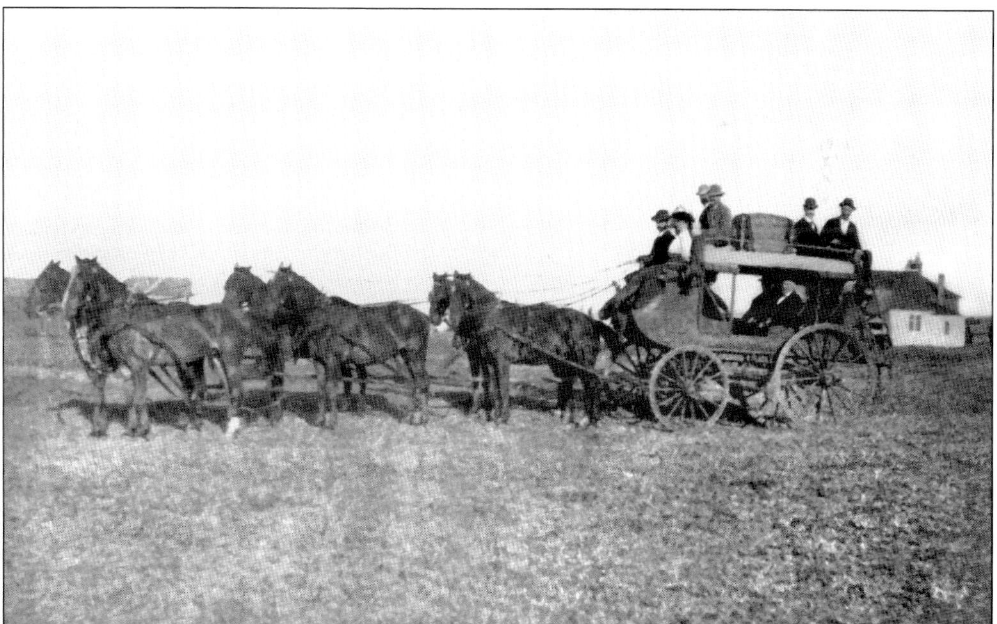

The stage was an important mode of travel through Cassia County. The stage stations, spaced about 12 miles apart, linked the area from Kelton, Utah, through the City of Rocks and Oakley and on to Boise, Idaho. Up until 1878, it was a four-day trip with stops only long enough to refresh drivers and horses. After that, the stage went through Albion.

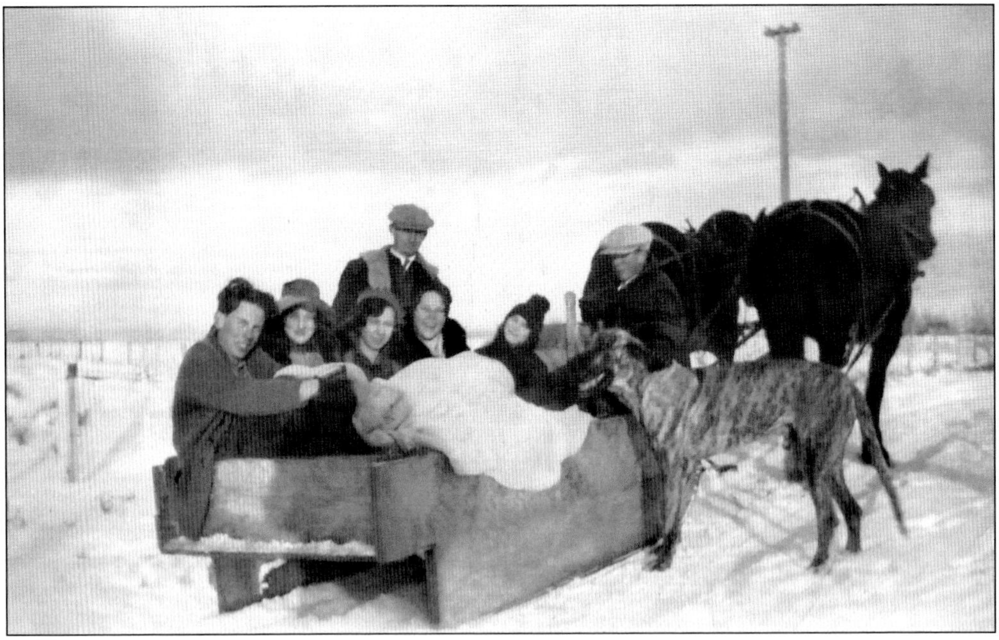

Pictured are Anita Gierisch, Duane Richins, and friends out for a ride in the country during the winter in the late 1920s. (Courtesy of Joyce McBride.)

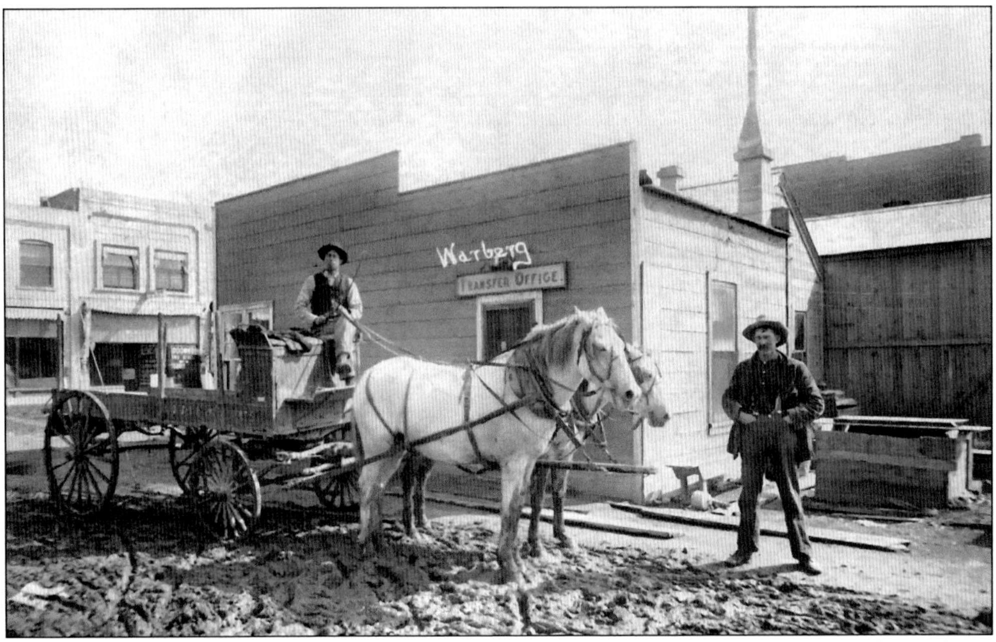

The Warburg Transfer Company conveyed goods from Burley to the towns throughout the county.

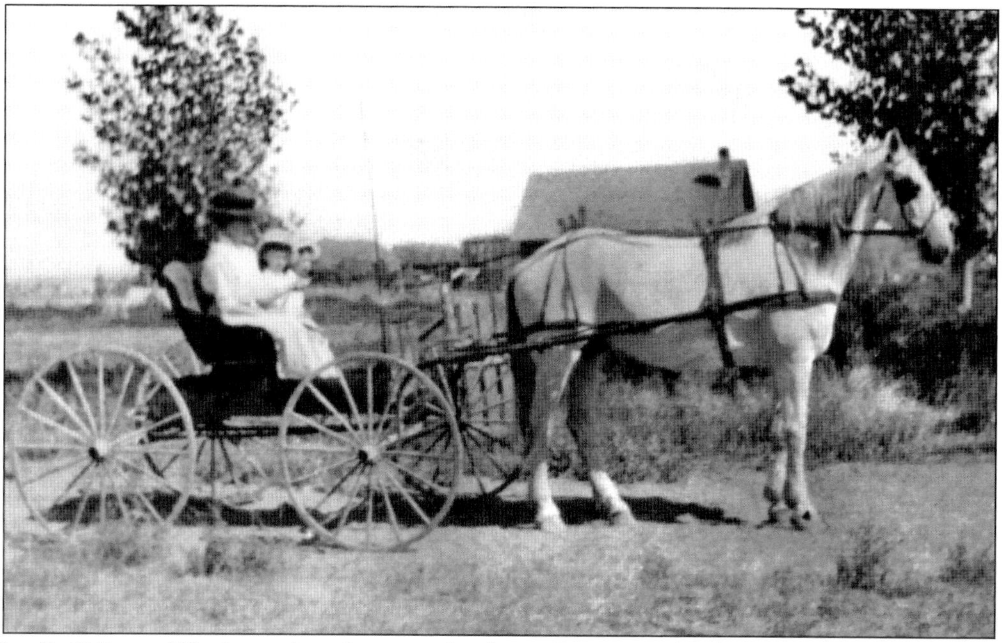

Luella Kellogg of Declo is taking her twin daughters, Frances and Helen, to church in this horse and buggy.

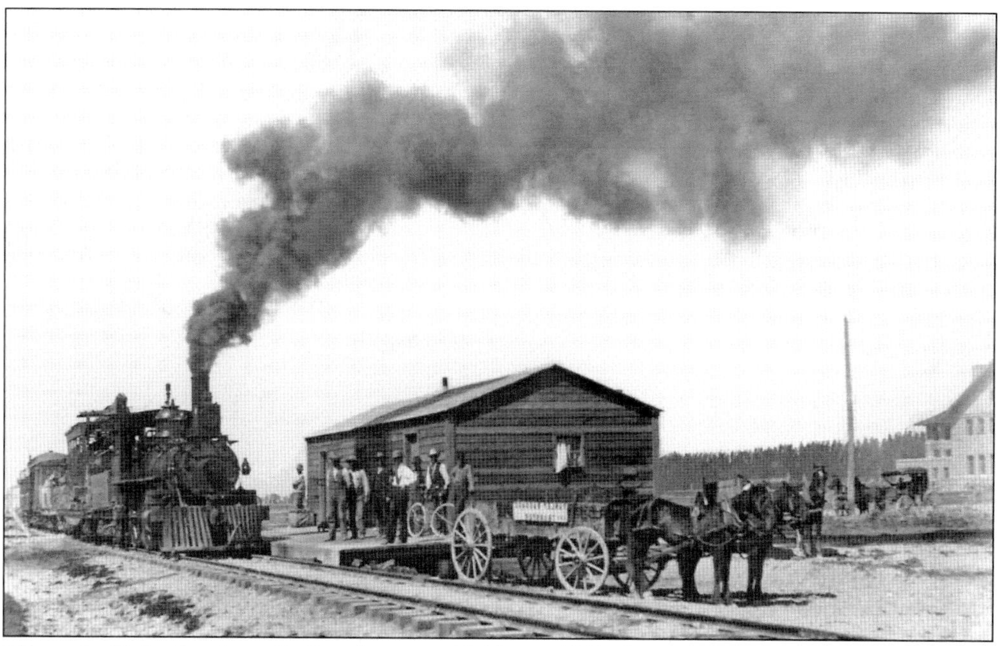

When the Idaho Southern Railroad came to Oakley in 1910, the community was finally connected to the balance of the world by rail.

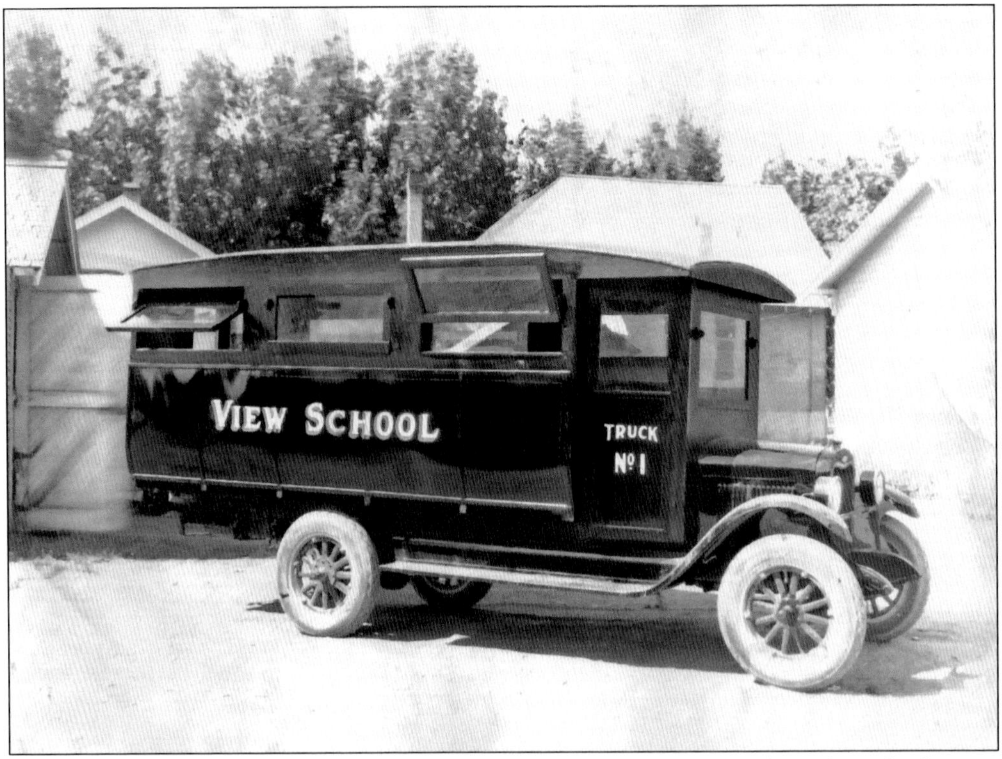

One of the first school buses, the View school truck No. 1 transported students from the farming area south of Burley.

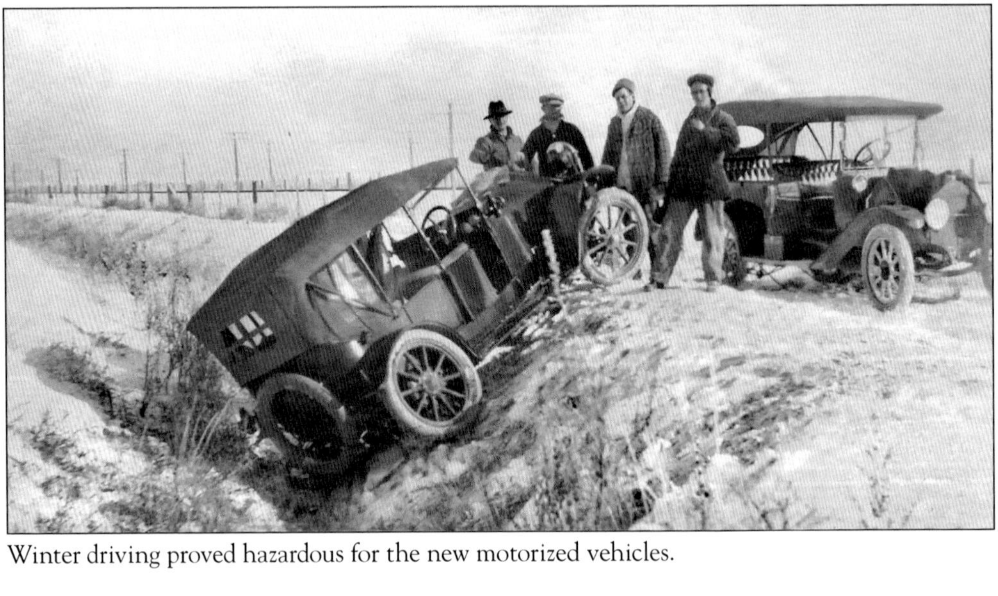

Winter driving proved hazardous for the new motorized vehicles.

Ten

Recreation

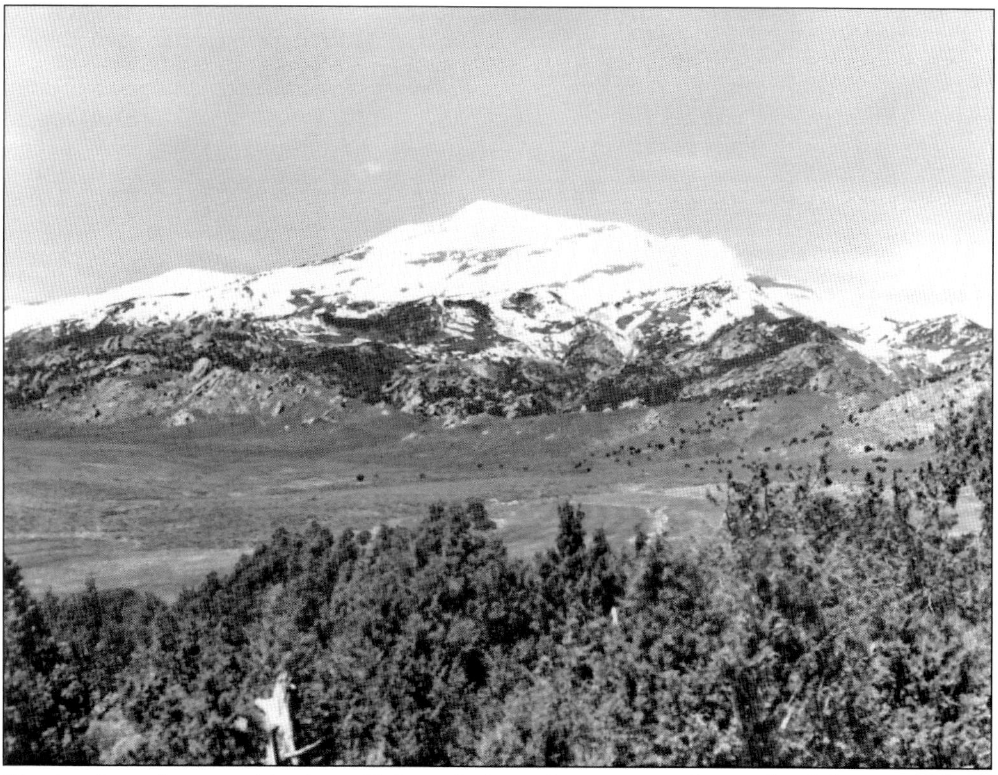

Coming from the east, this view of Mount Independence was to the north of the many wagon trains that made their way to California and Oregon in the 1850s. This high mountain range is of granite formation and is full of minerals such as coal, marble, gold, silver, copper, and lead. As one wagon train entered into the next valley, one California immigrant described in her journal seeing "a sublime, strange and wonderful scene."

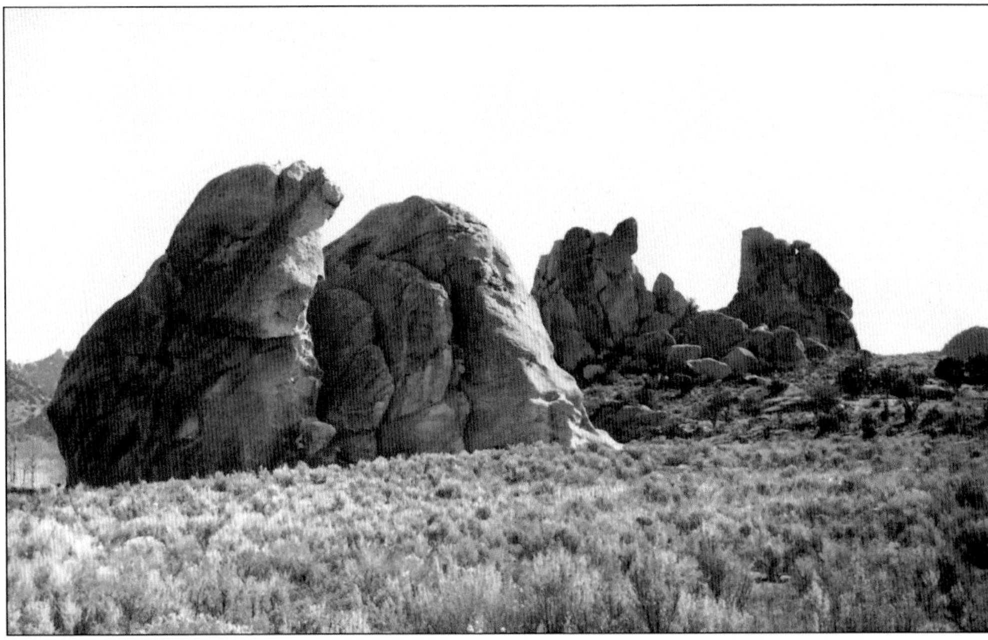

These formations are in the City of Rocks National Reserve. They were described in immigrant journals of the 1850s as "stone villages composed of huge isolated rocks of various and singular shapes." Immigrants called them such names as "Napoleon's Castle," "City Hotel," and "Sarcophagus Rock." This section of Cassia County is an area about 40 miles long by 10 or 15 miles wide. Many of these rocks rise to the height of 300 or 400 feet.

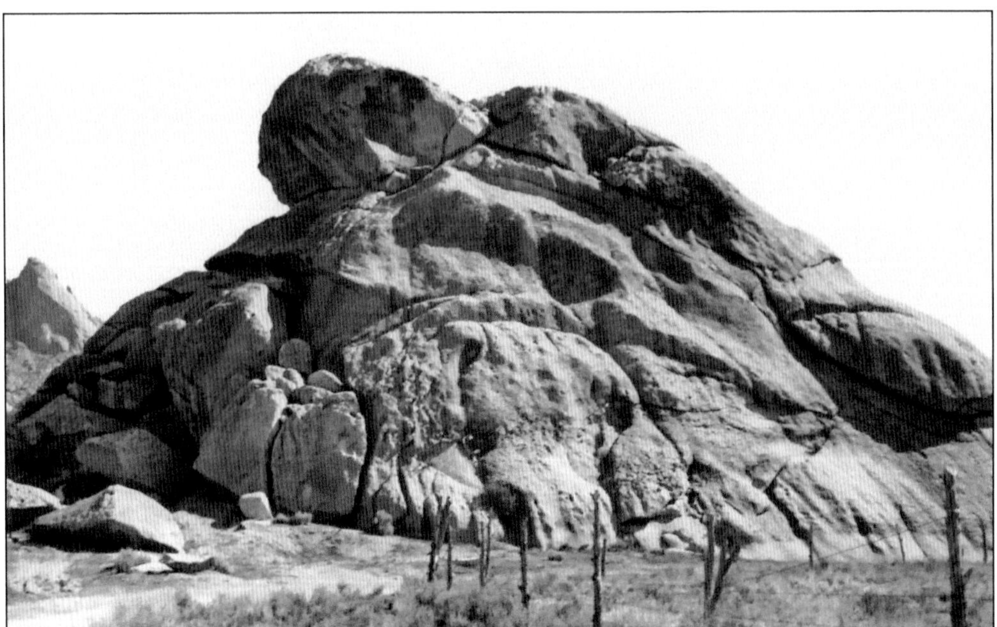

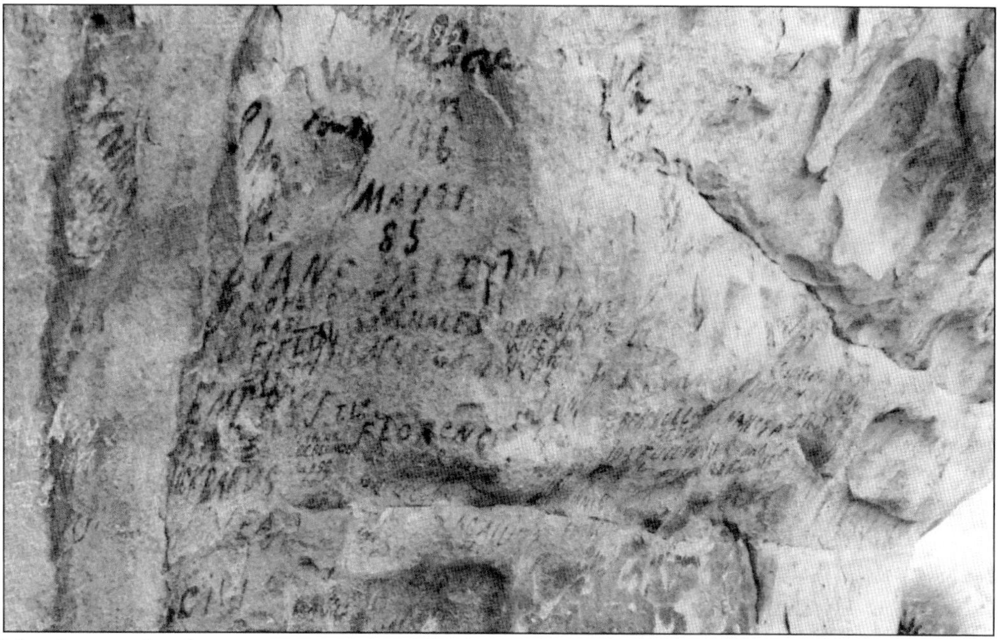

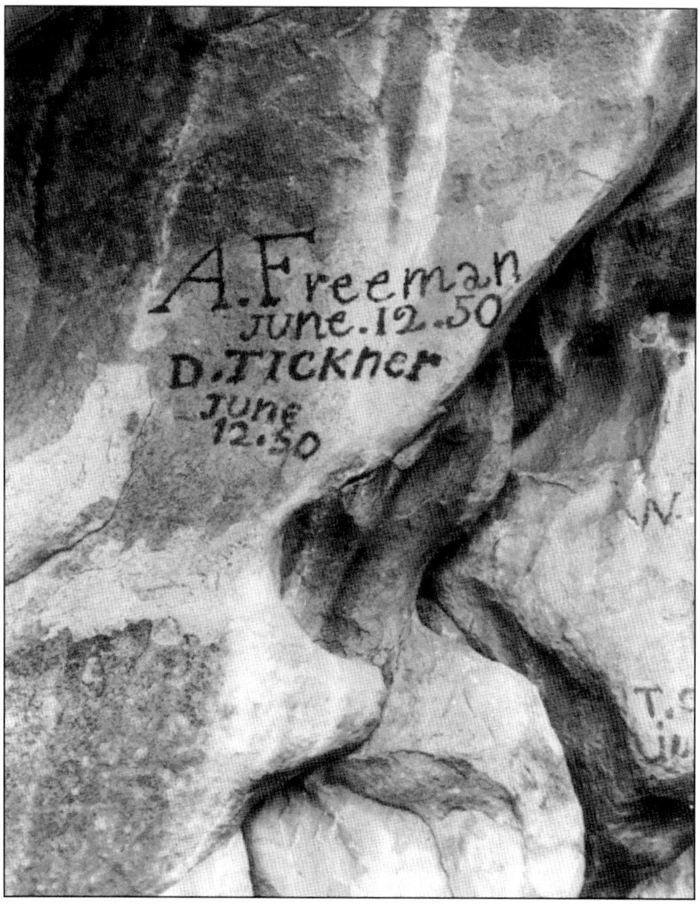

This huge rock is known as Register Rock. As the pioneer wagon trains came through the City of Rocks, they signed their names to the rock. The dates are from the 1800s, not the 1900s. A. Freeman and D. Tickner came through on June 12, 1850.

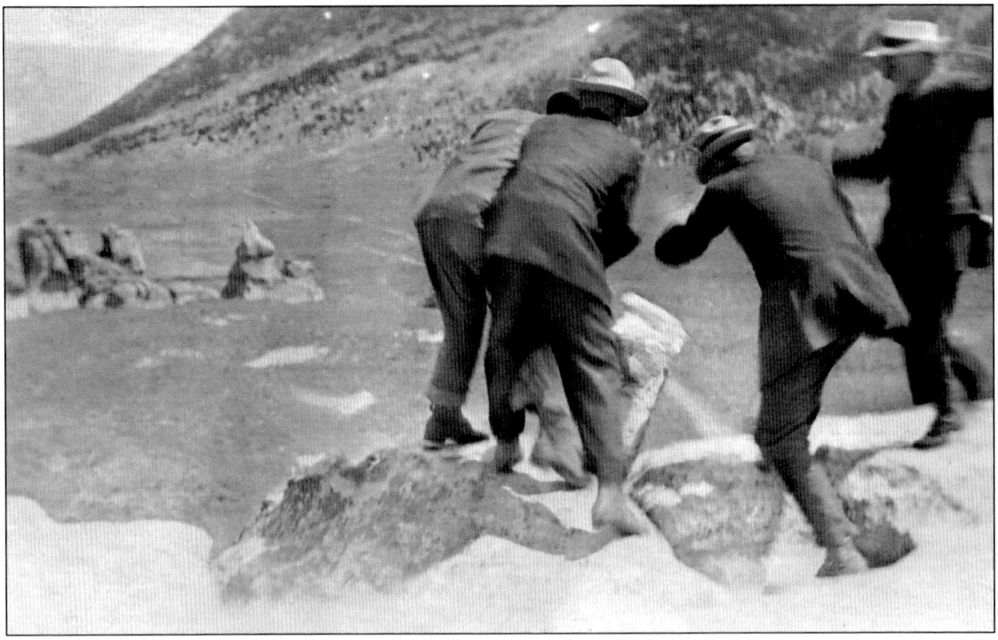

These scenes were common during the 1920s, as many outings were taken to the City of Rocks for picnics. The men were apparently trying to push a boulder off the side of the rocks.

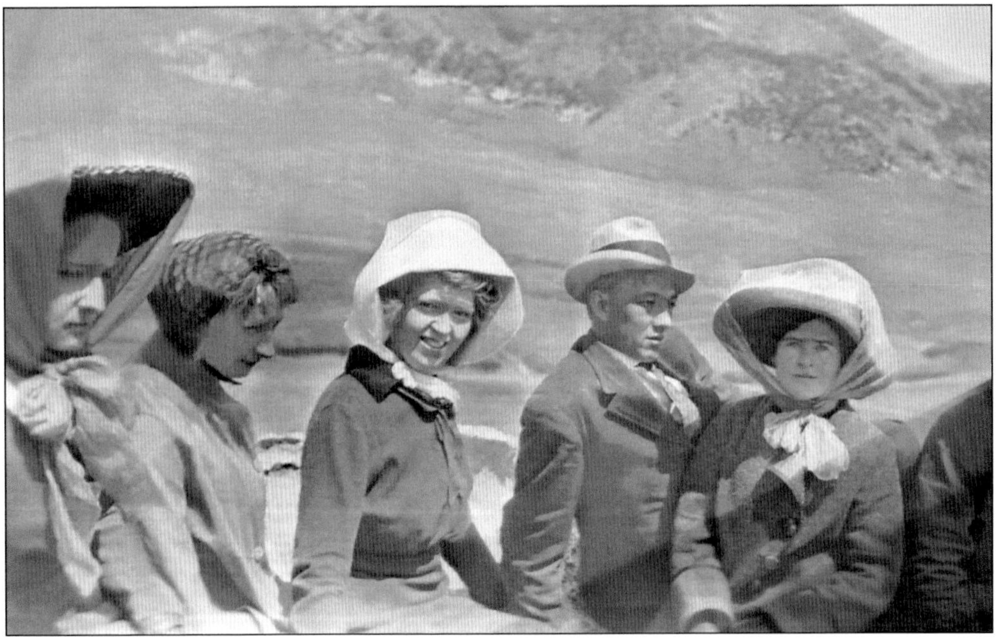

In these pictures, notice how the people were dressed for the day. This could have been a Sunday afternoon outing.

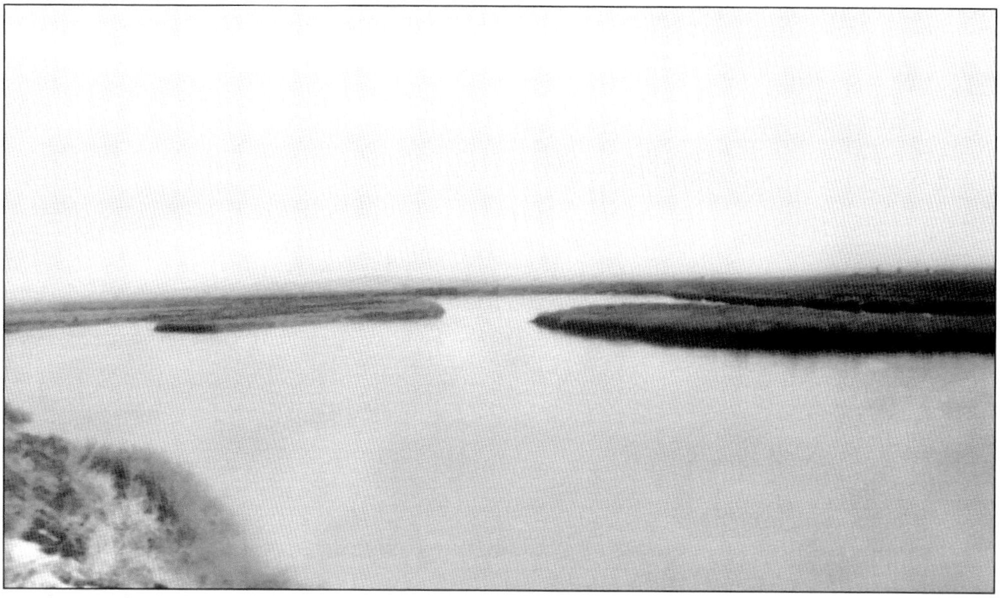

As the Snake River winds its way through southern Idaho, it opens out in Cassia County to a beautiful and calm expanse. Dredging for gold was done on the river here, and the Burroughs family lived on the dredge for a short time.

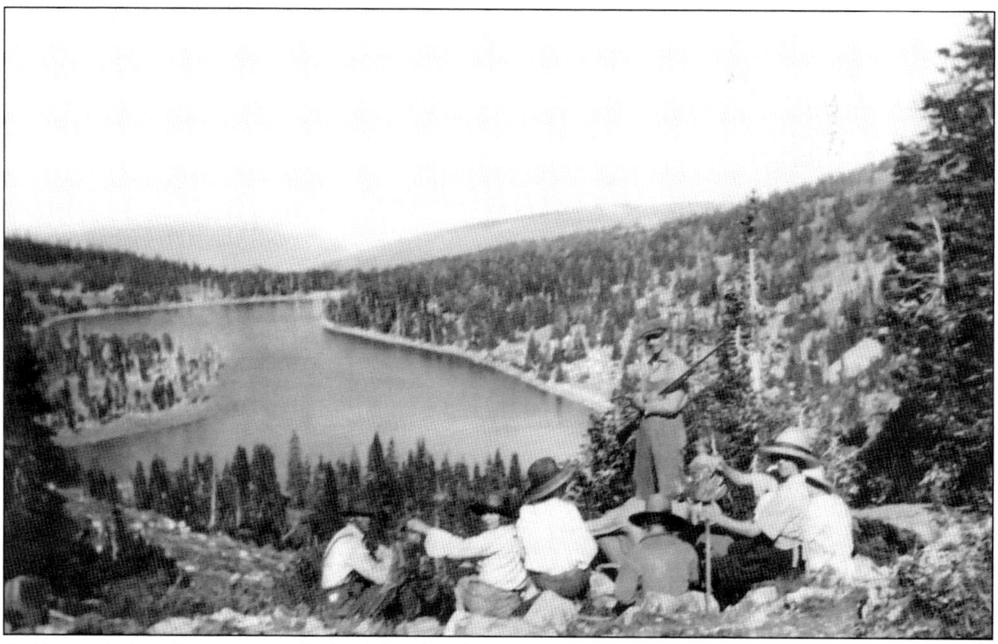

A Gierisch family outing to Lake Cleveland was quite an adventure. Before any roads went to the lake, the family would hike over the mountain from the Willow Creek area north of Oakley. This photograph was taken in the 1920s. (Courtesy of Joyce McBride.)

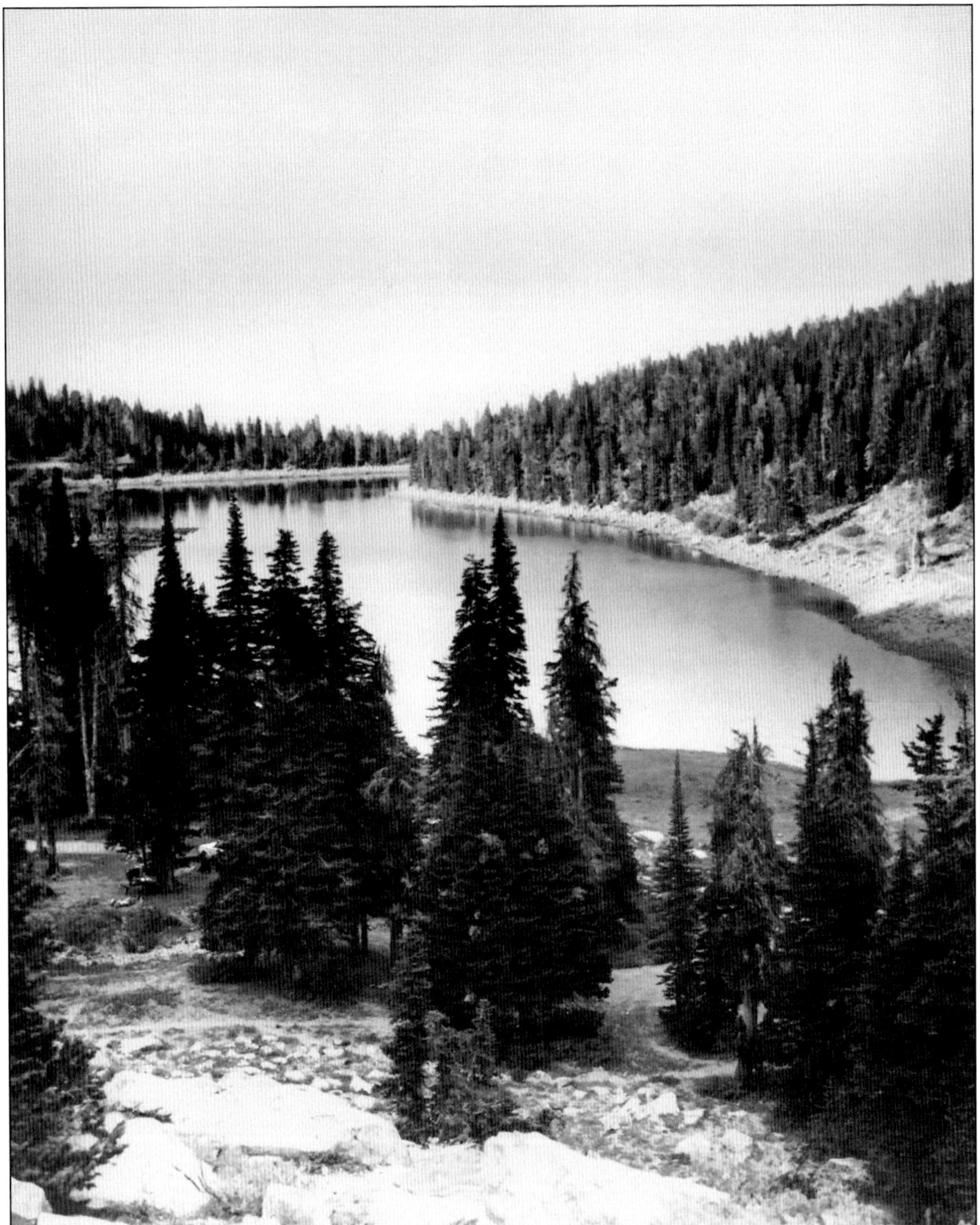

At a picnic held on the shores of this beautiful mountain lake during the presidential campaign of 1888, it was agreed to name the lake for the defeated candidate and the mountain for the successful candidate of the upcoming national election. William Henry Harrison won that year, and Grover Cleveland lost. At the picnic were Frank Riblett, county surveyor; Dr. and Mrs. Lindley; and Hardy Sears and Dan Stark, good friends but political opponents. Many people are still drawn to Lake Cleveland, nestled near the top of Mount Harrison.

Bibliography

Hale, Kent. *A History of Oakley, Idaho*. Self-published, 2003.

Declo History Committee. *Declo: My Town, My People*. Burley, ID: *Burley Reminder*, 1974.

Hedberg, Kathleen. *Cassia County, Idaho: The Foundation Years*. Burley, ID: Caxton Printers, 2005.

Powell, Verlene. *A History of Albion Pioneers*. Self-published, 2007.

Across America, People are Discovering Something Wonderful. *Their Heritage.*

Arcadia Publishing is the leading local history publisher in the United States. With more than 5,000 titles in print and hundreds of new titles released every year, Arcadia has extensive specialized experience chronicling the history of communities and celebrating America's hidden stories, bringing to life the people, places, and events from the past. To discover the history of other communities across the nation, please visit:

www.arcadiapublishing.com

Customized search tools allow you to find regional history books about the town where you grew up, the cities where your friends and family live, the town where your parents met, or even that retirement spot you've been dreaming about.

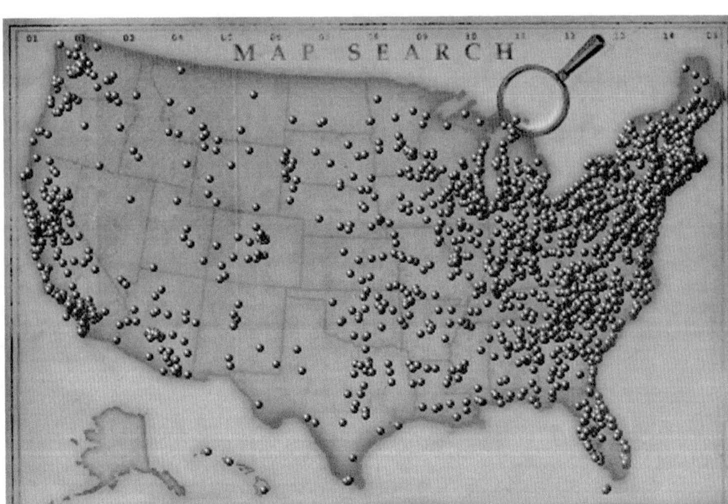